# THE THEORY OF

# POLITICAL COALITIONS

by William H. Riker

NEW HAVEN AND LONDON, YALE UNIVERSITY PRESS

*Copyright © 1962 by Yale University.*
*Third printing, January 1967.*
*Designed by Crimilda Pontes.*
*Set in Baskerville type and*
*printed in the United States of America by*
*The Carl Purington Rollins*
*Printing-Office of the Yale*
*University Press, New Haven,*
*Connecticut.*
*All rights reserved. This book may not be*
*reproduced, in whole or in part, in any form*
*(except by reviewers for the public press),*
*without written permission from the publishers.*
*Library of Congress catalog card number: 62–16239*
*Published with assistance from*
*the Mary Cady Tew Memorial Fund.*

*For MARY ELIZABETH*

# Preface

The specific purpose of this book is to construct, with the help of an existing general theory of coalitions (the theory of $n$-person games), a theory of coalitions that will be useful in studying politics. As such, it is not—most emphatically not—a book about mathematics, even though it makes use of some notions drawn from a mathematical theory. Since the audience I wish to reach is, primarily, political scientists and those laymen interested in the abstract interpretation of political events, I have, therefore, relegated those portions of the argument which make considerable use of mathematical symbols to appendixes, which, however, are summarized briefly in the text. Furthermore, I hasten to add that even the material in the appendixes, while occasionally using mathematical methods of notation, is not really mathematical in nature. Rather, this argument is simply reasoning about curves in a geometrical model, somewhat after the fashion in which economists reason about supply and demand curves.

This rather emphatic disclaimer is intended to warn mathematicians that, despite the use of game theory, they will not find material of interest to them here and to disarm political scientists who are at the present time, unfortunately, largely unaware of the relevance of mathematical notions to politics and, even more unfortunately, likely to be impatient with the kind of abstract reasoning about behavior in a model which can make use of mathematical symbolism to illuminate behavior in the real world of politics. The last chapter, especially, is intended to suggest the relevance of model-building to an understanding of action in the real world and, in content, this chapter is actually directed to those persons who must make policy on the basis of the theory of politics.

The more general purpose of this book is to add another (putative) example (to the several that already exist) of the fact that it is or may be possible for political science to rise above the level of wisdom literature and indeed to join economics and psychology in the creation of genuine sciences of human behavior. There is considerable intellectual ferment among political scientists today owing to the fact that the traditional methods of their discipline seem to have wound up in a cul-de-sac. These traditional methods—i.e., history writing, the description of institutions, and legal analysis—have been thoroughly exploited in the last two generations and now it seems to many (including myself) that they can produce only wisdom and neither science nor knowledge. And while wisdom is certainly useful in the affairs of men, such a result is a failure to live up to the promise in the name political *science*.

Conscious of this failure, students of politics have embraced a variety of new causes. Some have rejected the notion of a science altogether, asserting that all sentences about politics (even supposedly descriptive ones) are in fact normative and thus totally refractory to scientific use. Others, recognizing that much of the literature of political science reads like a set of wise proverbs, have embraced this fact and described the study as a "policy science." A third group, eager still to fulfill the promise of the name political science and envious of the achievements (under a behavioristic theory) of psychology, sociology, and economics, have adapted the methods and theories of these disciplines to the study of politics and hence have described their work as the study of political behavior. Finally, a fourth group has diagnosed the failure of traditional political science as the result of gathering information about political events without a theory of politics and has therefore been eager to create specifically *political* theories of behavior to serve as a base for a future *political* science. It is to this latter group that I belong, and it is my hope that this book will provide some theoretical orientation for the study of politics and thereby serve as an example of the possibilities of a genuine political science. There is, I suppose, in any scientific field, an outrageous immodesty implied in offering one's confreres a purportedly general theory and such immodesty is probably displayed in this book. In extenuation, I can only say that, in another sense, I offer it modestly. I am fully conscious, on the one hand, of the immodesty of the assertions of advantage and, on the other hand, of the possibility that the theory may turn out to be false or unusable. But I hope that, if the theory should turn out to be true, it will provide a part of the foundation on which others can build and that, if it should be false or unusable, it will inspire others to join in the work of creating a new political theory for a new political science.

I take the opportunity of this preface to offer thanks to many who have helped me. First, I offer thanks to the Social Science Research Council, which gave me a summer free for the development of an earlier version of Appendix I and to Lawrence College and the Center for Advanced Study in the Behavioral Sciences which together gave me a whole year at the Center to write this book. The Center is a magical place to which I owe much merely for the privilege of being there; and I owe a very special debt to one of its employees, Mrs. Irene Bickenback, for interpreting my scrawls into readable typescript. To my companions at the Center, even (and perhaps especially) to those in very different fields, I owe an immeasurable debt, for they again and again helped me to perceive my subject in a more illuminating way. A number of friends have commented on the manuscript of this book and I have often incorporated their comments without specific acknowledgment. To these friends I now offer thanks, especially to Professors Carl Christ, Charles Sellers, Duncan MacRae, Gordon Tullock, Glendon Schubert, and James Buchanan and Messrs. Robert Rossow, Robert DeLapp, and Richard Niemi. Most of all, however, I thank the gracious and graceful person to whom this book is dedicated.

*Appleton, Wisconsin*                    WILLIAM H. RIKER
*January 28, 1962*

# Contents

# THE THEORY OF POLITICAL COALITIONS

# CHAPTER 1

# The Prospect of a Science of Politics

The intellectual edifice of contemporary physical science —certainly the most impressive achievement of the human psyche in this or any other age—serves as a steady source of both inspiration and envy to scholars interested in the behavior of people rather than the motion of things: inspiration, because it is easy to dream of accomplishing in one field of thought what has already been accomplished in another; and envy, because it is hard to translate such dreams into reality. Driven by these motives, however, students of human behavior have repeatedly over the last century or so emulated the techniques of students of physical nature—but without conspicuous success and often with conspicuous failure.

What social scientists have so greatly admired about the physical sciences is the fact that these latter actually measure up to our notion of what science should be. That is, they consist of a body of related and verified generalizations which describe occurrences accurately enough to be used for prediction. Generalizations within each science are *related* because they are deduced from one set of axioms, which, though revised from time to time, are nevertheless a coherent theoretical model of motion.

Generalizations are *verified* because, drawn as they are from a carefully constructed and precise theory, they have themselves been stated in a way that admits of verification by experiment, observation, and prediction. Of course, very few generalizations, which consist of an assertion that a subject class is included in a predicate class (e.g., "the class of distilled water belongs to the class of things that boil at 100°C. at sea level"), can ever be fully verified. Verification involves showing that particular members of the subject class actually belong also to the predicate class; hence complete verification involves a demonstration that *every* member of the subject class belongs to the predicate. Since for the sake of uttering predictions, most subject classes in scientific generalizations are constructed so as to allow for future members, complete verification is seldom possible. Instead scientists content themselves with verification of a sufficient number of particular instances of members of the subject belonging to the predicate to give confidence in the generalization. How many such tests of particular instances are necessary to give confidence varies, of course, with the subject matter. (In general, the more precisely defined is the subject class the fewer are the necessary tests, which is why precision is a scientific virtue.) But despite the frequent impossibility of complete verification, enough verification for accurate prediction is often achieved and this is what behavioral scientists so much desire to emulate.

Numerous obstacles stand in the way, however, of direct emulation. For one thing, in the study of human affairs normative considerations often and easily intrude (sometimes unconsciously) into what were intended to be purely descriptive sentences. Leaving aside entirely the much controverted question of whether or not normative sentences can be verified, it is at least certain that they cannot be verified in the same way as descriptive sentences. Certainly, if normative verification occurs, it does not involve predictability. Hence the inclusion of normative elements in a descriptive generalization renders it scientifically unfit. (This, for example, is where Marx's endeavor to be scientific went astray. The main proposition of *Capital* can be summarized as "Capitalism is theft"; and since theft—when divorced from a positive legal system—is a normative notion, verification of this sentence as a description of nature is literally impossible.)

Again, human action is itself enormously more complex than the motion of things, especially when whole human beings are included in the action studied—whole human beings with their distorted perceptions, half-conscious emotions, and selective memories that bind over some (and only some) segments of the past into the immediate present. To make matters worse, while the gradation of language makes it easy to slice up physical reality into tiny bits for perception, our verbal patterns usually present social reality to us in great big slices. Thus the primitive physicists, even prior to the development of an elaborate special vocabulary, were still presented with rather small events for study, at least after they agreed to call the study of the origin of the universe *meta*physics. Thus, they were left with manageable problems (with some precisely defined subject classes) such as the explanation of the operation of the lever. Primitive social scientists (that is, we of this century, who are just beginning to develop a special vocabulary) are, on the other hand, presented with vast events such as wars and depressions, love affairs and character formation, elections and systems of jurisprudence, etc. These classes of events are doubtless of great human interest, but they do not admit of that precise definition which is so necessary in science.[1]

1. William H. Riker, "Events and Situations," *Journal of Philosophy*, 54 (1957), 57–70.

For still a third obstacle, social scientists are deprived of that notion of causal determinism which played so important a part in the development of the physical sciences. Even if physical scientists may now avoid or revise the idea of causality, still it cannot be denied that they were aided immeasurably by this idea to carry through a dynamic analysis of motion. Social scientists, on the other hand, are presented with subjects who, even if they do not have free wills, at least can make choices so unexpected in the present state of our knowledge that they in effect behave as if their wills were free.

As a consequence of these obstacles, the behavioral sciences are *sciences* only by the kindly tolerance of university faculties who are willing to put up with our pretensions and ambitions in appropriating the name. Facing this situation, some scholars (e.g., Karl Mannheim, Arnold Toynbee, et al.) have abandoned the search for scientific knowledge and substituted for it a flight into poetic imagination, which, however, they would still (doubtless for hortatory purposes) like to call scientific. It seems to me, however, somewhat premature to forego the scientific enterprise, especially when some of the behavioral sciences have for the last generation or so been beginning to develop into genuine sciences. Economics and psychology stand out among them as studies which, after 150 years of empirical investigation and refinement of theory, now have some coherent theory and verified generalizations. And this very fact offers hope to the other and younger branches of the study of society. Even political science, which as a subject separated from political philosophy and comparative jurisprudence has existed only in this century and within which the obstacles of normative sentences and oversized events loom larger perhaps than in any other study, can take some hope from the fairly recent achievements of economics and psychology. Instead of abandoning the effort to create a science, students of behavior generally and political behavior in particular ought rather to examine the procedures of the physical sciences to abstract from them their techniques of success. Some nineteenth-century students of politics (Bagehot, for example) thought they could take over bodily certain sentences from physics. Such slavish imitation of course led into a cul-de-sac. But there is no reason why the general methods of formulating provisional generalizations, of rendering them susceptible to verification, etc., cannot be taken over. This is what economics and psychology have done and it is what probably accounts for such success as they have had. Those who are interested in creating a science of politics must, therefore, first become students of scientific method in the hope that they can use it in their own concerns.

Fortunately, physical scientists of the last generation have been sufficiently curious about their own enterprise to try to explain it to others and many behavioral scientists have amplified upon this in sufficient detail that some understanding of method has been embodied in our common intellectual heritage. The essential feature of this method is the creation of a theoretical construct that is a somewhat simplified version of what the real world to be described is believed to be like. This simplified version or model is a set of axioms (more or less justifiable intuitively) from which nonobvious general sentences can be deduced. These deduced propositions, when verified, become both an addition to the model and a description of nature. As more and more sentences are deduced and verified, greater and greater confidence in the validity of the axioms is felt to be justified. Conversely, the deduction of false or inconsistent sentences tends to discredit the axioms.

The main advantage of a model is, of course, that it is a

convenient way of generating hypotheses and something of a brake on inconsistency. Not that a model is any substitute for creative imagination—the scientist, like the poet, must utter new words and sentences—but the model can guide him in imagining hypotheses and deciding whether or not they are useful. Beyond this main purpose, however, models are helpful in overcoming the special obstacles that stand so firmly in the way of a science of politics. Thus, by carefully excluding normative features from the axioms (or, alternatively, by rendering them conscious), normative elements in generalizations can, possibly, be excluded (or controlled). Again, although there is no necessary reason why models should cut behavior up into more manageable units than are given in common speech, still models have repeatedly had that effect—perhaps because they tend to enforce precision of statement. For example, the original impulse in the modern study of economics was to specify the conditions for the wealth of nations and, as indicated by the liveliness of Keynesian economics and the economics of underdevelopment, this remains an important concern today. But in the process of developing models, the units of study were enormously simplified. Either individual transactions were studied or behavior (such as that summarized by a demand curve) was abstracted out of its institutional and personal setting. Similarly, the development of models enormously simplified psychology. When, as in the nineteenth century, psychologists tried to generalize about whole human personalities, few generalizations could be verified. But with behaviorism and the stimulus-response model, psychologists no longer had to speak of "minds" and other features of whole people. Instead, the model led to precision of statement based on more precisely definable subject classes. Finally, the use of models occasionally permits one to transcend the obstacle of the existence of choice. The very act of choosing may be subjected to study by an axiomatic method so that the obstacle is thus transformed from a barrier to a boost.

So I conclude: the main hope for a genuine science of politics lies in the discovery and use of an adequate model of political behavior. In the next section, therefore, I turn to the problem of discovery and in the following chapters to the problem of use.

## A MODEL OF POLITICAL BEHAVIOR

Whether or not there is a distinctively political kind of action is a much controverted question. Many sociologists and economists have been inclined to interpret political life as simply an extension of the respective kinds of behavior they study.[2] But the common usage of English (and most other modern languages) distinguishes repeatedly between politics and other kinds of social life. This common sense abstraction has been reinforced in the last century by the appearance of a set of scholars who call themselves political scientists, presumably because they sense that politics is a distinct kind of activity deserving of a special scientific discipline. There now exists, for example, an International Political Science Association, which even has members in countries where official dogma insists that all political activity is mere superstructure supported by the really fundamental activity of economic life. On the basis, therefore, of the organization of scholars as well as of the perceptions of common usage, one can, I believe, assume that political behavior has unique features and that these may be studied by a special science.

Despite the rather general agreement that some action

2. Talcott Parsons, Edward A. Shils, et al., *Toward a General Theory of Action* (Cambridge, Mass., Harvard University Press, 1951), pp. 28–29. The classic example of the reduction of politics to some other study is, of course, the work of Marx.

is distinctively political, there is not much agreement on what the distinguishing feature of politics is. Some say it is action in the name of the state or government (i.e., public as distinct from private action); others say it is the struggle for power; still others, that it is the realization of moral ideals. Recently David Easton has offered a definition that combines all these and, besides, fits politics into the general scheme of the social sciences. Politics, he said, is the authoritative allocation of value. By emphasizing allocation, which is a kind of action, he made it clear that politics is social behavior, a study of dynamics and not primarily a study of such static things as forms of government. Thereby he fit political science into the tradition that selects motion and action as the proper concern of science, a tradition that has increasingly dominated Western scientific thought for the past century and a half. Furthermore, since the usual definition of economics is "the allocation of scarce resources," he showed both the parallelism and divergence of the two kinds of activity by the parallelism and divergence of the definitions. Along with all this, he managed to subsume all three of the older traditions in his definition. In its emphasis on authority, it subsumed the study of government (which is the center of authority in society); in its emphasis on allocation, it subsumed the struggle for power, or at least the public struggle for power; in its emphasis on value, it subsumed the study of morality, or at least public morality. Because his definition so neatly combined older traditions and fit them into the scheme of contemporary social and physical science, it might well, I believe, be generally used by political scientists. Certainly I shall use it here.[3]

Now if, as Easton asserts, politics is the authoritative allocation of value and if, as I interpret it, "allocation"

3. For a fuller exposition of its meaning, I refer to Easton's work, *The Political System* (New York, Knopf, 1953), pp. 90–232.

refers not to a physical process but to the social process of deciding how a physical process shall be carried out, then the subject studied by political scientists is decision-making. But, despite the somewhat uncritical enthusiasm of some recent writers for "decision-making," not all decision-processes are political or of any concern to the political scientist. Excluded, for example, are decisions on the application of rules (e.g., decisions on whether a sum is correctly cast up or whether a given individual belongs to a particular species), a kind of decision-process which is properly studied by philosophers of science and students of scientific method. Excluded also are decisions by individuals about their future behavior, a subject in the realm of social psychology. Indeed, the only decisions in the scope of politics are those which concern value and are assumed to be authoritative.

Authoritative decisions on allocations of value may be classified thus:

A. Those made by individuals
B. Those made by groups
   1. Those made by conscious processes
   2. Those made in a quasi-mechanical way

By far the largest and most significant of these categories is B1. There are doubtless some societies in which genuinely dictatorial decisions (category A) are produced; but often the societies we pejoratively describe as monarchies or tyrannies or dictatorships are really operated as oligarchies wherein decisions are in category B. Even true monarchies seldom endure for long because the king or dictator dies or is deposed and then is replaced, temporarily at least, by a junta. Just as category A is smaller than B, so B2 is smaller than B1. In the modern world, even in Communist countries, one important device for economic decisions (i.e., allocations of scarce resources) is the market and price system, which is a quasi-mechanical decision-process. But relatively few authoritative allocations of value are made so automatically. It is true, of course, that the market itself allocates values as well as resources and that in some societies these allocations are regarded as authoritative. But it is relatively rare that a society debases itself as abjectly to mechanical decisions as, for example, the United States did in the latter part of the nineteenth century. More typically, authority is believed to rest in determinate persons and the automatic allocations by institutions are believed to be subject to review by those in authority. Hence, in some contrast to economics, politics consists mostly of decisions in category B1.

The interesting thing about conscious decisions by groups (category B1) is that, if groups are more than two persons, the process of making them is invariably the same. It is a process of forming coalitions. Typically some part of the authority-possessing group comes together in alliance to render a decision binding on the group as a whole and on all who recognize its authority. This decisive "part" may be more or less than one-half, indeed it may be two persons or the whole group itself. But regardless of the number of persons conventionally believed to be decisive, the process of reaching a decision in a group is a process of forming a subgroup which, by the rules accepted by all members, can decide for the whole. This subgroup is a coalition.

Thus, much the greater part of the study of the authoritative allocation of value is reduced to the study of coalitions. And for this study, a model is at hand. It is the Von Neumann–Morgenstern theory of $n$-person games, which is essentially a theory of coalitions. This theory is, of course, not restricted to coalitions formed for authoritative decisions about value, but it is sufficiently applicable to political behavior to offer political scientists—for the first time since Aristotle tried to generalize about politics over two millennia ago—a model sufficiently descriptive and sufficiently unambiguous to occasion some hope for a genuine science of politics.

Most parlor games are constructed so as to represent in simplified form some of the more serious affairs of life. Amateur anthropologists have often commented that the American businessman's fondness for poker is occasioned by its similarity (in bluffing and betting) to activities in the market place. Chess, for another example, bears some slight resemblance to warfare. Many of its terms (e.g., "knight," "queen," etc.) are drawn from the vocabulary of war and government and conversely the politico-military vocabulary has been enriched by words from chess (e.g., "pawn," "checkmate," etc.). But although men have for centuries been inventing games that mirror the serious affairs of life, no one until John Von Neumann had the wit to realize that these serious affairs might themselves be investigated through a study of the play of games.

Von Neumann and Morgenstern's work, *The Theory of Games and Economic Behavior,* was greeted quite enthusiastically by statisticians and economists and in the 1950s a number of political scientists discovered its relevance to their work.[4] They were, I believe, chiefly im-

4. John Von Neumann and Oskar Morgenstern, *The Theory of Games and Economic Behavior* (Princeton, Princeton University Press, 1944; I hereafter cite the second edition of 1947). For the discovery by political scientists of the relevance of game theory to their concerns see Martin Shubik, ed., *Readings in Game Theory and Political Behavior* (Garden City, Doubleday, 1954); Richard Snyder, "Game Theory and the Analysis of Political Behavior," in Stephen K. Bailey et al., *Research Frontiers in Politics and Government* (Washington, The Brookings Institution, 1955); Herbert A. Simon, *Models of Man* (New York, John Wiley, 1957), especially the introduction; Morton A. Kaplan, *System and Process in International Politics* (New York, John Wiley, 1957), pp. 223 ff.; James Buchanan and Gordon Tullock, *The Calculus of Consent* (Ann Arbor, University of Michigan Press, 1962), passim.

pressed by the fact that this new branch of mathematics made possible rigorous quantitative discussion of situations in which existed free (and heretofore presumably unpredicable) human choice. But as the initial enthusiasm wore off, both economists and political scientists have begun to express doubts about the relevance of game theory to social science.[5] While some of this doubt arises out of a legitimate disagreement with some of the axioms of game theory—a disagreement that will be considered a few paragraphs later on—most of the doubt is simply disappointment that the minimax theorem did not help to solve many problems. As such, the disappointment is premature and rests on a misunderstanding of exactly what the resources of game theory really are.

It is certainly true that, in the mathematical theory of games, the major emphasis is placed on the minimax theorem, which was Von Neumann's first contribution to the theory and which proves the existence of a rationally "best" way to play any zero-sum, two-person game. (These technical terms will soon be explained.) The development of the theorem is, of course, technically elegant and its application in statistics and linear programming exceedingly important. Not surprisingly, therefore, the chief textbook on the mathematics of game theory, McKinsey, *Introduction to the Theory of Games,* devotes 14 out of 18 chapters to the theory of two-person, zero-sum games.[6] Most of the popular accounts of game theory also emphasize the minimax theorem.[7] So it is quite to be expected that social scientists tend to identify all of game theory with the theory

5. Thomas C. Schelling, *The Strategy of Conflict* (Cambridge, Mass., Harvard University Press, 1960).

6. J. C. C. McKinsey, *Introduction to the Theory of Games* (New York, McGraw-Hill, 1952).

7. J. D. Williams, *The Compleat Strategyst: Being a Primer on the Theory of Games of Strategy* (New York, McGraw-Hill, 1954); John McDonald, *Strategy in Poker, Business, and War* (New York, Norton, 1950).

of two-person, zero-sum games. And it is quite true that this specialized theory has little relevance to social situations. For the minimax theorem to be relevant, at least the following conditions must be satisfied:

1. The two-person condition: There must be exactly two participants (or two teams of participants), although one participant may be "nature."
2. The zero-sum condition: The interests of the participants must be in direct and absolute conflict so that the gains of one participant exactly equal in absolute amount the losses of the other. This, of course, also assumes that gain and loss can be quantified and measured.
3. The knowledge condition: Every possible course of action open to the participants and its rewards to them must be known to them and the scientist. Note, however, that it is not necessary to know exactly which choices are or will be made among the possible courses of action—it is this leap over choice that renders the minimax theorem so powerful when it is applicable.
4. The rationality condition: Given a choice of courses of action one of which brings greater rewards than the others, it must be assumed to be possible that some participants will prefer the course of action with greater rewards.

Quite evidently social situations satisfying all the conditions are rarely met with outside of games themselves. Economic life, for which Von Neumann and Morgenstern thought their model especially suited, usually involves some mutuality of interest in violation of condition 2— e.g., buyer and seller each gain something from a sale. In political life, although it is sometimes possible to satisfy 2, it is usually impossible to satisfy conditions 1 and 3. About the only kind of social situation that really does satisfy all four conditions is total war, when each side demands the unconditional surrender of the other. And this is admittedly an infrequent circumstance.

But even though the minimax theorem is usually irrelevant to the study of society, this theorem is only a part of game theory. In *The Theory of Games and Economic Behavior* only 134 out of 632 pages are devoted to two-person, zero-sum games. The remaining four-fifths deals mostly with the theory of *n*-person games. Again, in Luce and Raiffa, *Games and Decisions,* the one textbook in game theory written for social scientists, only one chapter out of fourteen is concerned with the minimax theorem.[8] In short, it seems entirely unreasonable to reject game theory as a whole simply because of disappointment over applications of the minimax theorem. There are other resources in game theory; none, perhaps, so mathematically elegant, but many doubtless of more direct relevance to social affairs. It is these other resources that I shall tap here. Whether or not they hold as much promise as I hope for a model leading to a genuine science of politics will have to be determined by the reader when he assesses the volume as a whole.

## THE ASSUMPTIONS OF THE MODEL

### The Condition of Rationality

The detailed development of the model of *n*-person games is of course contained in the works of Von Neumann and Morgenstern, McKinsey, and Luce and Raiffa. I shall not repeat it here, although when I draw on details of the model I will, of course, explain what I am doing. But, al-

8. R. Duncan Luce and Howard Raiffa, *Games and Decisions* (New York, John Wiley, 1957).

though the whole model is not restated here, some of its axioms are so controversial that it seems wise to explain the controversy and justify the use of these disputed axioms.

The crucial controversy is, clearly, over the notion of rationality, which Von Neumann and Morgenstern define, perhaps a little loosely, in the beginning of *The Theory of Games*, thus:

> We shall . . . assume that the aim of all participants in the economic system . . . is money, or equivalently a single monetary commodity. This is supposed to be unrestrictedly divisible and substitutable, freely transferable and identical, even in the quantitative sense, with whatever "satisfaction" or "utility" is desired by each participant. . . . The individual who attempts to obtain these respective maxima is also said to act "rationally" [pp. 8–9].

It is true that in the more formal portion of the theory, what is established is a standard of rational behavior (i.e., a technique of maximizing) for one person alone regardless of how others behave; but in applying the standard as part of a model of the economy, the expectation of rationality on the part of all participants reappears.

This is a strong and possibly dubious assumption. We all know of instances in which persons behave as if they prefer less money to more (i.e., strictly irrationally) such as employees who refuse promotion to better paying jobs or entrepreneurs who continue to operate in high-wage areas when they could easily move to low-wage areas or consumers who out of friendship buy from a seller who charges higher prices than his neighboring competitor. It is not clear, however, that such behavior is irrational, for it may be simply a conflict between the utility of money and the utility of other things such as neighborliness and friendship. There is also some experimental evidence which suggests that considerable numbers of people consistently prefer less money to more. Edwards, for example, has shown that in a gambling situation both Harvard undergraduates and Cambridge national guardsmen prefer bets with less expected value and more exciting odds to bets with more expected value and less exciting odds.[9] In their calculations of preference they apparently considered the excitement of the play as well as the monetary rewards and sought to obtain some of both values. Hence, supposedly, they did not behave as the model of economic man assumes they would. As Coombs has shown, however, such inconsistency results, not from a rejection of rewards, but from an attempt to maximize two not necessarily commensurate rewards simultaneously. If subjects (University of Michigan students) are allowed to consider odds and expected value separately, no irrationality appears.[10] Thus irrationality of the sort Edwards supposedly discovered may be a function of the experiment rather than of the people.

One ingenious way of meeting the criticism implied by such (possibly unfair) experiments is to redefine the condition of rationality into an irrefutable tautology. Following the work of Luce and Raiffa, the revised condition may be stated thus:

> *Given a social situation in which exist two alternative courses of action leading to different outcomes and assuming that participants can order these outcomes on a subjective scale of preference, each participant*

9. Ward Edwards, "Probability-Preferences in Gambling," *American Journal of Psychology, 66* (1953), 349–64, and "Probability-Preferences among Bets with Differing Expected Values," *American Journal of Psychology, 67* (1954), 56–67.

10. Clyde H. Coombs and Dean Pruitt, "Components of Risk in Decision-Making: Probability and Variance Preferences," *Journal of Experimental Psychology, 60* (1960), 265–77.

*will choose the alternative leading to the more pre-
ferred outcome.*

In this formulation it is simply asserted that, if a person
can decide what action will suit him best, then he will
choose that action. If, for a particular person, the greatest
satisfaction would come from giving away all his money
and taking a vow of poverty, then that is the action he will
take and it falls within the definition of rationality. Since
the only objective evidence we can gather about other persons' scales of preference is the evidence of their behavior,
the very act of following a chosen course must indicate
that this course led to a preferred outcome. Hence, it follows that all choices leading to action are rational and irrationality would appear to be equivalent to indecision.

The great advantage of this formulation is that it avoids
the obvious pitfall of asserting that individuals' scales of
utility are isomorphic with the scale of some objective
measure such as money or even power. Furthermore, it
changes the nature of the research problem from one
which is possibly beyond human capacity to one which
can at least be broken up into manageable pieces. As Luce
and Raiffa have pointed out, it is no longer necessary to
try to prove the general validity of the notion that men
seek to maximize money or power, when it is already well
known that the statement in its full generality is untrue;
rather the research problem is "to devise suitable empirical
techniques to determine individual preferences," that is,
individual scales of utility.[11]

But there is a disadvantage to this formulation also, for
it weakens the condition to the point that all choices resulting in action are said to be rational. And at this point
the rationality condition becomes no more than the condition for the existence of participants who behave in a
social situation. If the behavior of all participants possesses

11. Luce and Raiffa, p. 50.

the stated characteristics, then the existence of this characteristic is clearly implied in the assertion that participants exist. So if the rationality condition is to be useful in models of behavior, one is forced to go back to the cruder and already somewhat discredited notion of an economic or political man who maximizes a utility that is scaled about the same way as money or power. So the model builder is faced with the problem: How can the rationality condition be stated in such a way that it is more than a tautology but not subject to the criticisms implied in those experiments which show that the scale of individual utility is not the same as a scale of money?

If there is an answer to this question, it must lie, I believe, in the notions of summation and marginality. It must not be asserted that all behavior is rational but rather merely that some behavior is and that this possibly small amount is crucial for the construction and operation of economic and political institutions. But first a note of caution: In referring to the notion of summation I do not mean to support the argument rather commonly used by economists that, although individuals may not maximize, the market appears to be rational because *in sum* the deviations by buyers and sellers tend to "cancel out." The trouble with such an evasion is, of course, the fact that there is no reason to suppose (aside from the well-known symmetry of economics such that every purchase is a sale) that the sum of deviations cancel to zero. It may well be, as, for example, in the instance reported by Edwards, that all deviations are in one direction so that a summation magnifies the deviations rather than eliminating them. Hence, in using the notion of summation, I shall not be attempting this rather mystical arithmetic, but rather simply treating institutions (whose operations consist of many small units of individual behavior) as whole units.

In the dynamics of pricing in a competitive market,

there may be (and often are) sellers who offer at prices markedly different from that on which the market finally settles. Those who sell at less than the stabilized market price or who do not sell at all (and who in both instances may fail to maximize like economic men) may well constitute the vast majority of the sellers. But it is not their behavior that counts; rather it is the action of those sellers who do manage to offer at what turns out to be the stabilized price that, from the supply side, determine the nature of the market. If the market is thus controlled by those persons (possibly a minority) who behave in a maximizing way, then it can be said that the market institution selects and emphasizes rational behavior.

So, I believe, do other institutions, such as election systems, warfare, and other decision-making processes in which several persons must, for the sake of winning, come together for common action without much regard for considerations of ideology or previous friendship. Politics, in the old saw, makes strange bedfellows—and the very strangeness is the triumph of the maximizing motive in some (though far from all) participants. Since elections, warfare, etc., are decision-processes in which the stronger side wins, they place a premium on a side becoming stronger by any means possible which does not too flagrantly violate accepted canons of behavior. (Canons of behavior may be more or less restrictive on the choice of means in coalition-making. Thus a coalition including both the U.S. and the U.S.S.R. was felt to be appropriate in an effort to defeat Hitler but a similar coalition today to control the military use of nuclear energy is felt by the governments of both nations to be inappropriate.) At any rate, these institutions that work by coalitions select and reward with success behavior which is apparently motivated by the intention to maximize power.

(Admittedly power is a rather queer relationship, one

which political scientists have not been able to define in such a way that the full range of common usage is brought into its scientific meaning. One political scientist defines power as the means to force other people to do what they would not otherwise do. Another defines it as the ability to exploit a situation to one's own advantage. A third defines it as the probability of success in a given situation. These definitions are partially overlapping, partially not; and no one has yet seen a way to combine them in one general definition. For this reason, I am inclined to think that the word "power" means so much as to be meaningless. And hence, I prefer a definition of rationality that does not use this imprecise notion. As an alternative, I suggest the notion of winning. What the rational political man wants, I believe, is to win, a much more specific and specifiable motive than the desire for power. Furthermore, the desire to win differentiates some men from others. Unquestionably there are guilt-ridden and shame-conscious men who do not desire to win, who in fact desire to lose. These are the irrational ones of politics. With these in mind, therefore, it is possible to define rationality in a meaningful way without reference to the notion of power. Politically rational man is the man who would rather win than lose, regardless of the particular stakes. This definition accords with the traditional sense of the rational political man having the character of a trimmer and it is consonant with all the previously mentioned definitions of power. The man who wants to win also wants to make other people do things they would not otherwise do, he wants to exploit each situation to his advantage, and he wants to succeed in a given situation.)

Now if in fact the market, election systems, warfare, etc., do place a premium on rational or winning behavior, the condition of rationality may be thus restated in a possibly defensible and certainly nontautological way:

*Given social situations within certain kinds of deci-*
*sion-making institutions (of which parlor games, the*
*market, elections, and warfare are notable examples)*
*and in which exist two alternative courses of action*
*with differing outcomes in money or power or success,*
*some participants will choose the alternative leading*
*to the larger payoff. Such choice is rational behavior*
*and it will be accepted as definitive while the be-*
*havior of participants who do not so choose will not*
*necessarily be so accepted.*

This revised form of the rationality condition can be
verified in only one way: that is, by showing that a model
using it permits the deduction of nonobvious hypotheses
which can themselves be verified by experiment, observation, and prediction. In positive economics (which, I believe, actually uses the rationality condition as here formulated and which is, certainly, the only well-developed
theory of institutions now in existence) the rationality condition has been partially verified by some successful predictions. With respect to other institutions about which
there is almost no positive theory, the condition is neither
verified nor proved false. Some decision about its validity
awaits the development of the kind of theory toward which
a start is attempted in this book. And until a substantial
body of such theory exists, the rationality condition must
be accepted as a necessary assumption in a model which
may or may not turn out to be useful.

There are some writers, however, who on entirely a
priori grounds reject the rationality condition, even in
the modified and more modest form in which I have stated
it. They prefer to reject all models using the condition—
even before they know whether or not the models are useful—because they are so firmly convinced on intuitive
grounds that very few, if any, people seek to maximize
money or to win. In order to allay some of the doubts oc-

casioned by these writers, then, it seems desirable to point out some a priori reasons for believing that the condition is not altogether inapplicable and that some people do actually seek to maximize and to win.

Although our cultural heritage contains many canons of behavior that serve to restrain the impulse to maximize and win, still there is one kind of situation in which these canons are understood not to prevail in quite the same way. This is the fiduciary relation. Therein the consistent choice of more money or power over less or winning over losing is definitely encouraged by a special brand of morality. Of course, many fundamental restrictions on individual behavior apply just about as much to the person qua trustee as to the person qua individual and attempts by trustees to maximize in violation of these canons is just about as self-defeating as similar attempts by individuals who are caught and go to jail. But even these fundamental restrictions undergo some transformation, even softening, in fiduciary relationships so that the fiduciary morality is something different from individual morality.

The one duty of the fiduciary agent is to guard the position of the beneficiary of the trust. And since this is a world of change, "guarding" means more than mere safekeeping. It means as well improving the beneficiary's fortune and position. For this interpretation of the duty, we have not only the authority of law books but also that ultimate source of Western morality, the teachings of Jesus. In the parable of the three servants who were placed in a fiduciary relation when the master, departing on a journey, left five talents with one, two talents with a second, and one talent with a third, the first and second each doubled their money, while the third buried his. On his return the master praised and rewarded the first two, while from the third, by way of condemnation of his sloth, he took the unused talent and gave it to the first. While the metaphorical sense of this parable probably is that one ought to use one's gifts in the service of the Lord, what concerns us here is simply the fact that the parable accepts and builds upon the notion that in mundane affairs the fiduciary's duty is to further as much as possible the beneficiary's interests. Indeed, the parable is nonsense unless its auditors agree that the fiduciary has a special duty. Hence we find, in the very center of the Western ideas of morality, set forth explicitly, albeit rather incidentally, the notion of the trustee as promoter.

One main inference from the parable is that the fiduciary is not permitted the luxury of deciding what is right and wrong. Instead he is given one overriding moral standard: Promote the interests of the beneficiary. In the Western tradition many kinds of behavior which are morally indifferent and even morally approved when performed by individuals are actually culpable when measured by the standard of fiduciary morality. It is, conventionally, a morally indifferent matter if, for example, a farmer produces no more than he himself needs out of land that is wholly his own; but as trustee for a beneficiary, say, a minor nephew, it is conventionally believed that he ought to make the same land produce as much as it will. Again, it is felt to be entirely one's own business if one wastes one's own substance in riotous living or gifts to the poor; but if the substance wasted is the trust fund one manages, one can be prosecuted for either riotous living or charity. With a moral tradition of this sort, a fiduciary agent, given two alternatives of action one of which produces a larger outcome than the other (assuming, of course, equal risk), is morally bound to choose the alternative leading to the larger outcome. That is, the fiduciary agent operates under a duty to behave rationally, a duty that is enforced with legal sanctions.

Not only is the fiduciary morally obligated to maximize

money and to win, but also many of the cultural limitations on maximizing and winning are relaxed in the fiduciary relation. The individual is in the Western tradition
strongly encouraged to give alms to the poor, but this
moral imperative does not exist for the trustee. Penny-
pinching is pejoratively named miserliness when the pennies are one's own; but when the pennies belong to governmental units like school districts or to private eleemos-
ynary institutions like colleges, the erstwhile miser is a
"devoted public servant" or "the man who really keeps
the college alive." Doubtless both kinds of penny-pinching
stem from the same miserly emotions, but in one circumstance it is condemned and in another commended. Most
startling of all such shifts of moral judgment is in the at-
titude toward killing other people. This is held to be
highly illegal almost everywhere when it is done for personal gain or to satisfy personal aggressiveness. But when
done as a soldier in organized warfare for the sake of "the
nation" or "the folks back home," it is acclaimed even to
the point that the best killers get the greatest honors.

So I conclude: Not only are fiduciary agents obligated
to behave rationally but also the alternatives for maximizing and winning are greater for the agent than for the
principal. I pass no judgment on the social value of this
special system of ethics—I simply note that it exists in the
cultural tradition of the West, and probably also of the
East.

The significance of this morality for the condition of
rationality in the game theoretic model is simply this:
Most of the decisions in economics and political life are
made by persons acting in a fiduciary relation. Since the
economy of the modern world in both capitalist and Communist places is dominated by monopolies and oligopolies,
many decisions on prices are made by managers, who are,

of course, agents either for owners or for governments. And so bureaucratic is this economic life that, even if one manager alone might out of gentleness or stupidity attempt to behave irrationally, the bureaucratic checks and balances tend to enforce the obligation to maximize and to win. Political decisions are similarly controlled by agents rather than by their putative principals. There was a time long ago when rulers regarded the realm as their household. But now elected officials are, by reason of the very process of their selection, representatives or agents and even dictators claim to act in the name of "the nation" or "the folk" or "the masses." In democracies, the dialectic among political parties acts as a powerful sanction to enforce the fiduciary morality on politicians who might otherwise behave irrationally and in some dictatorships at least the bureaucracy performs the same enforcement function. (In Hitler's ultimately unsuccessful dictatorship, however, the bureaucracy was not even allowed to encourage rational behavior and this fact is believed by some to explain some of Hitler's fortunately disastrous decisions, such as when, out of an irrational contempt for Slavic peoples, he divided his eastern army, sending some to defeat at Baku and the rest to defeat at Stalingrad.) [12]

If, as seems pretty clear, the fiduciary morality imposes an obligation to behave rationally and if, as also seems pretty clear, most economic and political decisions are made by agents rather than principals, then it must be the case that rational behavior is at least striven for in most areas of business and public life. Since most of the evidence by which the rationality condition is discredited comes from situations where individuals act wholly for

12. Alexander Werth, *The Year of Stalingrad* (New York, Knopf, 1947), p. 202; and George Fischer, *Soviet Opposition to Stalin* (Cambridge, Mass., Harvard University Press, 1952), pp. 176 ff.

themselves (e.g. gambling), it may be quite irrelevant to the kinds of decisions with which politics and economics are mostly concerned. At any rate, as long as the fiduciary morality exists, there seems to be some justification for using models containing the rationality condition, at least until we can discover whether or not they are useful for economic and political science.

## The Zero-Sum Condition

In the game theoretic model generally, there is no need to impose the zero-sum condition, except for the fact that it is essential if one wishes to use the more powerful portion of the mathematics. In the studies to be pursued here, however, the zero-sum condition will be imposed, partially out of mathematical considerations and partially out of a desire to simplify the model. Since the condition has, like the rationality condition, been subjected to much criticism by social scientists, its degree of relevance to the analysis of society deserves some preliminary investigation.

The zero-sum condition is the requirement that the gains of the winners exactly equal in absolute amount the losses of the losers. If there are players 1, 2, . . . , $n$ and if the payoffs to each are real numbers represented by the symbols "$v(1)$," "$v(2)$," . . . , "$v(n)$," then

$$v(1) + v(2) + \ldots + v(n) = 0.$$

Manifestly, if any $v(i)$ is not zero, then some $v(i)$ must be positive and some $v(i)$ must be negative. If, for example, $v(1)$, $v(2)$, . . . , $v(6)$ are positive and $v(7)$, $v(8)$, . . . , $v(n)$ are negative, then

$$\sum_{i=1}^{6} v(i) = - \sum_{i=7}^{n} v(i)$$

(read: "the sum of the values for player $i$, when $i$ ranges over the players numbered one through six, equals the negative of the sum of the values for player $i$, when $i$ ranges over the players numbered seven through $n$).

In application to society the zero-sum condition is the requirement that social situations be abstracted for study in such a way that only the direct conflicts among participants are included and common advantages are ignored. In relation to games themselves, for example, this means that the individual pleasure in exercising skills and the mutual pleasure in companionship are simply not considered as a part of the game situation. Yet these pleasures, perhaps even more than the desire to win, are what generate the game situation to begin with, are what reconcile losers to their losses, and are what induce winners to risk their gains and reputations in repeated engagements. The justification for ignoring such mutual advantages is, of course, that by abstracting only conflict it is possible to concentrate on one important and precisely stated problem, namely, how to win. But does a similar justification apply to other social situations besides games? Can one justifiably study direct political and economic conflict alone without considering the context of cooperation in which the conflict usually occurs?

Although some of the initial enthusiasm for game theory was based on an intuition about the pervasiveness of conflict, longer reflection has led many social scientists to doubt that pure conflict ever occurs. Attempts to apply the minimax theorem to bargaining situations (to which at first it seemed most obviously suited) quickly revealed that bargaining involves some sort of gain for both parties. In the most frequent circumstance—a sale-purchase—both buyer and seller gain at least a portion of their objectives. Hence in the 1950s a theory of two-person non-zero-sum games was created, mostly by economists interested in game theory.[13] Enthusiasm for this new approach, which is less mathematically elegant but more immediately applicable to bargaining circumstances, has even led some to suggest that zero-sum theory should be banished from economics.[14] In a similar way, pure conflict also seems rare in political affairs. As Buchanan and Tullock have pointed out, one very interesting thing about political societies is that people consent to remain in them, even when they are on the losing side in particular decisions. This fact, which has impressed political philosophers at least since the time of Plato and which is the observational basis for the innumerable and drearily repetitious theories of social contract, cannot be expressed in terms of a zero-sum game. When even the losers on a particular decision gain more than their loss by reason of the participation in the society, only a non-zero-sum model can be used. Thus, for the analysis of constitutions, that is, of the continuing association over lifetimes, a model such as that developed by Buchanan and Tulloch out of non-zero-sum theory seems particularly appropriate.

But even though in the long run we all gain from society and civilization, still we do frequently perceive what we imagine to be pure conflict situations. In a sense, we hold the mutual gains as a constant, just as Von Neumann did when he investigated the problem of winning at poker. When we think about roll-calls in a legislature or elections, we ignore the gains that we know will accrue to everyone from the continued existence of civilized society and consider only the immediate problem of winning. Such decisions as those made by voting or fighting have a winner-take-all character. In contrast to money or utility which can be divided up into parts and distributed among

13. See Luce and Raiffa, pp. 88–153, for a review of this theory.
14. See Schelling, pp. 81 ff.

the players of a non-zero-sum game, victory is an indivisible unit. If one person wins, the others do not win. Furthermore, to speak of victors implies the existence, or previous existence, of the vanquished. By emphasis on winning what is often an indivisible prize, in these matters, as in games, the common imagination abstracts pure conflict for which the zero-sum model is entirely appropriate.

Thus, whether or not one should use the zero-sum model depends entirely on the way one's subject is commonly perceived. In discussing bargains, which are perceived as mutual gain, of course a non-zero-sum model is probably best. On the other hand, in discussing elections and wars, which are perceived as requiring indivisible victory, the zero-sum model is probably best and I shall use it here when I wish to talk about these and other essentially political decisions.

# CHAPTER 2

# The Size Principle

In this chapter some notions from the theory of games are used to derive a fundamental principle concerning the size of coalitions. (The argument of the chapter is entirely verbal and quite sketchy. For those who wish a more exact derivation, the size principle is considered in detail in Appendix I.) Specifically, the following statement is derived from the model:

> In n-*person, zero-sum games, where side-payments are permitted, where players are rational, and where they have perfect information, only minimum winning coalitions occur.*

(The precise meaning of the technical terms in this statement will be explained in the subsequent discussion and in Appendix I.)

In the next chapter this statement about behavior in the model will be translated into a descriptive statement, or sociological law, about the natural world and observational evidence will be adduced to verify it:

> In social situations similar to n-*person, zero-sum games with side-payments, participants create coali-*

*tions just as large as they believe will ensure winning and no larger.*

At first glance this law may seem an obvious truism. "Common sense" might argue that the greater the number of losers, the greater the sum of their losses and hence the greater the gains of the winners. Or conversely, the fewer the winners, the more each can expect to win. But if one considers that Downs, *An Economic Theory of Democracy,* one of the few significant attempts to develop a formal, positive political theory and certainly one of the half-dozen outstanding works of political theory in this century,[1] is based on two axioms, one of which is in partial contradiction with the just-stated law, then the nonobvious character of the generalization is apparent. Downs assumed that political parties (a kind of coalition) seek to maximize votes (membership). As against this, I shall attempt to show that they seek to maximize only up to the point of subjective certainty of winning. After that point they seek to minimize, that is, to maintain themselves at the size (as subjectively estimated) of a minimum winning coalition.

## A SKETCH OF THE CONTENT OF THE THEORY OF GAMES

Without entering here into the intricacies of the theory of games, it is still possible to indicate in outline both the nature of the model and the route by which the size principle is derived from it.[2]

While in popular speech the word "game" is ambiguous (referring, as it does, both to a set of rules and to the play

1. Anthony Downs, *An Economic Theory of Democracy* (New York, Harper, 1957).

2. For a more detailed introduction to the theory of games, see Luce and Raiffa, *Games and Decisions,* which is written especially for social scientists, and, on a more technical level, McKinsey, *Introduction to the Theory of Games.*

of a particular match under these rules), in the theory of games the word "game" refers only to the set of rules themselves. "The game is simply the totality of rules which describe it," say Von Neumann and Morgenstern. Particular matches are "plays" of the game. The rules specify the *number of players,* the *moves* (that is, the occasions on which each player can act—note that a move is an occasion for choice, not the choice itself), the *set of alternatives* from which each player can choose at each move, each player's *state of information* at each move (that is, the amount he can know about the choices made at previous moves by each player and by chance), the amount of *collusion* permissible among players, and the *payoff* (that is, the gains and losses for each player for every possible arrangement of choices at the several moves).

It is possible to classify games into categories created around each one of these features of rules. Thus, categorizing about the payoff, games can be zero-sum or non-zerosum; categorizing about the state of information, in some games players may have perfect information (that is, they know all the choices made at previous moves) or they may not; categorizing about the amount of collusion permitted, in some games players can reach private agreements about the division of the payoff (i.e. side-payments) and in other games they cannot; categorizing about the number of players, games may be one-person, two-person, . . . , *n*-person; etc., etc. There has been much controversy, some of it quite irrelevant, about which set of categories is in some sense "fundamental" and which categories are most deserving of study. To resolve this controversy, I simply assert that, as a strategy of model-building with ultimate reference to understanding society, the categories most immediately useful for the social sciences are those involving the number of players.

Von Neumann and Morgenstern distinguish sharply

among games according to the kinds of problems that arise with differing numbers of players. In one-player games, the problem is simply that of maximizing gains against a given range of chance in nature (pp. 86–87). And nature is assumed to be neither benevolent nor malevolent, but simply indifferent. In two-person games, the problem for each player lies in getting along with or getting the best of somebody else, at least assuming there is some conflict of interest. And when the two-person game is also zero-sum, then the conflict of interest is total. Each player is, of course, seeking to maximize, but his maximization is against an opponent who is similarly seeking to maximize against him. Hence maximization against a malevolent rather than indifferent opponent is the concern for both players. In three-or-more-person games, the problem lies in the parallelism of interest. Conflict exists, of course, especially when the game is zero-sum, but it is a conflict complicated by the possibilities of alliance and collusion. In the one-person game, the activity of the player is to choose a technique of maximization. In two-person games, the activity of the players is to select a *strategy* (that is, a complete plan of choices to be made at each move) such that the player guarantees himself at least as much as the amount that his opponent can hold him down to if his opponent uses his best strategy. And in the three-or-more-person game, the main activity of the players is to select not only strategies, but partners. Partners, once they become such, then select a strategy.

Since the concern in this book is with coalitions, which are partnerships, we shall limit our discussion to three-or-more-person games (or more conveniently, "$n$-person" games). What, basically, we wish to know about such games is the kind of coalitions that will be formed. For a given $n$, there are $2^n$ possible coalitions (including, for formal and exhaustive description, the coalition with all players and the coalition with no players). If all of these coalitions are equally likely, then there is little point to further analysis. But from everyday experience we know that persons in real situations analogous to $n$-person games do not seriously consider the formation of each and every one of the $2^n$ possible coalitions. Evidently there are some restraints operating on such persons so that the actual choice among coalitions is limited. The task of $n$-person game theory is to specify similar restraints in the model in the hope that they can then be discovered in reality. More hopefully still, the theory will define sufficient restraints so that one and only one coalition is left. Were that goal to be attained, then for every real situation analogous to an $n$-person game it would be possible to assert that a one best coalition exists. Unfortunately, while a number of restraints have been defined and discovered, no one has been able—perhaps because it is impossible—to define restraints to eliminate all but one coalition.

In the discussion of limits on coalition-making, Von Neumann and Morgenstern devised two main concepts: *characteristic function* and *imputation*. A characteristic function, referred to by the symbol "$v(S)$," is the statement of the total payment to each coalition possible in the game. The relevance of this notion to limitations on coalition-formation is obvious: If, in specifying the list of payments to coalitions, it is apparent that some coalitions are distinctly more profitable than others, then it can, provisionally, be supposed that, ceteris paribus, the less profitable ones will not be considered by the players. There is more in the players' universe of interests, however, than the payoff to coalitions. Each player is, in addition, and more significantly, interested in the payoff to himself. For the discussion of this consideration, there is available the concept of an imputation, which is referred to by the symbol "$\overset{\rightarrow}{\alpha}$". An imputation is a list of the payments to each player in a given structure of coalitions. If the set of $n$ players is divided up into disjunct or nonoverlapping subsets so that each player belongs to some subset (even if it contains no other player besides himself), each such division is a coalition structure or a partition. While the number of possible partitions is very large, much larger, of course, than the number of possible coalitions—the same coalition can appear in many distinct partitions—still it is finite. But for each partition there is an infinity of possible imputations. Presumably, however, only some of these several infinities of possibilities are considered by the players owing to the fact than many of the imputations are less advantageous than others for some selected subset of the players. Hence, if one can put limitations on the admissible imputations, that is, on the imputations that will be seriously considered by the players, then one also puts limitations on the process of coalition-making—inasmuch as imputations are related to particular partitions into coalitions.

Most of the discussion of coalition-making has heretofore centered on imputations. Von Neumann and Morgenstern devised a "solution" of $n$-person games which consisted of a limitation on admissible imputations and hence of a specification of admissible coalition structures. Unfortunately, this limitation did not result in either a unique winning coalition or a unique imputation. They said, in effect, that there is a certain set of imputations or divisions of gains and losses, each one of which is associated with a different particular coalition-structure and any one of which is a reasonable outcome for rational players to arrive at. Much dissatisfaction has been expressed with the concept of a solution, however, because for some games there is no set of "equally desirable" imputations and for other games the set is infinite. Hence, other writers have sought to impose other limitations. Luce, for example, suggested that, from a given coalition structure with a given imputation, only certain restricted changes in structure be regarded as admissible.[3] (For example, in some Western European parliaments in recent years, it has been an unwritten rule that cabinet-selecting coalitions not include the Communist party even though it might be quite large. Thus, winning coalitions including the members of this party were effectively prohibited.) As Luce has pointed out, however, his notion of specific restrictions on change (which he called "$\psi$-stability") depends on the specific sociological conditions of each game and is not much help as a general limitation on coalition-structure and imputations. For another example, Milnor has devised some definitions of "reasonable" outcomes, which are limits on admissible imputations, somewhat, but not quite, in the spirit of Von Neumann and Morgenstern's limitations.[4] The net effect of a study of these attempts to limit the number of admissible imputations is to leave one with a sense of dissatisfaction. Not enough limitations have been successfully imposed to limit the possibilities in a way that admits of useful application in the study of real coalition-making. It may be, of course, that the reasonable outcomes in an $n$-person model or an $n$-person real situation are in fact so numerous and diverse that systematic analysis and prediction is impossible. But it may also be that game theorists have not asked the questions most useful to social scientists and that by exclusive emphasis on the attempt

3. See R. Duncan Luce, "A Definition of Stability for $N$-Person Games," *Annals of Mathematics, 59* (1954), 357–66. This notion is explained in nontechnical terms in Luce and Raiffa, pp. 166–68, 220–36. An institutional explanation and application of the notion is to be found in R. Duncan Luce and Arnold A. Rogow, "A Game-Theoretic Analysis of Congressional Power Distributions for a Stable Two-Party System," *Behavioral Science, 1* (1956), 83–95.

4. J. W. Milnor, "Reasonable Outcomes for $N$-Person Games," *Research Memorandum RM-916,* The Rand Corporation, 1952. This publication is not generally available; fortunately, however, it is summarized and criticized in Luce and Raiffa, pp. 237–45.

to delimit admissible imputations they have overlooked the possibility of delimiting coalition-structures directly.

## SOME LIMITS ON CHARACTERISTIC FUNCTIONS

Assuming that the latter is the case and that useful information may be obtained by a study of characteristic functions somewhat in isolation from imputations, an effort is made in Appendix I to analyze, verbally rather than mathematically, the consequence for the size of winning coalitions, and hence for the coalition-structure, of restrictions on characteristic functions. Limiting the game model to that of the $n$-person, zero-sum game with perfect information and with side-payments permitted, the main features and conclusions of the argument in the Appendix can be summarized thus:

1. Let the sum of what the winners gain be equal to the sum of what the losers lose. (This is the zero-sum condition.)

2. When a coalition includes everybody, the winners gain nothing simply because there are no losers. Note: It must be assumed—and this is a highly significant assumption—that the members of a winning coalition have control over additional entries into their coalition. If they have no such control, all losers could invariably join the winners and thereby both produce a valueless coalition of the whole and nullify the winners' victory.

3. The worst a player can do is to enter a coalition of himself alone. The rationale of this assumption is that, if other players in a coalition try to force some one player to lose more than the amount he would lose alone, he can always avoid this result by resigning from the coalition and forming a coalition of himself only. Customarily this maximum loss is designated by the symbol $-\gamma$.

4. A coalition of all but one of the players can win at

most the amount $\gamma$ inasmuch as there is only one loser.

5. Let a *winning coalition* be defined as one which is as large as or larger than some size arbitrarily stated in the rules. All coalitions that are not winning are either *blocking* or *losing*. The complement of a winning coalition is a losing one. The complement of a blocking coalition is a blocking coalition. A *minimum winning coalition* is one which is rendered blocking or losing by the subtraction of any member.

6. If there are $n$ players in the game, a winning coalition of $k$ players, where $k$ is some arbitrary number, can win at most $\gamma\,(n - k)$. That is, the best a coalition can do is collect the sum of the maximum that each of the players outside the winning coalition can lose. But the structure of the game may be such that the winning coalition can only win less than the maximum amount.

7. The diagram in Figure 1 describes the possible ways that the values of the characteristic function for winning coalitions can be arranged in any $n$-person game. On the horizontal axis is measured the size of winning coalitions from the minimum size, $m$, to the maximum size, $n$. On the vertical axis is measured the amount won by the coalition. By reason of statement 2, the measurements on the vertical axis start with zero; by reason of statement 3 the entry next above zero is $\gamma$; by reason of statement 5, the highest entry is $\gamma\,(n - m)$. The line from point $(0, \gamma\,(n - m))$ on the vertical axis to point $(n, 0)$ on the horizontal axis connects a series of points, each one of which is a maximum value or (maximum payoff to) a coalition of a given size, that is $\gamma\,(n - k)$. All similar lines connecting values of winning coalitions for any game must lie within the space enclosed by the two axes and the line from point $(0, \gamma\,(n - m))$ to point $(n, 0)$. Examples of such lines are shown in Figure 1. Note that the lines may have positive,

negative, or zero slopes, that is, as one moves from left to right, they may slope upward (positive) or downward (negative) or they may run parallel (zero slope) to the horizontal axis.

8. Given these possibilities of shapes for the lines connecting points of the characteristic function in the range of winning coalitions, one wishes to know if, for various

## FIGURE 1

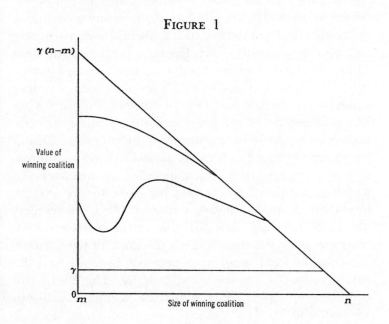

classes of shapes, there is any restriction on the kind of coalitions that will be formed among rational players. Define a coalition, *S,* as *realizable* if $v(S)$ is such that rational players will accept it. On the other hand, define a coalition, *S,* as *unrealizable* if the $v(S)$ is such that rational players will not accept it. Divide the possible shapes for the line of the characteristic function into three classes:

1. Those with negative slope throughout,
2. Those with portions having a zero slope,
3. Those with some portions having a positive slope.

Considering class 1, it is apparent that, for any coalition larger than minimum, its members can, by ejecting one or more of their members, increase the amount to be divided among them. Since the ejection is presumably costless, in such a game only minimum winning coalitions can be expected to occur. Hence only minimum winning coalitions are realizable. Considering class 2, members of a winning coalition the value of which lies on a portion of the line where the slope to adjacent values is zero, can by ejecting members make it possible to divide the fixed winnings among fewer people and thereby increase the gain of at least one member of the winning coalition. Since the complement (i.e., the losing coalition) of the winning coalition is presumably trying to break it up and to form an alternative winning coalition which includes its members, the winning coalition has a strong incentive to prevent the formation of an alternative coalition. This the winners can do by reducing their coalition to the minimum winning size, or to the size at which the slope to the adjacent value on the left is positive or negative, in which case the considerations of classes 1 and 3 apply. The alternative considerations aside, only minimum winning coalitions are realizable for class 2. Considering class 3, note first that any jaggedness in the shape of the line may be smoothed out, owing to the fact that players in a winning coalition can expand to the size at which the value is greatest and need not stop increasing at some intermediate point. Thus, if the actual graph of the characteristic function is as pictured in Figure 2, one may simplify this to that pictured in Figure 3. (Of course, if the line is as pictured in Figure 4, it can be smoothed into a case falling in class 1.)

If a winning coalition is at some size equal to or greater than $m$ but less than $k$, it can costlessly add members and increase its value up to size $k$. Since it is in a dictatorial position, it can be expected to do so. On the other hand, it will not expand beyond $k$ in size, for to do so would bring into play the considerations mentioned in the discussion of class 1. Thus for games in class 3, only coalitions at the maximum of $v(S)$ are realizable and the maximum of $v(S)$ does not occur at size $m$.

FIGURE 2

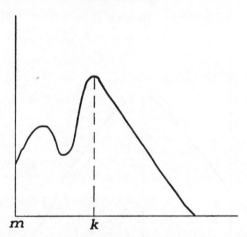

9. The analysis in the previous paragraph permits the statement of a condition to identify, when it appears in nature, a game for which the characteristic function for winning coalitions has a positive slope and a maximum value at some size other than $m$. This condition is: *Even though the members of a winning coalition know they have indeed formed a winning coalition, they keep on adding members until they have reached some specific size larger than the minimum.*

10. The condition in paragraph 9 is extraordinarily re-

strictive. No natural social situations with which I am familiar exhibit it, although of course such situations might conceivably be created in the laboratory. (It is true that members of winning coalitions try to increase the size of their coalition, when the members do not know they have made a winning coalition. But that is an entirely different matter to be considered in Chapter 4. And it is also true that in some kinds of natural situations—e.g. roll-calls in legislative bodies—the members of a winning coalition do not fully control admission to the coalition, so

FIGURE 3

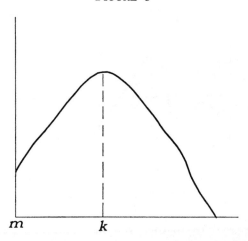

$m$        $k$

that some prospective losers can minimize their loss by joining the winners. But again, this is a different matter, exhibiting no more than the obvious consequences of the failure to meet the condition, mentioned in paragraph 2, of control over admissions.) The high degree of restrictiveness of the condition stated in paragraph 9 is perhaps more vividly revealed if it is stated this way. For a natural situation modeled as a game in which the slope of the characteristic function is positive in the winning range and in which the maximum $v(S)$ is at some size larger than the minimum, there must be (a) a smaller majority which is required under the rules but which is never arrived at in play and (b) a larger majority which is not mentioned in the rules but is invariably arrived at in the play. In other words, players who know they have won may not be content with winning but must continue to build up their coalition to the larger majority. There may exist in nature some situations that display these features, but if they do exist, they are so rare and obscure that one who has searched diligently to find them has been unable to do so.

FIGURE 4

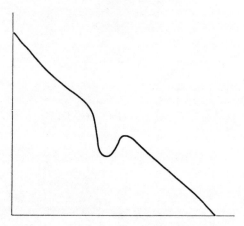

As the argument in Appendix I (pp. 247 ff.) indicates, the most commonly used rules for the division of the winnings among the winners in games in which $v(S)$ has in part a positive slope lead to paradoxical results. That is, although a coalition with the maximum $v(S)$ is said to be realizable, with these rules, however, only minimum winning coalitions are realizable. This paradox suggests that even in the abstract such games are difficult to imagine and in concrete reality are probably nonexistent. I conclude, therefore, that little is lost by assuming that $n$-person, zero-sum social situations can always be represented by games in which the graph of the characteristic function in the range of winning coalitions has a negative or zero slope. And if one assumes that only class 1 and class 2 games appear in nature, then one may say further that, among rational players with perfect information, only minimum winning coalitions occur. While this conclusion, which is the assertion with which the chapter started, does not pick out a one best coalition or in any way provide a solution for $n$-person games, it does serve as the base, as I believe the following chapters will demonstrate, for a nonobvious sociological law—the size principle—which can be tested by empirical methods.

CHAPTER 3

# Evidence about the Size Principle

Whether or not the just-stated conclusion is of any scientific value depends on whether or not an analogous statement about the real world can be verified. The analogous statement is:

> *In social situations similar to n-person, zero-sum games with side-payments, participants create coalitions just as large as they believe will ensure winning and no larger.*

For convenience, this statement will be referred to as the *size principle*.

In the model, it was assumed that players had perfect information, that is, that they knew precisely who belonged to which coalition. With this knowledge they could, of course, aim at creating exactly minimum winning coalitions. In almost no situations in the natural world, however, do participants possess such extensive or certain information. At best the manager of a bill in a legislature, the candidate seeking office, or the diplomat assessing an alliance can only estimate the degree of loyalty of his allies and often he does not know certainly how many allies he actually has until after a decision has been made. In order to take account of this fact about the real world, therefore, the notion of an actually minimum winning coalition must be supplanted by the notion of a subjectively estimated minimum one. Otherwise the conditions of the model need not be weakened, even the condition of rationality.

But this one change renders verification extraordinarily difficult. Since the members of a winning coalition may be uncertain about whether or not it is winning, they may in their uncertainty create a coalition larger than the actually minimum winning size. When this occurs, the members cannot be said to have behaved irrationally for their behavior can be interpreted as a purely rational attempt to ensure that they win rather than lose. In the (possibly misapplied) words of Pastor Tyndale, words spoken in defense of the tyranny of Henry VIII and words drilled into me as an elementary principle of politics by Professor McIlwain: "It is better to have somewhat than to be clean stripped out of altogether." In short, the rejection of an optimal payoff in favor of a subjectively certain payoff may be regarded as a rational act of maximization in an uncertain world.

Conversely, the mere fact that minimum winning coalitions do actually appear in the real world is not good evidence that the members of them were behaving rationally. In every situation in which two sides oppose each other for an indivisible victory in a decision, the maneuvering of each to make itself a winning coalition may result in the—essentially accidental—occurrence of a minimum. Simply that one occurs does not preclude the possibility that its members would have allowed it to grow to a nonoptimal size had they been able to do so, although it may perhaps suggest that the decision-system forces rationality on them.

Owing to these considerations, given some oversized winning coalitions, it is seldom possible to distinguish between those occasioned by irrational motives such as loyalty and those occasioned by a rational intention to ensure "somewhat." Conversely, given some actually minimum winning coalitions, it is seldom possible to distinguish between those deliberately planned and those occurring by accident of maneuver. And this feature of analysis renders verification extraordinarily difficult.

There is some experimental evidence collected for testing another theory of coalition-formation which tends to support the size principle. The theory in question, Caplow's, is similar to the dynamic theory set forth in Chapter 6, below, and a detailed comparison of the two theories is to be found in the note to Table 1 of that chapter. The main difference is, interestingly, that Caplow does not fully perceive the significance of size. Vinacke and Arkoff, seeking to test Caplow's theory, found it in error in exactly that point at which it conflicted with the size principle. Where Caplow predicted either a minimum winning coalition or a slightly larger one, the minimum one occurred two-thirds of the 88 times the experiment was run.[1] This evidence is indirect, however, and much more of this kind of experimentation is necessary before one can have confidence in the results.

I have made some attempt to distinguish among kinds of winning coalitions in small groups, but I regard my results as even less definitive than those of Vinacke and Arkoff. Indeed, these results are not even very relevant to the size principle, but I report them here simply for the indications they give of some directions for further re-

1. Theodore Caplow, "A Theory of Coalitions in the Triad," *American Sociological Review, 21* (1956), 489–93; and W. E. Vinacke and A. Arkoff, "Experimental Study of Coalitions in the Triad," *American Sociological Review, 22* (1957), 406–15.

search. One experiment involved a three-person, zero-sum
game, which college students were hired to play in order
to study not the size of the coalitions but the range of imputations. Since its rules permitted only one size for a
winning coalition, namely, two persons, naturally the
problem of arriving at a minimum did not arise. All coalitions arrived at were necessarily minimum. Nevertheless,
it quickly became apparent that factors were present in the
bargaining which would probably have led, in a larger
game, to nonoptimal coalitions. The game can be described briefly thus:

1. Each of the three players was given two dollars for
   playing capital for three to five plays of the game.
   (It was assumed, doubtless improperly, that the
   utility of money was approximately equal for all
   the players.)
2. The players were instructed that, after several ses-
   sions of face-to-face negotiations between each pair
   of players, they would be asked to choose another
   player as a partner. If two players chose each other,
   the third player would be required to give the
   pair fifty cents, which the members of the pair
   could divide in the way they chose during the
   negotiations. If no players chose each other, then
   no payoffs were to be made.

This game was played from three to five times per group
and the negotiations were tape recorded. (The players
knew, of course, that their conversations were recorded,
but since the experiments were conducted in the relaxed
atmosphere of a fraternity house, the obviousness of the
recording did not, I believe, seriously influence either
their behavior or their conversation.) Though the number
of games played were far too few to support any definitive
conclusion, it appeared to those who heard the tapes that

only in those groups in which the players knew each other quite well—well enough to treat the experiment entirely as play—was there a serious attempt to maximize. When the players were only slightly acquainted prior to the game—since this was done in a small college, all knew each other at least by sight—then there seemed to be a very strong tendency to form a three-person coalition against the experimenter so that each player could take home exactly the two dollars he was given as original capital. This coalition against the experimenter usually took the form of a master plan for three plays or trials of the game: The players agreed that player 1 would lose on trial one, that player 2 would lose on trial two, that player 3 would lose on trial three, etc. In other words, the only slightly acquainted players placed a higher subjective utility on avoiding possible future animosities and conflicts than they did on the one or two additional dollars they could acquire by rational play. In short, they refused to perceive this as a zero-sum situation and proceeded to imbed it in the much larger situation of college life. Thus they did not have the motives assumed by the theory. I think it likely that in the decision-making of most small groups similar motives are regularly called into play. Especially in small groups making genuine decisions rather than playing what they know is a game, considerations of maintaining the solidarity of the group and the loyalty of members to it probably often dominate considerations of maximum victory on particular decisions. In general it is quite possible that participants in small groups seldom, if ever, perceive situations arising in the group as zero-sum. If so, then little evidence relevant to the size principle is to be found in the study of small groups.

For what it is worth, however, I report an additional experiment, if it can be so called, involving a five-person parlor game in which the object of the players is to form a winning coalition to take an amount of money specified in the course of the play away from the losers. In brief outline this game, called Talleyrand, consists of the following rules: [2]

1. There are five players whose object is to form a winning coalition of three or more players to take money from the losers.

2. The first player, chosen by chance, proposes to take an amount, $a_1$, from each loser and at the same time passes notes offering amounts, $b_{1,2}$, $b_{1,3}$, $b_{1,4}$, $b_{1,5}$, to other players to join him in the coalition (the first number of the subscript of $b$ refers to the offering player; the second to the receiving player). By making offers, he becomes a "leader." The second player in a clockwise direction responds by (1) accepting 1's offer by passing a note of acceptance, or (2) leading a new coalition in the manner just described for player 1, or (3) acting as if he were a leader when in fact he is accepting 1's offer. Players 3, 4, and 5 have the same options with respect to offers as do players 1 and 2. All offers are for one full round of moves unconditionally binding on the leader if and only if the coalition actually forms during that round; but acceptances are not binding on the accepting players.

3. Once each player has had a move of this sort, the first player has the option of announcing a coalition. If the members of his coalition agree that it exists, then the announcer collects $a_1$ from each loser and pays $b_{1i}$, $b_{1j}$, etc. If the members do not agree, 1 forfeits the amount $a_1$ to the pot where it may subsequently be claimed by the leader of the winning coalition. After this forfeiture, 1 may

2. *Talleyrand,* copyright 1958 by William H. Riker.

move in the fashion described for player 2 in paragraph 2 above. During the second and third rounds of moves each leader has the option of announcing a winning coalition if he chooses, collecting $a_i$ and paying $b_{ij}$ if it forms and forfeiting $a_i$ if it does not.

4. A hand consists of at most three rounds of moves. If no winning coalition has been formed in a hand, all leaders must forfeit to the pot the amounts $a_i$ and the money in the pot remains for the next hand of the game. In the second hand, player 2 must start the play; in the third hand, player 3; etc.

As is indicated by these rules, the excitement of the play is enhanced by the restrictions on communication so that leaders are never certain whether their offers have been accepted and no player knows just what offers have been made to others by others. I have induced many friends to play this game, and they have, of course, approached it as entertainment rather than as a serious enterprise. Again the number of matches for which records were kept is too few to admit of generalization. One feature, however, is interesting: At no time did any player even attempt to form a coalition larger than three persons. Since they all clearly understood this to be entertainment, however, their consistent attempts to behave rationally must, I fear, be understood in terms of their temporary release from the obligations of maintaining polite society.

If behavior in small groups is not likely to produce much information about behavior under the zero-sum condition, evidence about the usefulness of a model containing it must be found in the behavior of persons in large groups. Here it is probably impossible to obtain experimental evidence and one must rely on observation. And in this circumstance it is even more difficult to distinguish between intentional (i.e. certainly irrational) and accidental (i.e. possibly rational) excess majorities. There is, however, one kind of situation in large groups in which the observer is able to bypass this difficulty. Occasionally in the operation of institutions conceived of as zero-sum, it happens that a winning coalition becomes much over-sized, perhaps as a result of purely adventitious influences. Presumably, then, the leaders are subjectively convinced that they have more in the coalition than they need to win. Their conviction is, of course, a certainty if their winning coalition is a coalition of the whole or a grand coalition. When this occurs one would expect, if the size principle is a valid description of behavior, that they would make strenuous efforts to reduce their oversized coalition in the direction of a minimum winning one. To the extent that they do in fact so behave, the size principle is verified and confidence is increased in the validity of the model. Conversely, to the extent that they do not so be-have, the principle is proved false and confidence in the model is shown to be unjustified. So I now turn to an examination of some instances of overwhelming majorities in what are popularly conceived of as zero-sum situations.

### OVERWHELMING MAJORITIES IN AMERICAN POLITICS

The evidence that I am about to offer is rather more compelling than may at first appear to persons accustomed to the anecdotal method so customarily used in the dis-cussion of historical examples. I have devised two classes of situations in which coalitions of the whole have been formed by reason of some accidental circumstance. Then I have shown that in *every* instance in these two classes of events the size of the coalition of the whole, which, ac-cording to the theory, has no value, has been reduced to a smaller size that has some value. Thus the validity of the size principle has been *proved* for these two classes and, to the degree that these classes are representatively drawn from zero-sum situations, it is strongly implied that the size principle holds in all other classes of events likely to occur in the situations from which these classes are drawn.

To begin, I shall assume that American politics on a national scale, where the stakes are the control of the decisions by the national government, is popularly perceived as a zero-sum situation. It is, of course, true that in many parts of the system there are institutions which, clearly, operate as non-zero-sum. Many decision-making bodies in local government, for example, are operated as if the participants believed their body was in competition with other local bodies for the control of governments at a higher level. Again these local bodies are often operated as small groups in which considerations of loyalty and local solidarity outweigh rational calculations of advantage. Even at the state level, governments may be perceived as non-zero-sum (e.g., in the black belt of the South, where the really zero-sum game is between the government controlled absolutely by whites and the Negroes outside the governmental system). But in general at the national level, politics is perceived as zero-sum, at least in times of Presidential elections with their indivisible victory and other bifurcating features. As a consequence of the extreme zero-sum interpretation of national politics, such non-zero-sum notions as a bipartisan foreign policy are in practice difficult to entertain or apply. The minority inevitably believes it is ignored, which is, of course, evidence of the zero-sum perception. And so, even though there admittedly are many non-zero-sum situations in American politics, I shall assume that at the highest level politics is perceived as zero-sum. On that assumption, it is legitimate to use instances of overwhelming majorities at the highest level as a test of the size principle.

There have been three instances in the history of American politics when one of the two major parties substantially disappeared. These instances are: the "era of good feeling" (ca. 1820); the period after 1852 when the Whig party dissolved; and the period around 1872 when the Democratic party substantially disappeared from Presidential politics. While there have been other occasions of overwhelming victories (e.g. the Presidential elections of 1920 and 1936), none of these have involved the substantial disappearance of the losing coalition. Hence I limit the discussion to those three instances that involve a coalition of the whole or of what was for all practical purposes the whole. Although these three are gross events involving a vast amount of actors and action, still I shall try to analyze them briefly according to the following scheme: (1) the occasion for the disappearance of the losing coalition and (2) the action of the winning coalition with regard to its excess majority.

After the election of 1816, the Federalist party almost entirely disappeared from American politics, leaving the Republican or Jeffersonian party as almost a grand coalition. It is popularly said that the Federalist party was discredited and laid open to dismemberment by the fact that some of its leaders appeared to be traitors during the War of 1812. But other parties have had to put up with accusations of treason and have survived and prospered (e.g. the Democratic party after the Civil War and in more recent times). So one finds it difficult to attribute all the defections from Federalism to the facts that some of its leaders attended the Hartford Convention and that some Federalist governors refused to prosecute the war with proper diligence. Rather, I believe, the main events in the decline of Federalism had already occurred when the war broke out. The accusations of treason simply helped to finish off an already debilitated coalition. What hurt the party much worse than the war was the admission from 1796 on of a number of trans-Appalachian states and the gradual broadening of the right of suffrage in both the new states and the old. Without entering into the (possibly fruitless) controversy over precisely what ideologies and interests were gathered into the Federalist and Republican coalitions in the 1790s, it is apparent that the Federalist coalition was clearly a winning one in terms of the number of participants in the first part of the decade. The anti-Federalists and later the Jeffersonians, seeing that they could not win, managed to change the whole substance of politics by doubling (perhaps tripling) the number of participants. In the terminology of the model they changed games from $\Gamma$, an $n$-person game they couldn't win, to $\Gamma'$, a $2n$- or $3n$-person game they could win. Since the trans-Appalachian states were mostly organized by Republicans and since the new voters in the original states were more frequently Republican than Federalist, the dominance—and increasing degree of dominance—of the Republican coalition was ensured as it moved into larger and larger games. The only way in which the Federalists might have remained a winning coalition was by refashioning their ideology and recompromising their interests. This they refused or were unable to do and in this sense may be said to have behaved irrationally, thus almost by default permitting repeated Republican victories.

As a consequence of the disintegration of the party after 1816, the Republican party became for a number of years almost a coalition of the whole. According to the model, such a coalition wins nothing and I think it may reasonably be said that no national policy of which a substantial minority disapproved was devised or adopted during the administrations of Monroe and John Q. Adams. (The possible exception is the Monroe Doctrine, which, however, was not so much a national policy as a unilteral declaration by one official. Otherwise the crowning piece of legislation of this period is the compromise of 1820, by which it was agreed that no one would win, at least on the sectional issue.) As might be expected the grand coalition dissolved into a disorganized mélange of blocking coalitions. Most of Monroe's second administration was devoted to maneuvering by the factions of Crawford, Adams, Clay, and Jackson for control of a valueless coalition. This kind of maneuvering—I hesitate to call it an $n$-person game for the players (i.e. factions) were so disorganized—continued on through Adams' administration, with the gradual emergence of Jackson as the victor. So it may be said that when Jackson took office in 1829, he had command of a relatively valueless coalition to which nearly everybody claimed to belong. This is the situation Tocqueville described when he said that the "great parties" (i.e. Federalist and Republican) had been replaced with "minor parties." [3]

But at the very time Tocqueville observed this, Jackson was engaged in reshaping his grand coalition into a minimal winning one. While of course he could not carry through the kind of analysis undertaken here, still he could and did sense that nothing could be achieved without a loyal and devoted set of allies. And it turned out in practice that the only way he could obtain these was by expelling some lukewarm friends from the grand coalition. Viewed in this light some of the events of Jackson's administration that heretofore have been viewed as trivial or embarrassing are seen actually to be the crucial events of his revival of the two-party system.

In the American imagination Jackson is the great democrat. And this he was in the sense that he appreciated the folk. But he was not a simple citizen among citizens. He shared with Washington, it is true, a pride in playing the

3. Alexis de Tocqueville, *Democracy in America*, ed. by Phillips Bradley (2 vols. New York, Knopf, 1945), *1*, 175 ff.

role of Cincinnatus; but he also modeled himself on the great Whig lords. From the time of the battle of New Orleans, Jackson knew he was the chief man in the West, the magnate of the frontier, its greatest landowner, its greatest horse breeder, its greatest captain, its greatest representative. Thus occurred this curious combination: a man of the people with a sense of honor as delicate as a Tuscan count's. And it is exactly this combination of qualities that Jackson used to minimize his winning coalition. What Jackson asked of the people in his coalition was not primarily that they agree on a particular policy (although he asked that often enough) but rather that they agree with him. He expected first of all intense personal loyalty, which, since he was Old Hickory and a truly charismatic leader, was not an unmeetable demand. And so whenever he drew a line and asked all those who would be counted his friends to step over on his side of it, he was using his personal honor as a means of tightening up and rendering more valuable his winning coalition. It made very little difference to Jackson, apparently, and hence to politics generally, whether the line concerned the snubbing of Mrs. Eaton or South Carolina's nullification. I suspect, in fact, that the pro- and anti-Jackson controversy centered more on Clay's motion of censure and Benton's motion to expunge than on any other events in that time. Some historians have called these affairs trivial features of the fight over the bank. But in the interpretation offered here, it is these that are politically significant and the bank issue that is a trivial adjunct to the really serious business of creating a coalition that could win something. It did not in fact win much under Jackson and Van Buren; but in the hands of many state leaders and later in the hands of Polk this almost minimal winning coalition possessed real value, sufficient to fructify the Jacksonian ideals.

The second instance of an overwhelming majority occurred when the Whig party disintegrated after 1852. In a sense the Jacksonian coalition succeeded so well that it destroyed its opposition. Actually, however, it was not quite as simple as this. The particular conformation of the Jacksonian coalition (that is, its intersectional alliances among urban and rural, frontier and sea coast, native and foreign-born) rendered it almost invulnerable. When it lost strength in Virginia, for example, it gained strength in Illinois. When it lost in North Carolina, it gained in Pennsylvania. Furthermore, while it was a minimal winning coalition among the generations of the 1830s and 1840s, the young people, who in the American system have usually shown a predilection for the winners, made it a gigantic coalition in the 1850s. The Whigs, a minority to begin with and fighting on all fronts, faced an almost insuperable task. With its supple and subtle intersectional ties, the Democracy would probably have been beaten only in exactly the way it eventually was, namely, by a party and ideology so thoroughly sectional that it could upset the Democracy's intersectionalism. This, however, the Whig party could not do because it also was committed to an intersectional alliance. For the opponents of the Democracy, therefore, it was necessary to abandon Whiggery and construct a new and deliberately sectional coalition. The occasion for abandoning it came when Franklin Pierce, a hitherto obscure politician and a completely dark-horse candidate soundly defeated the Whig's best, General Scott, who was the second hero of the Mexican War and certainly a household name throughout the country. Quite abruptly, and probably as a result of this defeat, Whig organizations were simply allowed to die in many parts of the nation. Several new parties took their place so that in New England there were Know-Nothings, in the Middle Atlantic and Middle West there were Republicans, and in the border and the South there were old

Whigs. Disunited, these were severally even weaker than the Whigs had been—and in 1853–55 none of them appeared to be particularly significant. So, for the moment, the Democracy approached being a grand coalition, just as the old Republicans had been in the 1820s. And, as in the 1820s also, no new national policy with which a substantial minority disagreed was successfully adopted—this oversized winning coalition was incapable of winning anything of value.

Unlike the 1820s, however, no national leader appeared to break the deadlock inside the oversized coalition. Rather the Democracy developed two centers, one around Douglas, the other eventually centering around Buchanan. The difference between them was largely a question of whom the Democracy would expel. Douglas wished to base the party on the small farmer of the Middle West and frontier and to lop off the Southern extremists. Douglas' brainchild, the Kansas-Nebraska Act of 1854, was designed to accomplish just this: It provided the small farmer with effective control of the northern territories, while mollifying the moderate Southerners with a chance at the West. The Buchanan faction, however, wished to base the party on the South, while allowing the border and the urban North compensatory privileges. As a consequence of this division, the party lopped off both its extremes. The Kansas-Nebraska Act was passed, but Buchanan administered it in favor of the South. As a result, nobody was really satisfied. Northern Democrats flocked into the new Republican party and, when Douglas won the Democratic nomination for the Presidency in 1860, the Southern Democrats withdrew from the party. By then the Democracy was thoroughly disrupted and a losing coalition (i.e. the Republican party) was transformed into a winning one, by the rules of the game which allowed a plurality to win. The disgruntled Southerners completed the loser's victory by withdrawing from the game entirely. Thereby they determined a new game in which the previous losers (i.e. the sectionally based Republicans) were actually the winners.

In contrast to the events of the 1820s, the oversized and worthless winning coalition of the 1850s reduced itself too much. Its rational attempts at a reduction in size, attempts that would surely not have occurred had it had a strong opponent in 1854–55, occasioned a miscalculation. Or rather, when opposing factions wished to lop off members at opposite ends of the ideological spectrum, it turned out their neither faction could win. Hence, members were lopped off at each end; and the oversized winning coalition reduced itself to two losing ones, while the previous loser turned into a winner through no fault of its own. The very fact, however, that its leaders in both factions sought to reduce its membership (i.e. change the base of the alliance, which, of course, involved letting some people go) is evidence in favor of the size principle.

Turning now to the third instance of an oversized coalition, I observe that the Democracy was defeated but not routed by the Civil War. In fact, the technical victors of 1860 were in 1867 still pretty certain that technical victory had not yet been transformed into an actual victory. Lincoln had won by a minority vote in 1860 and in 1864 he was elected in a truncated nation, not as a Republican but as a Unionist, that is, as leader of an *ad hoc* party consisting of Republicans and war Democrats. As the election of 1868 approached, the Republican leaders were all too aware that, although they had controlled the national government for seven years, they had not yet won an election by a majority in the whole nation. Furthermore, they were not at all certain that they could do so. In the congressional election of 1866, Johnson, who was the Democratic half of the Unionist ticket of 1864, displayed every intention of reviving the old Democracy. It had been an overwhelming majority in the fifties and would quite probably still be at least winning in 1868, if it could be re-activated. What, specifically, Stevens and Sumner feared was that the now solidily Democratic border and Southern states might re-ally with the Democracy of New York, Pennsylvania, and the northern Middle West. If this happened, the Republicans were sure to lose. Hence followed the Stevens and Sumner plan of military reconstruction which was intended to and actually did transform the South from Democratic to Republican, thereby guaranteeing Republican victory in the whole nation. The technique of this plan was to forbid re-entry of Southern states into the union until it had been made certain that they would vote Republican—made certain, that is, by organization of Negro voters and disfranchisement of white voters (both under the supervision of a Republican army). Thus, by appropriate inclusion and exclusion of players, the Republicans made a new $n$-person game in which their coalition was assured of overwhelming victory. Their victory was in fact so overwhelming that in 1872 the Democratic party did not even feel capable of offering a candidate for the Presidency.

Unlike the other two overwhelming majorities, however, this one had some value. In a sense, two games were played simultaneously: one a game for Presidential office under the rules of Reconstruction, the other a game for public policy under the old rules as commonly perceived by most voters. In the first game the Republican majority was overwhelming, in the second close to minimal for, in the Congress, Republicans and Democrats were about evenly matched. By using the majority in the first game to win in the second, the Republican coalition could win substantially. Although the Grant administration is usually regarded as wholly corrupt and uncreative, the people who controlled it did make themselves rich and set the scene for the "robber barons," both of which were achievements of great value to them.

Even though the maintenance of this profitable coalition in the nation depended on the maintenance of an overwhelming majority in the game for office, still the tendency to minimize the overwhelming majority was too great to be resisted. Here the process consisted of allowing idealists to withdraw and the South to slip from their grasp. The Stalwarts, as the ex-Radicals surrounding Grant came to call themselves, could probably have kept both by appropriate compromises—but they made no effort to do so.

A substantial segment of the Republican party of the late sixties consisted of people imbued with abolitionist or populist idealism. But the leaders who stood for these ideals disappeared during Reconstruction. Stevens, though himself almost fanatically concerned about genuinely democratic ideals, still was thoroughly Machiavellian in his worship of expediency. So he surrounded himself with political hacks who accepted his discipline. When he died he left control in the hands of men like Conkling and Colfax whose noblest ideal was to enjoy power (which of course they had no intention of sharing with sentimental idealists). So began the drift out of the party of those who had been attracted by the idealism of men like Lincoln and Sumner. Some went back to the Democracy. Some tried to form a new party which nominated Greely for President in 1872. The Stalwarts did nothing to prevent this. Indeed they even encouraged it by making fun of the delicate consciences of the liberals. At the same time they were losing the liberals, they also allowed parts of the South to slip from their control. Possibly they believed they now had absolute control in the North; possibly they simply lacked the resources, the energy, or the rationale to continue Reconstruction. Whatever their motives, however, the fact remains that they did not prevent the election of some Southern Democratic congressmen and governors. Hence, by 1876 they were again a minimum winning coalition, indeed a minority that obtained technical control only by rigging the Presidential election of that year.

Reviewing the three instances of the substantial disappearance of the minority, it appears that, regardless of the reasons for the existence of an overwhelming majority or grand coalition—and they are quite different reasons in the three instances—still the leaders of each maximal coalition behaved in some way that minimized it. Jackson drove out all who would not follow him until he achieved a tightly organized and almost minimal winning coalition. Douglas and Buchanan, fighting for control, each drove out partisans of the other until their once overwhelming majority was, technically, a minority. The Stalwarts confidently allowed both liberals and the South to slip from their grasp and then, owing to a miscalculation, found themselves no more than a blocking coalition. Hence, in *every* instance in which an American party has approached becoming a coalition of the whole, the leaders of the party have in some way decreased its size, which is exactly what one would expect according to the size principle.

I do not suggest, of course, that these nineteenth-century statesmen appreciated this principle as a law of rational behavior. What I do insist, however, is that it describes their behavior, even though they probably perceived their problems thus: "With our overwhelming majority, there are so many and so conflicting interests in the party that none can be satisfied. As long as two conflicting interests remain in the party, neither can be satisfied [which, I add, is why a grand coalition is valueless]. For the sake of action for the interest we approve, we shall therefore decide to satisfy one interest, and, if others are offended, they may leave the coalition." Or one can put the problem in this less calculating way: Every coalition has internal conflicts over the division of spoils. When pressure from an opposing coalition is great, so great in fact that the opposition may win and thereby deprive the coalition of any spoils to distribute, these internal conflicts are minimzed. But when pressure from the outside diminishes, there is less urgency to settle the internal conflicts amicably simply because they are not so dangerous to the oversized winner as to the minimal winner. Those who lose in the intramural contests of an oversized winner tend to leave the coalition and the remaining members are on the whole content to see them go. Thus the excess size of the winning coalition is itself an essential condition of the reduction in size, which is what the size principle asserts. But, while most politicians probably perceived the problem in one of these ways, it has been pointed out to me that at least one nineteenth-century politician perceived the principle almost directly. Thomas Hart Benton, the Jacksonian leader in the Senate and Missouri, once described the political situation in Missouri of the early 1830s thus: "Our majority is *too large;* we shall be much stronger when the number is reduced, and when two or three newspapers shall *openly* act with the enemy which are now secretly doing it." [4]

## OVERWHELMING MAJORITIES IN WORLD POLITICS

The development in the sixteenth century of the system of European nation-states and the fairly recent extension of this system to the whole world created a pattern of international politics which is very like an $n$-person game.

4. Quoted in William N. Chambers, *Old Bullion Benton* (Boston, Little Brown, 1956), pp. 262–63, emphasis in the original. I am indebted to Professor Charles G. Sellers for pointing out this beautifully appropriate quotation.

The players are the nations, but otherwise the rules are rather vague. Often, and especially now when there is threat of nuclear war, the game has seemed non-zero-sum, that is the common benefits of peace and civilization have seemed greater than any possible gain from conflict. But occasionally international politics turns into a zero-sum game as when total war has occurred or when politics is practiced inside an institution like the United Nations with its essentially zero-sum decision-processes. If it does become an analogue of a zero-sum game, the experience of international politics also becomes relevant evidence about the model.

The customary definition of total war includes two features: (1) war such that the object is the complete destruction of the government(s) on the losing side and (2) war such that all great powers in the system participate. This is a behavioral version of the zero-sum condition in a simple game. The game is simple because all the losing players—which are governments even though they may claim to be mere agents for the people they govern—lose their existence, presumably the worst loss they could sustain individually. It is zero-sum because precisely the loss of the losers, i.e., their destruction, is the announced object of the winners. The gain is the exact reverse of the loss. Furthermore, the zero-sum condition in an $n$-person game involves the notion of complementary coalitions and this notion is roughly represented by the second part of the definition of total war.

Total war has further this interesting feature: If one side actually wins, that is, if one side is exhausted before the other, then victory, by removing the losers, transforms a (probably minimal) winning coalition into a grand coalition. And, if we accept characteristic function theory, grand coalitions are worthless. Assuming, as I shall, that winners in total war retain for some time after victory the zero-sum habits of thought engendered by their very participation in it, then they will reject a coalition of the whole and begin to squabble among themselves. Presumably they will seek to substitute for it something that approaches a minimal winning coalition. If, in fact, they actually do so, their action constitutes further verification of the size principle. Let us, therefore, examine diplomacy just after the conclusion of total wars to see whether or not victors have fallen out.

There have been three instances of total war in the modern nation-state system: the Napoleonic wars and the First and Second World Wars. The Napoleonic wars qualify, first, because they included all the great powers in the (then mostly European) nation-state system: France, Spain, Austria, Prussia, Russia, and England. And second, they involved as a major feature the implied intention to destroy governments. Napoleon frequently dethroned kings and replaced them with republics or Bonapartes; and, while objectively the thrones of Austria and England may have been safe from him, his opponents did not think so. His opponents on the other hand announced their intention of dethroning Bonapartes and restoring legitimate claimants everywhere. The First World War qualifies, first, because not only were all the European great powers involved but also the United States, Turkey, and Japan. And second, whatever may have been the somewhat obscure intentions of the Central Powers, the Allied Powers intended—or so one can read Wilson's insistence on self-determination of nations—to destroy the governments of the Central Powers. In fact, the empires of Austria, Germany, and Turkey were dismembered and the emperors and sultan were deposed. The Second World War qualifies, first, because along with all the European great powers the United States, China, Japan, and British Commonwealth nations were involved. And second, the United Nations announced their intention of exacting unconditional surrender which was understood clearly to mean the deposition of Hitler and Mussolini and the Japanese military clique, though not necessarily of Hirohito. While the intentions of the Axis were not clearly announced, presumably they included at least the deposition of Stalin and some sort of subordination of the chief governments in the United Nations.

The Napoleonic wars ended with a victorious coalition of the governments of Great Britain, Austria, Prussia, and Russia, which destroyed Napoleonic France and its satellites by deposing the Bonapartes in France, Spain, and elsewhere. This winning coalition constituted itself the Concert of Europe with the announced intention of maintaining the status quo ante indefinitely. Here, then, was presented a direct clash between the conservative ideal (which is irrational in a continuing zero-sum game) and rational calculations of advantage. And so, even before Waterloo, the winning coalition with its conservative ideals was broken up. Over questions of whether or not Russia would retain that portion of Poland it had acquired in the Napoleonic era and whether or not Prussia would acquire Saxony, the Congress of Vienna split into two camps: on the one hand, Russia and Prussia who supported each other's territorial ambitions and, on the other hand, Austria and England who supported the status quo ante. In this division, the weaker side (i.e., the Anglo-Austrian side because it had no army in Poland or next to Saxony) secretly allied itself with the defeated French in order to block Russian and Prussian aggression. Hence followed this astonishing result: Austria and England, both of whom had been fighting France for nearly a generation, brought a reconstituted French government back into world politics and allied with it against their own former allies in the very moment of victory. As it turned out, a compromise was reached so that the Anglo-Austro-French alliance never had to act; but transitory though it was, it marked the end of the anti-Napoleonic coalition and the re-entry of Talleyrand's France into winning coalitions in European politics. Thus, in this instance, the winners of total war fell out even before they had a chance to divide the spoils: The whole of the 100 days and Waterloo itself occurred after Castlereagh, Metternich, and Talleyrand signed their secret treaty against Russia and Prussia.

After the First World War, the Allied Powers tried to enshrine their wartime alliance in a League of Nations, which, incidentally, excluded the governments they had destroyed and reconstituted. It was not quite a grand coalition, but, considering the exhaustion of the Central Powers, it amounted to one. As such, it was worthless. Even at Versailles the disagreements among the Allies were apparent: England wished to revive Germany while France did not; and both of them wished to dampen Wilson's sentimental idealism. In the ensuing few years, that Germany which England had sought to revive effectively broke the Allied coalition by flirting (as in the Treaty of Rapallo) with the dreaded Bolsheviki of the U.S.S.R. This maneuvering culminated in the Locarno Pact of 1925, which may be regarded as the definitive end of the wartime coalition and the beginning of the maneuvering that led to the Second World War. In this instance, as in the Napoleonic one, a reconstituted loser was brought back into world politics in order to break up a wartime coalition which, after victory, turned out to be worthless. Even though the almost grand coalition of the victors had been institutionalized in the League, the calculations of diplomats searching for national advantage resulted in a winning coalition considerably less than maximum.

The breakup of the wartime coalition after the Second

World War was even swifter than after the First. The anti-Axis coalition of the United States, United Kingdom, and Soviet Union was uneasy enough to begin with owing to the bitter ideological differences between the two former and the latter. Not unreasonably, therefore, this uneasy coalition of the whole did not long survive the victories which rendered it grand. Having defeated the Axis, the winners had nothing to win from unless they split up and tried to win from each other. At Yalta, even at Potsdam, the heads of the three victorious governments planned a continuation of their wartime alliance under the very name they had used to fight the war, i.e., the United Nations. But within less than a year after Potsdam, indeed even before it occurred, the United States and the Soviet Union were scrambling about the world to gain the allegiance of the uncommitted nations to one of the two hostile coalitions they were forming. And at the time of the Korean episode the United Nations itself came to be regarded by the Soviet Union as part of the United States' network of alliances.

From these three instances of the end product of total war one can readily conclude: the winning coalitions of total war do not long survive victory. Both in the model and in actuality they have become valueless. They die because victory renders them nugatory. To win something of value in the next phase following total war, the size of the winning coalition must be reduced. From the evidence of total war also, the size principle is thus additionally verified.

## A NON-WESTERN INSTANCE OF AN OVERWHELMING MAJORITY

The overwhelming majorities previously discussed were chosen on a systematic basis. That is, two institutional environments in which they might occur were chosen (of course subjectively) for examination; but then *all* actual occurrences in these environments were analyzed. This latter part of the procedure adds, I hope, a little objectivity to the analysis. Although only six instances are involved, the fact that they were systematically chosen renders them more valuable as evidence than if they had been chosen on a wholly subjective basis (e.g., as in the case method). While in general I wish to avoid evidence that is anecdotal in form, still I cannot forbear discussing one entirely isolated instance that has come to my attention. It is of interest for it is drawn from a non-Western environment, India. Although some of the actors in the event have been deeply influenced by Western culture, still Indian society is as far from Western in tone as it is possible to find among complex societies in the contemporary world. The fact that Indian politicians behaved in the instance here recounted in accordance with the size principle suggests that the law and the model are not culture-bound but apply to human affairs generally.

In 1948 the Congress party in India suddenly found itself in what was substantially the position of a coalition of the whole and certainly an overwhelming majority. This was a new experience and one for which the leaders had not planned. Yet, within a fairly short time after the discovery of their curious position, they began to behave as rational men, increasing the value of their coalition by expelling members and thereby creating a losing side.

Prior to 1947, the Congress had been only one among several centers of power in India. Of course, the English administration was the greatest and winning coalition for it possessed most of the physical force, however much it lacked moral authority. The strength of the English coalition regularly diminished, however, after 1914. The progress of Indian nationalism, especially in the form of passive resistance, made the use of force more and more difficult. Thereby the one main advantage the English had was gradually taken from them. Furthermore, the English themselves gradually cut the ground from under any pretensions they may have had to racial or intellectual superiority: they educated an Indian middle class. At the same time a self-conscious English liberalism, in the hands of writers like E. M. Forster and George Orwell, castigated the whole imperial enterprise. Gradually, thus, the English were losing the will to rule. In the vacuum left by the dissipation of English power, several indigenous coalitions appeared. The Congress, led by Gandhi and the Nehrus, father and son, was the greatest but not the only one. The Muslim League also grew rapidly, not only because the English sometimes tried to bolster their own position by exacerbating Hindu-Muslim strife but also because the Gandhian emphasis on religious nationalism tended to exclude Muslims and arouse consciousness of their faith. The Indian princes, puppets established over about one-fifth of India, tried to develop enough independent power to survive the collapse of English rule. A number of other parties aimed at enlisting the masses, but actually enlisted only relatively small portions of the middle class, e.g., the Communist party, the Hindu Mahasabha (an ultra-conservative religious party), and the Scheduled Castes Federation (the untouchables' party).

The English coalition had sufficient weight to remain (barely) in control up to the end of the Second World War. But then, poverty-stricken and exhausted by the war and now governed by the anti-imperialist Labour party, the English withdrew. Perhaps because they despaired of producing an agreement among Indian parties, perhaps because they could not resist, even in the collapse of empire, a final application of *"divisa et impera,"* they partitioned India in several ways. Quite accidentally, thereby, Congress became almost a grand coalition.

The major partition was, of course, Pakistan which included the main centers of Muslim population and hence removed most of the Muslim League from Indian politics. While the English provided that the states might become independent, or join one of the partitioned nations, independence was not a real alternative as the struggle between India and Pakistan intensified. Within a few months all the states had been absorbed and reorganized and their princes had been deposed. Even Kashmir, the one holdout with a chance of success, acceded to India just as it was invaded by Pakistan. Thus, the princes were quickly eliminated as an effective force in Indian politics.

In equally unexpected ways some of the minor parties disappeared. While Indians (or at least nationalists) perceived the struggle with England as zero-sum, they did not so perceive the founding of a new government. This was presumably an activity from which all gained and in which all could participate. But since Congress controlled the government-under-construction, participation was only possible by accepting the leadership of Congress. This is exactly what, for example, Dr. Ambedekar, the leader of the Scheduled Castes Federation, did. The Hindu Mahasabha was removed from politics in an entirely different and even more unexpected way. Less than six months after independence, an ex-member of this party shot and killed Gandhi. By the assassination of a saint, the parties of religious extremism were so discredited that they became politically insignificant for several years. Finally, the Communist party, then weak but, of course, potentially important, was eliminated by police action. The party threw most of its resources into a revolt in Hyderabad, which was easily subdued. Hence during the formative years of the republic the Communist voice was muted.

Owing to this concatenation of circumstances, all effective opposition to the Congress disappeared and, shortly after independence, it found itself a coalition of the whole. The leaders of the Congress, however, perceived their national politics in a zero-sum fashion, as well they might, considering both their adoption of Western voting devices (legislatures, elections) which encourage zero-sum perceptions and their heritage of Indian culture with its incessant factionalism among castes, families, villages, etc. Hence they proceeded to add value to their coalition by expelling members from the right and left.

While the bulk of the Congress consisted of followers of Gandhi, there were at least two reasonably clearly defined factions in 1948. One was the Socialist group led by Nehru and Narayan; the other was a religiously and economically conservative group led by Sardar Patel. The controversy from 1948–50 concerned the question of which group would expel the other. Patel, who was more a party organizer than a propagandist, had the initial advantage. He had never hid his dislike of the Socialists but always previously, since their help was necessary in the struggle for independence, he had tolerated their presence in the party.[5] In 1947, however, he maneuvered a number of Socialists out of positions of leadership and managed to have the Congress forbid the use of the word "Congress" in the phrase "Congress Socialist Group." Presumably their help was no longer necessary and he preferred to see them leave the party. This is exactly what many of them did in the spring of 1948. Having expelled the Socialists, Patel sought in 1950 to take over leadership of the Congress by electing as its president one of his own faction, Purushottamdus Tandon, whose success resulted in the

5. Myron Weiner, *Party Politics in India: The Development of a Multi-Party System* (Princeton, Princeton University Press, 1957), p. 56.

expulsion or resignation of even more of Nehru's supporters. Then Patel died and Nehru, who had hesitated
to break with Patel, now took a hand in running the party
as well as the government. He forced the resignation of
Tandon and was himself elected pressident of the Congress, from which vantage point he could proclaim a secu-
lar and socialist policy for the party. His proclamations
perhaps attracted back some Socialists; but, since they now
had their own party, many were permanently lost for the
Congress. More significantly, his proclamations alienated
conservatives who now drifted out of the Congress to support "independent" candidates. The consequence of expulsions on both the right and left was that by 1951 the
Congress had much opposition. In the election of that
year, its candidates received only 45 per cent of the popular vote—although because the opposition was scattered,
the party won 74 per cent of the seats in Parliament. It
had become almost a minimal winning coalition, at least
on the basis of the popular vote.

# CHAPTER 4

# Research on and Applications
# of the Size Principle

The evidence adduced in the last chapter in support of the size principle is entirely historical in nature. More directly behavioral evidence is, unfortunately, not easily available. It is, however, possible, or so I believe, to obtain such evidence. In this chapter, therefore, I shall outline some directions of research on the size principle as well as indicate the relevance of the principle to the interpretation of institutions and to descriptive theory generally.

## THE INFORMATION EFFECT

As was pointed out in the last chapter, the uncertainty of the real world and the bargaining situation forces coalition members to aim at a subjectively estimated minimum winning coalition rather than at an actual minimum. In decision-systems large enough so that participants do not know each other or what each is doing, the actual size and weight of a coalition may be in doubt, if only because of lack of communication or because of participants' inability to estimate each other's weights. Even in smaller systems, however, where participants communicate easily and know precisely their weights, still the minimum size for winning may be in doubt if side-payments (i.e. bargaining) are permitted. Bargaining necessarily involves bluffing, which in the *n*-person situation means either a refusal to commit oneself or treachery (that is, pretending to belong to one coalition while actually belonging to another).

To describe the full range of doubt about size, it is desirable to have a special vocabulary of technical terms. The following are derived from two-person theory and are, I believe, reasonable extensions of the usage there:

> *Complete Information:* If one participant, *a*, knows precisely the weight of another, *b*, and if *a* knows precisely how much the addition of *b* to a coalition will alter its value, then we shall say that *a* has *complete information* about *b*.

> *Systematically complete information:* If every participant has complete information about every other, we shall say that the decision system is characterized by *systematically complete information*.

> *Perfect information:* Interpreting a *move* as the act of joining a coalition, if one participant, *a*, knows what move or moves another, *b*, has made, then we shall say that *a* has *perfect information* about *b*.

> *Systematically perfect information:* If all participants have perfect information about each other, we shall say that the decision system is characterized by *systematically perfect information*.

(In order to make it easier for readers to remember these definitions, I shall sometimes speak redundantly of "complete information about weight" and "perfect information about moves.") In applying these definitions to imaginary games or real situations of conflict, the limiting cases are (a) a system in which systematically complete and systematically perfect information exist and (b) a system in which no participant has either complete or perfect information about any other. The model used and developed in Chapter 2 is an instance of the former limiting case, for it was assumed that all players had complete and perfect information. There does not seem to be any natural situation characterized by this degree of information, except perhaps some laboratory situations established by experimenters. The other limiting case of no information is equally nonexistent in nature, at least in all natural situations involving bargaining. Bargaining necessarily involves some communication among participants and communication necessarily develops and reveals some information. Most natural instances of decision-systems stand somewhere between these two extremes, with information verging in varying degrees toward completeness or perfection. Some examples of the variation follow:

1. Prior to the invention of nuclear armaments, international politics was a decision-system in which no participants had complete information about the weight of any other, except that, in the case of very small and unarmed governments, their weight was known by all to be zero. As indicated by the numerous and abortive attempts to measure war potential, no large government had complete information about any other. Nuclear bombs and intercontinental missiles have, however, presumably increased the degree of completeness of information available about the governments that possess them. These make for complete information in the sense that we can say that a government so armed can destroy any opponent(s). As more and more governments acquire these weapons,

systematically complete information may be approached in international politics. In this situation the calculations of diplomats may be expected to be more precise, though hardly less dangerous. On the other hand, while in the traditional system of international politics information was highly incomplete about weight, it was often perfect about moves, although seldom systematically perfect. The existence of neutrals or balancers who made no move or who behaved treacherously (e.g. "perfidious Albion" of the nineteenth century) determined that there be some departure from perfection, except in times of total war. Nevertheless, information did approach perfection and diplomats have often deluded themselves with the belief that they possessed systematically perfect information. (Often these delusions have had disastrous consequences for the people of the world, as when Hitler assumed in 1939 that the United States would remain neutral in any European war or when Chamberlain assumed in 1939 that the Soviet Union would remain neutral or ally with France and England.)

2. Something of the reverse situation exists in decision-making bodies like democratic electorates or legislatures. Since votes are counted equally, the weight of each potential voter is known. Hence if all participants vote, systematically complete information exists. Even if all do not vote, one can still speak of the information as in effect systematically complete if and only if the nonvoters are randomly self-selected (i.e., sufficiently randomly that, had they all voted, the outcome would have been the same). On the other hand, no matter how large or small the electorate, information is seldom perfect and almost never systematically perfect. The vast amount of energy devoted to public opinion polling testifies to the imperfection of information in large electorates and C. P. Snow's novel, *The Masters,* contains many examples of imperfect information about moves in a small electorate. In both situa-

tions, the moves of some participants are unknown until the moment of decision, at which time the information is useless, except, of course, when it is possible to make the decision over again.

The significance of incomplete and imperfect information in natural decision-making bodies is that coalition-makers tend to aim at forming coalitions larger than the minimum winning size. This effect can be appreciated with an example:

Assume a zero-sum game, $\Gamma$, of 101 players in which the object is to form winning coalitions of 51 or more members whose decisions are binding on the whole set of players. The winners of course take something of value away from the losers. Weights of the players are equal and all participate so that information is systematically complete about weight. In this example, the players are partitioned into seven sets: two sets, $S$ and $T$, of 48 players each and five sets, $A$, $B$, $C$, $D$, and $E$, of one player each. Information about the moves of the 96 members of $S$ and $T$ is perfect (that is, they are both publicly and privately loyal members), while information about $A$, $B$, . . . , $E$ is wholly imperfect and remains so until the moment of decision. Bargaining is a sequence of simultaneous offers by $S$ and $T$ of payments to $A$, $B$, . . . , $E$ for their allegiance at the moment the umpire calls for a decision. (These conditions of bargaining may initially seem unrealistic; but they are intended to simulate the usual conditions in the real world where (a) bargaining is continuous and hence simultaneous and (b) coalitions cannot know what "last" offer has been effectively communicated to the uncommitted and hence cannot know at what subjective stage of bargaining the decision occurs.) These offers are conditional on the success of the offering coalition; that is, losing and blocking coalitions do not actually pay up. For simplicity in this example, offers are in terms of money, although in most natural decision bodies the offers are in

terms of promises on policy. Later on, this and other sim-
plifying conditions will be removed in order to reveal the
full complexity of coalition-formation.

What concerns us in this imaginary situation is the prospective behavior of $S$ and $T$ in the event to follow. Will
they seek to form minimum winning coalitions or larger
ones?

Since they must try to purchase the allegiance of the
uncommitted, they must first collect from their own members promises to contribute to an operating fund. Each
member pledges to pay out of his prospective winnings an
amount that varies with his subjective utility for (a) winning and (b) money. No interpersonal comparison of utility is here involved, however, for each person translates
his utility into a pecuniary scale; but it is convenient to assume that players' utility functions are linear with money.
Having assumed that the members of $S$ and $T$ are loyal,
it must also be assumed that their pledges put no strain
on their loyalty. Hence, each player's maximum pledge
can be no more than the loss he would sustain by losing.
Since each wishes to win, the pledges approach the maximum. The utility of money won and lost varies, however,
among persons; so the operating funds of $S$ and $T$ are different absolute amounts, although, owing to the zero-sum
feature of the game, they do not vary widely.

Each coalition can, of course, distribute its fund in an
infinity of ways and each of these is a pure strategy. But in
terms of our immediate problem, these strategies may be
categorized into two classes:

> 1. Those in which offers are made to exactly three
> players, and
> 2. Those in which offers are made to four or five
> players.

A strategy in the first class is clearly preferable if $S$ or $T$
can induce three players to accept an offer unconditionally.

But three such acceptances violate the requirements of the example for they generate systematically perfect information. Here the question is: which class of strategies is preferable when uncommitted players do not move until the moment of decision? If the operating funds are identical, then there are probably strategies in each class which assure each coalition of an equal chance to make a better offer on a simultaneous bid. (By *better offer*, I mean one which is higher than the opponents for at least three of the five uncommitted. Expressing the offers as fractions of the operating fund, each of the following offers is better than the preceding one: ($\frac{1}{3}$, $\frac{1}{3}$, $\frac{1}{3}$, 0, 0), ($\frac{1}{2}$, 0, 0, $\frac{1}{3}$, $\frac{1}{6}$), (0, $\frac{1}{6}$, $\frac{1}{6}$, $\frac{1}{3}$, $\frac{1}{3}$), etc.) But I have postulated a slight difference in the operating funds. Hence, the problem is, for the coalition which has or believes it has the larger fund, how to exploit its advantage best. Where "$F_s$" and "$F_t$" designate the respective operating funds and where $F_s > F_t$, coalition S can expect to have an equal chance (assuming it uses its best strategy) to make a better offer that T for the allegiance of three players, *when* S *itself uses only the amount* $F_t$. But S has in addition the amount ($F_s - F_t$) which it can use to increase its chance of winning. If S uses this amount to offer to more players than T, then S can increase its expectation of winning. Hence, S must prefer a strategy in the second class.[1]

1. An example of this preference can be exhibited easily when there are exactly three players at issue between S and T. Assume S has $7 and T has $6 and that their offers to A, B, and C must be in multiples of $1. Otherwise the rules are the same as in the example in the text. Then S has the following strategies: to divide the money in ratios of (7,0,0), (6,1,0), (5,2,0), (4,3,0), (3,2,2), (3,3,1), (4,2,1), (5,1,1) and all the permutations of these. Similarly T can divide thus: (6,0,0), (3,3,0), (4,2,0), (5,1,0), (2,2,2), (3,2,1), (4,1,1) and all the permutations. (The divisions [7,0,0] and [6,0,0] need not be considered, however, for they can produce at most one ally, when two are needed.) The expected value of each of these classes of strategies can be readily computed if "expected value" is defined as S's chance of winning (where winning is defined as making a better offer to two or three players) with a particular class of strategies (i.e., with a ratio and its permutations) minus T's chance of winning with a particular

class of strategies. These expected values can be put in matrix form as in the analysis of two-person games, where the entries in each cell are the expected values for S and the values for T are the negative for those of S. This matrix is as follows:

T's strategies (read down)

| | | 1 | 2 | 3 | 4 | 5 | 6 |
|---|---|---|---|---|---|---|---|
| | | (3,3,0) | (4,2,0) | (5,1,0) | (2,2,2) | (3,2,1) | (4,1,1) |
| S's | 1 (6,1,0) | 0 | 0 | $\frac{1}{6}$ | $-1$ | $-\frac{2}{3}$ | $-\frac{1}{3}$ |
| strategies | 2 (5,2,0) | 0 | $\frac{1}{6}$ | $\frac{1}{6}$ | 0 | 0 | $\frac{1}{3}$ |
| (read | 3 (4,3,0) | $\frac{1}{3}$ | $\frac{1}{6}$ | 0 | 1 | $\frac{2}{3}$ | $\frac{1}{6}$ |
| across) | 4 (3,2,2) | $-\frac{1}{3}$ | $\frac{1}{3}$ | 1 | 0 | $\frac{1}{3}$ | 1 |
| | 5 (3,3,1) | 0 | $\frac{1}{3}$ | $\frac{2}{3}$ | 1 | $\frac{1}{3}$ | $\frac{1}{3}$ |
| | 6 (4,2,1) | $\frac{1}{3}$ | $\frac{1}{6}$ | 0 | 0 | $\frac{1}{6}$ | $\frac{1}{3}$ |
| | 7 (5,1,1) | $\frac{1}{3}$ | $\frac{1}{3}$ | $\frac{1}{3}$ | $-1$ | $-\frac{1}{3}$ | 0 |

According to Von Neumann and Morgenstern's theory, the best way for each player to play a game with this set of outcomes is to choose among the strategies by a random device which is so arranged that the strategies are chosen in the following ratios:

| For S | | For T | |
|---|---|---|---|
| 1 | .00 | 1 | .54 |
| 2 | .00 | 2 | .00 |
| 3 | .31 | 3 | .25 |
| 4 | .05 | 4 | .01 |
| 5 | .17 | 5 | .03 |
| 6 | .24 | 6 | .17 |
| 7 | .23 | | |

(These strategy-mixes were calculated for me by Joseph Yeaton of the Radiation Laboratory of the University of California. I deeply appreciate his kindness in devising a program to solve this extraordinarily complex game.) By the use of these mixes of strategies, S can achieve an expected value of .24 regardless of what T does, while T can hold S down to no more than .24 regardless of what S does. The point of this illustration is that 69 per cent of the time S should use a strategy in the second class, that is, an offer to three players rather than two. It is only in this way that it can exploit its advantage of a larger operating fund. The disadvantaged coalition T, however, has a distinct preference for a strategy in the first class and should use one 79 per cent of the time.

So far we have considered only how $S$ and $T$ can make the best offers to uncommitted players. Since this is in effect a seven-person game and a genuine bargaining situation, we must also consider the responses of the uncommitted. Indeed, anticipations about their responses affect $S$'s and $T$'s choice of strategy. The uncommitted have two

FIGURE 5

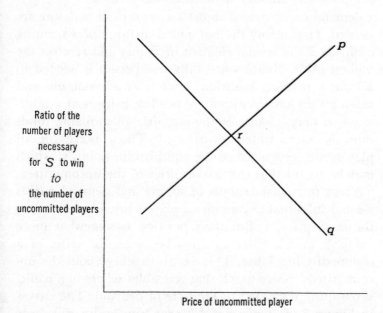

Ratio of the number of players necessary for $S$ to win *to* the number of uncommitted players

Price of uncommitted player

concerns: one is to maximize their receipts; the other is to enter a winning coalition. These considerations are in conflict with each other, for if one asks too high a price, he may be left out and, if he assures himself of winning, he may fail to maximize. This conflict may be depicted geometrically, after the fashion of a supply curve. See curve $p$ in Figure 5, where the price of each individual player rises as the chance of being included rises. On the vertical axis the chance of being included is displayed as the ratio of (a) the number of players necessary to render $S$ a winning coalition to (b) the total number of players not committed to either $S$ or $T$. As this ratio approaches unity, uncommitted players are almost certain of winning, while as it approaches zero most of them are almost certain to lose. In short, as $p$ rises uncommitted players are in short supply; as it declines, they are in excess supply. To complete the analogy with economic analysis, curve $q$ is a demand curve, which shows a rise in price as fewer are needed. Presumably the last added member of a winning coalition is the crucial element in victory and receives the highest price. Hence when only one person is needed to fill out a winning coalition, price is at a maximum and when all the uncommitted are needed, price is at a minimum, if only because of the fact that all available funds must be more widely distributed. The concerns of all players are recognized in the equilibrium point, $r$, which may be regarded as the market price of the uncommitted.

From the usual analysis of supply and demand curves we may infer that uncommitted players initially seek about the same price, $r$. But their position is somewhat more complex than a seller in a market, even the seller of a commodity like labor. There is an urgency about the uncommitteds' desire to sell that resembles sellers in a panic, yet is quite unrelated to the state of demand. The curves in Figure 5 are somewhat different from ordinary supply and demand curves in that the measure on the vertical axis is not an absolute quantity but a ratio of need to quantity, a difference in measurement that reflects the profound differences between economics and politics. This difference involves the fact that, quite apart from the considerations of supply and demand, the uncommitted wish to ensure that, when they do join a coalition, it is a winner. Indeed, they may prefer a lower offer to a higher one, if the lower comes from a more probable winning coalition.

Prior to their choices at the moment of decision, they can have only these objective indications of the relative prospects of $S$ and $T$: the relative size and relative number of offers tendered by $S$ and $T$ to uncommitted players. The relative size of the offers is obviously indicative of the relative amount of resources and the relative desire to win. Less obviously, but no less surely indicative of relative resources and desire is the relative number of offers tendered. If, for example, $S$ has made more offers that $T$, then the uncommitted can infer that $S$ has a larger operating fund and can be expected to win. Furthermore, both $S$ and those uncommitted who have received offers from $S$ and not from $T$ have an obvious incentive to publicize this inferential evidence on the size of the operating funds. If, then, it happens that more players have received offers from $S$ than from $T$, all players who have received offers from $S$ should, rationally, prefer $S$ even though some may have received higher offers from $T$.

This preference for a strategy in class 2 (i.e. offers to four or five players) has in turn an effect on the choice of strategy by both coalitions. Neither dares to reveal to the uncommitted that its operating fund is smaller than the other's. Hence, for the coalition which actually has the smaller fund and which might therefore prefer to use a strategy in class 1, still a strategy in class 2 is preferable simply in order to avoid disclosing weakness. Even if operating funds are exactly equal—as in extreme instances they might be owing to the pressure of the zero-sum feature—both coalitions have an incentive to use a strategy in class 2. In fact, by logical extension, both coalitions have an incentive to reveal opponent's weaknesses or conceal their own by offering to *all* the uncommitted.

From the foregoing rather contrived example, it seems reasonably clear, although unfortunately I cannot demonstrate it formally, that imperfection of information inspires not-yet-winning coalitions to seek more additions than they need to win. If one removes some of the restrictions imposed in the example, then the compelling nature of the incentive is even more clear. In most natural decision-making bodies the operating fund consists not of money but of promises on policy. In such case the chances of different subjective valuations of the contents of the operating funds may occasion wide differences in the effective size of the funds. A concession pledged by a member of S at very little personal cost might be valued by an uncommitted player at an extremely high rate—and vice versa. All such possibilities increase the uncertainty over the size of the operating funds and hence increase the pressure to enroll more than the amount needed to win. Or again, in the example the coalitions S and T were assumed to be the same size. But this too is a rarity in natural decision bodies. If in fact they differ in size or weight, then it may be expected that they will also differ in the amount of the operating fund. And this too increases the pressure on both coalitions to tender offers to all the uncommitted. And for all these reasons, as well as the reasons adduced in the example, imperfections in information lead to nonminimum winning coalitions. In a similar and much less subtle way, incompleteness of information has the same effect. If coalition-makers do not know how much weight a specific uncommitted participant adds, then they may be expected to aim at more than a minimum winning coalition.

Out of this static analysis, one can formulate an hypothesis about a static relationship of covariation in coalition-formation:

> *The greater the degree of imperfection or incompleteness of information, the larger will be the coalitions that coalition-makers seek to form and the more fre-*

*quently will winning coalitions actually formed be greater than minimum size. Conversely, the nearer information approaches perfection and completeness, the smaller will be the coalitions that coalition-makers aim at and the more frequently will winning coalitions actually formed be close to minimum size.*

## DIRECTIONS OF RESEARCH ON THE INFORMATION EFFECT

The information effect is an hypothesis that can be investigated more directly than the size principle. But since the former is a qualification of and inference from the latter, evidence validating or invalidating the information effect is also relevant to the size principle. Fortunately, there is much material available for the systematic study of the information effect and one might hope that it will be investigated by students of politics. For that reason, I shall here indicate some of the directions in which I believe such research might feasibly be undertaken.

Since the information effect involves the covariation of the amount of information and the size of coalitions, empirical verification depends on the discovery of decision-making organizations which carry through a series of decisions with substantially the same participants but varying degrees of information. While many such organizations exist (e.g., families, boards of directors or trustees, labor unions, etc.) the most obvious and available are governmental organizations such as legislatures and electorates. In democratic countries, at least, these are sufficiently public that they may be observed and often they are sufficiently large that participants perceive controversies in them as zero-sum. Hence they provide adequate natural conditions for the study of the information effect, especially if something like a two-party or two-faction system exists.

One area in which some empirical work has been done is the study of the behavior of the American electorate from 1820 or so to the present. The recent interest in the notion of a critical election is one starting point. Key has defined a *critical election* as one "in which the depth and intensity of electoral involvement are high, in which more or less profound readjustments occur in the relations of power in the community, and in which new and durable electoral groupings are formed." [2] In actual use of this definition to discover critical elections by statistical methods, only the last of these three criteria was used by Key and later by MacRae and Meldrum.[3] This is perhaps all to the good, however, for it is doubtful if "relations of power" can be measured at all and any criterion of "involvement" (such as one I constructed for another purpose but applied to Presidential elections) is likely to pick out entirely different elections from those picked out by a criterion of "new and durable groupings." [4] MacRae and Meldrum have refined the notion of critical elections to a *period* of critical elections. Although their evidence relates only to Illinois from 1888 to 1956, the extension seems a priori to be reasonable for all states and the nation as a whole. The American electorate is many-faceted and its government is only slowly responsive to reshuffling of coalitions. Since a new winning coalition is not likely to have significant effects on public policy until an old winning coalition is thoroughly broken up, one would expect a reshuffling of

2. V. O. Key, jr., "A Theory of Critical Elections," *Journal of Politics, 17* (1955), 1–18; see also, V. O. Key, jr., and Frank Munger, "Social Determinism and Electoral Decision: The Case of Indiana," in Eugene Burdick and A. J. Brodbeck, eds., *American Voting Behavior* (Glencoe, Free Press, 1959), pp. 281–99.

3. Duncan MacRae and James A. Meldrum, "Critical Elections in Illinois: 1888–1958," *American Political Science Review, 54* (1960), 669–83.

4. William H. Riker, "A Method of Determining the Significance of Roll Call Votes in Voting Bodies," in John C. Wahlke and Heinz Eulau, eds., *Legislative Behavior* (Glencoe, Free Press, 1959), pp. 377–83.

coalitions to extend over enough elections to bring some payoff or prospect of payoff (in terms of revision of public policy) to the changelings.

For our purposes, the significance of the notion of a period of critical elections is that during such a period the amount of information in the system declines. When voters previously loyal to one party switch to another, information is decreased in at least two ways: First, by the very act of switching, the changelings destroy information about themselves, for their loyalty to *any* party is in doubt until they have proved it in several elections. Second, the reception of switching voters into their new party may occasion the departure of some of its previously loyal adherents. Hence, substantial switching by one bloc of voters may have a cumulative effect in a series of elections. Regardless of the precise causal influences at work in a critical period, however, it is clear that such a period is characterized by a decrease in the amount of information.

If critical elections can be identified—and MacRae and Meldrum's use of factor analysis to do so shows the existence of a fairly adequate technique for the purpose—then some fairly direct tests of the information effect seem to be possible. One can divide a series of national or state elections into two classes: those in a critical period and those in an immediately subsequent noncritical period. If the information effect is a valid proposition then, on the average, elections in the noncritical period should display closer margins between the parties than those in the critical period.

MacRae and Meldrum found that in Illinois between 1888 and 1956 there were two critical periods, the mid-1890s and 1924–36. Their data as presented is not directly usable for the purpose of testing the hypothesis, but it appears to support it for the period 1924–56 and not to do so for the period 1894 to 1922. Owing to the interaction of state and national politics, the fact that evidence from one state in one period does not support the hypothesis should, of course, occasion some suspicion, but should not, I believe, be regarded as definitive disproof. Key found, by the use of a simpler but probably less revealing method, that the elections of 1896 and 1928 were critical in New England and that 1928 was critical in Indiana. Again his data is not presented in a form directly usable here, but if it is assumed that these elections are high points in a critical period, then his data appear to support the hypothesis. If one can assume that it takes politicians several years after a critical election to be certain that the switches are permanent (i.e., that the new information is perfect) and if, further, one can assume that this data on several states indicates that the six years before and after 1900 and 1930 were critical periods in the nation as a whole, then national election results (Presidential and congressional elections considered together) clearly support the hypothesis. But before one can have much confidence in this evidence one way or another, critical elections must be precisely identified in the nation and the states and the tests I have suggested must be applied. This is, of course, a major research undertaking.

Although collected from an entirely different orientation, a similar kind of evidence about electoral behavior is available in the work of Benson.[5] He studied voting in New York from 1826 to 1900 searching for cycles which he defined as a "recurrent pattern of fluctuation in county party percentages." Furthermore, he divided each cycle into a "fluctuation phase" and a "stable phase." In the former, there were marked changes in county party percentages in a large number of counties and in the latter fairly few such changes. It is apparent that Benson's "fluc-

5. Lee Benson, *The Concept of Jacksonian Democracy: New York as a Test Case* (Princeton, Princeton University Press, 1961), pp. 126 ff.

tuation phase" is substantially equivalent to Key and Mac-Rae's period of critical elections. Hence, his calculations also ought to provide the basis of a test of the information effect. While his data is also not in a directly usable form, it does suggest the validity of the hypothesis. He found that stable phases were longer in duration then fluctuation phases, which clearly fits the latter into the category of critical elections. Furthermore, he found that there was a tendency, during a stable phase, for the major parties to gain strength in counties where they were weak and lose strength in counties where they were strong. This is, of course, precisely equivalent to what the hypothesis asserts. In most counties the stronger party, completely and almost perfectly informed about its strength, behaved in accordance with the size principle. Benson's study of the 1844 election in New York, which occurred at the height of the stable phase following the fluctuation phase of 1827–36, shows that between 1840–44 no more than 25,000 voters out of 500,000 switched parties in this period, most of them going into minor parties. This means that politicians had in that period an extraordinarily high degree of perfection of information. As compared to 1832, when the margin between winners and losers was 3 per cent, in 1840 the margin was 1.2 per cent, and in 1844 it was 2 per cent (or if the losing Whigs have the other losing party added to them) the margin was 1.1 per cent. By counties, the difference is even more striking. Between 1832 and 1844 the number of strong Democratic counties (57.5 per cent and above) declined from 17 to 3, the number of strong anti-Democratic counties (42.4 per cent and below) dropped from 9 to 5, and the numbers of middling counties (42.5 per cent to 57.4 per cent) rose from 29 to 46.[6] This seems to be pretty good evidence for the existence of the information effect, although, since it is limited to only one state

6. Ibid., pp. 138 ff.

in one period, it is not at all conclusive. Here again major research is indicated for other states and the whole nation.

It thus appears that American voting data, available as it is for a period of about 150 years, provides a fertile source of evidence about the information effect. So, I suspect, would voting data from other countries with a fairly lengthy experience with democratic or at least public elections, e.g. England, France, Canada, Australia, New Zealand, the Scandinavian countries.

But elections are not the only kind of political and zero-sum decisions for which coalitions are constructed. Persons elected engage regularly in making decisions, often under zero-sum conditions. Each contested vote in a legislature provides data for the investigation of the information effect. Since legislatures usually involve much more face-to-face contact than state or national elections, the relationship between information and coalition size cannot be studied exclusively with statistical methods. Observation of the degree of information is, therefore, more difficult to make and yet, under favorable conditions in which observers get the full confidence of rival coalition-makers, one might expect the observation to be much more accurate. In such a test, the procedure would be to state the degree of information possessed by coalition-makers on each legislative decision (either nonunanimous votes or roll-calls) and then to determine whether or not the decisions in which more information was available were also decisions with a closer margin between the winners and losers. Casual observation of well-publicized close votes in legislatures (such as the votes in the House in 1941 on extending the Selective Service Act of 1940 or the several votes in the Senate in 1954 on the Bricker Amendment) suggest that it is indeed true that very close votes are also votes with a high degree of information; but again extensive empirical investigation is necessary before one can have much confidence one way or another in such evidence.

## RELEVANCE OF THE SIZE PRINCIPLE AND THE INFORMATION EFFECT TO OTHER DESCRIPTIVE THEORY

If it is to be useful and even valid, a general theory must pass two pragmatic tests: (1) it must be able to subsume hitherto observed but unexplained facts and relationships and (2) it must be able to reconcile conflicts between more particularistic or casuistic theories developed to explain observed phenomena. (In the recent jargon of social scientists, it must be able to reconcile conflicting "middle level" theories.) The theory developed here is capable of both these things and, without listing its numerous applications, I shall in this section simply demonstrate that in two instances it passes these pragmatic tests.

First, let us consider an unexplained relationship resulting from a first-order observation, namely, that relationship, discovered by Key, between the existence of a Republican minority and the persistence of organized factions in Democratic parties in Southern states. Key observes, "The cohesiveness of the majority faction [within the Democratic party] in these states [Virginia, North Carolina, and Tennessee] points to the extraordinary influence of even a small opposition." [7] Although this statement is defended by a number of causal arguments drawn from the cases themselves, it nevertheless seems surprising and hard to defend on theoretical grounds. Actually, of course, the theoretical defense of it is a simple inference from the size principle. When the Democratic party is a coalition of the whole, it is worth nothing. But when an opposition exists, the coalition is worth something. Hence, a majority fac-

7. V. O. Key, jr., *Southern Politics in State and Nation* (New York, Knopf, 1950), p. 300.

tion inside the Democratic party appears to take charge of the winnings. It then expels some of these not necessary to win in order to divide the gains among fewer persons. Similarly, the size principle explains the persistence of the dual factionalism that Key observed in Louisiana and Georgia where popular leaders polarized politics. Once Long and Talmadge introduced factions that could really win something, close-to-minimum winning coalitions appeared. What the size principle does not explain is the fact that in six states Key studied, no persisting factions appeared and the margins of winning in particular elections were often very wide. Quite obviously other factors are at work here that prevent the full operation of the size principle (although it does, of course, sometimes operate in particular elections even when there are not persistent factions). Key suggests what these factors may be when he says: "the grand objective of the haves is obstruction. . . . Organization is not always necessary to obstruct, it is essential, however, for the promotion of a sustained program for the have nots. . . . It follows . . . that over the long run the have nots lose in disorganized politics." [8] Put in game terms, players who are pretty certain to lose if the coalition of the whole is broken up, have an interest in maintaining a grand coalition in which, if they do not win, at least they do not lose. But this casuistic explanation and the behavior it concerns is outside the application of the size principle and a still more general theory of coalition formation, to be developed in Chapter 5 and subsequently, is needed to subsume it.

Turning now to the second pragmatic test, that is, whether or not a general theory can reconcile conflicts in particularistic interpretations of phenomena, let us consider the continuing debate over the ideology of political parties in the United States or any other two-party system.

8. Ibid., p. 307.

This debate, which often arises journalistically, concerns whether or not there is a discernible ideological difference between the parties. In particular elections there are indisputable differences, of course, if only the differences in the character of the candidates. But in several elections, especially several simultaneous elections but also even in elections over time, it may well be that no discernible difference exists. Lord Bryce once quoted with approval a journalist's observation that the parties in America were like two bottles with different labels but both empty. The metaphor might be more expressive if one said they were both filled with the same mixture of liquids (perhaps with molasses as the main ingredient). But to conserve the conventional metaphor, I shall speak of the "empty-bottles theory" by which I mean the assertion that there is no discernible ideological difference between the two parties and that such ideology as each has is utterly incoherent. There is much opposition to the empty-bottles theory. Each individual act of straight-ticket voting, for example, expresses the voter's belief, which of course may be false, that he or she can discern a difference. Many scholars have tried to buttress this common belief by verbalizing the difference precisely. That is, they have tried to show that affiliation with a party amounts to rational satisfaction of an interest rather than a delusion manipulated by politicians for their own advantage. Unfortunately the competition among these several definitions of the difference betrays their inadequacy. One scholar asserts that the difference is that Republicans embrace commercial values and Democrats reject them. Another scholar asserts that Republicans embrace Calvinist values and Democrats reject them. A third asserts that Democrats are humanistic and libertarian while Republicans are materialistic and conventional. A fourth asserts that Democrats are progressive while Republicans defend the status quo. The very failure to definitively establish any one of these supports the empty-bottles theory, while the very effort to establish them discredits it. There is, apparently, no reconciliation.

The most direct statement of the irreconcilability of these two positions is found in Downs' work, *An Economic Theory of Democracy*. For him the problem arises thus. His model is based on two axioms: (1) that all citizens are rational in the sense that they seek to maximize utility from governmental actions and (2) that parties are rational in the sense that they seek to maximize votes. He then imagines a situation in which citizens, taken together, have diverse interests and in which two parties are each allowed to appeal to as many interests as they wish in order to maximize membership. As a consequence, in this situation there is a tremendous overlapping of the policies of the two parties (and, as he points out, the overlap is even greater when there are more than two parties). Of this situation he remarks: "Clearly both parties are trying to be as ambiguous as possible." [9] From this he infers: [10]

> Ambiguity thus increases the number of voters to whom a party may appeal. . . . Political rationality leads parties in a two-party system to becloud their policies in a fog of ambiguity. . . . Naturally, this makes it more difficult for each citizen to vote rationally; he has a hard time finding out what his ballot supports when cast for either party. As a result, voters are encouraged to make decisions on some basis other than issues, i.e., on the personalities of the candidates . . . etc. But only parties' decisions on issues are relevant to voters' utility incomes from government, so making decisions on any other basis is irrational. We are forced to conclude that rational be-

9. Downs, *An Economic Theory of Democracy*, p. 135.
10. Ibid., p. 136.

havior by political parties tends to discourage rational behavior by voters.

This is, of course, a contradiction between the two axioms. Downs deserves great credit for having pointed it out, although he did argue that the model is "not necessarily contradictory."

If one wishes to retain the model, one must find one's way out of the cul-de-sac of contradiction. To eliminate the contradiction one must revise the axioms. Since the axiom that parties seek to maximize members is at the root of the trouble (that is, it is the rational action of parties that prohibits rational action by voters), this is the axiom that needs revision. It can be revised in two ways: one can either relax its generality or change its definition. Downs uses the first alternative, but, as I shall try to show, the second is preferable, even in terms of his own analysis.

Downs points out that parties have a powerful incentive to achieve complete ambiguity. Indeed, if they behave rationally, they must. Furthermore, voters have, as he points out, no adequate defense against rational behavior by parties. Nevertheless, he concludes that the model is "not necessarily contradictory" and speaks of the situation in which parties actually succeed in beclouding their policies as a "rationality crisis." From this I infer that he supposes parties will not always succeed in beclouding, even though under the axiom of their rationality they must. Since he has imagined no institutional reason why they might not succeed, I conclude that the only reason they might not is that they might not try. And this amounts to relaxing the requirement that all parties behave rationally.

This is, of course, a perfectly acceptable alternative. But if it is chosen here, it must be chosen elsewhere. And this Downs does not do for the very good reason that it would undermine most of his arguments about the behavior of parties. (For example, if he chose this alternative consistently, he could no longer use the axiom to derive the propositions that parties in the model must be honest and reliable.) Hence, even from Downs' own point of view, this is an undesirable way to resolve the contradiction.

A much easier and much less discommoding way to resolve it is the second alternative, that is to change the definition of rationality. Instead of simply asserting that parties seek to maximize votes, one could assert instead the size principle: that parties seek to increase votes only up to the size of a minimum winning coalition. If the axiom is revised in this way, parties no longer have an incentive toward absolute ambiguity. Including the information effect in the axiom makes the resolution even easier. Then parties have an incentive to becloud issues only in the case of issues that are of concern to the voters about whom they have imperfect information. For the voters, both those for them and those against them, about whom they have perfect information, there is no need whatsoever to becloud the issues. Furthermore, as Downs points out elsewhere, parties have an incentive to develop an ideology in order to economize in the process of building coalitions. Hence, with some incentive to clarify by ideology and without an absolute incentive to becloud, one can expect parties in his model to present the voters with an artistically devised mixture of ambiguity and clarity which are varied in amounts according to the degree of information available.

Indeed, I think this is what actually happens in American politics. The empty-bottles theory is advanced by those who observe the beclouding. The definitions of difference are advanced by those who perceive the clarity and coherence of party ideology. Since, according to the size principle and the information effect, coalition-builders are actually engaged simultaneously in clarifying and

rendering ambiguous (for, however, different voters), it should surprise no one that both theories are advanced. When the analysis is raised to a more general level, however, it is apparent that both theories are partially correct and partially wrong and that their correct parts are entirely consistent with each other.

# CHAPTER 5

# The Dynamic Model

In order to discuss the process of coalition-building with some agreement between author and reader about what is under discussion, an appropriate introduction to the analysis of the dynamics of forming coalitions is a brief statement of the assumed model of the process.

## THE MODEL IN OUTLINE

The model of course involves a decision-making body, $I$, of $n$ members, operating under the rules of an $n$-person, zero-sum game with side-payments allowed. Although in this body there are a number of *roles* (which will be defined subsequently), the members themselves are personally indistinguishable and may adopt any role, if circumstances permit. Since the weights (or influence or power or significance) of members are assumed to vary, it is also assumed that some roles are particularly appropriate for members of heavy weights and others particularly appropriate for members with low weights. The rule of decision, with respect to any point at issue, is that a coalition with weight $m$, where $m > \frac{1}{2} \sum\limits_{i=1}^{n} w_i$ and where $w_i$ is the

weight of a member, $i$, can act for or impose its will on the body as a whole. Superficially, there is no limit on the subjects or outcomes of decisions; but, in fact, the zero-sum condition implies a limit, namely that no outcome can disrupt the body. That is, no decision can be taken in such a way that losers would prefer to resign rather than acquiesce. (There are, of course, in the natural world, zero-sum situations, such as total war and revolution, in which one side deliberately sets the stakes as the lives of the losers so that no resignation is possible. In such instances, then, even the zero-sum condition sets no limit on the outcomes. Typically, however, what we perceive as zero-sum situations are those in a continuing body where, presumably, the losers of today continue to participate in the hope of becoming the winners of tomorrow.)

In such a body as this, coalition-building begins when a *leader*, who is defined simply and circularly as a member who manages the growth of a coalition, undertakes to form one on a particular issue for decision. In order to form a coalition a leader must attract *followers*, who are also defined simply and circularly as those members of the body who join the association which the leader forms.

Now that the discussion is concerned with a dynamic rather than static analysis, it is important to distinguish between what a follower joins and the end product of coalition-building, both of which kinds of subsets of $I$ have heretofore been called coalitions. To distinguish, therefore, the word "coalition" will be reserved for the end product of the process and it will be appropriate to modify it with the adjectives "winning," "losing," "blocking," "grand," etc. Since, presumably, no moves can occur after a coalition is in fact winning (or indeed after *any* coalition formed around a prospective decision is winning), the association that a follower joins cannot appropriately be described with these adjectives. The weight of this association is smaller than $m$ and hence it cannot be winning. Since no other association with a weight of $m$ exists, it is not losing. Nor is it blocking, for blocking coalitions can occur only when all the unattached members have been absorbed into two coalitions (and thus when no further moves are possible). Hence, the association which a follower joins cannot be described with the adjectives one uses for coalitions, a fact which suggests that these associations are not coalitions at all, when dynamically observed. For these reasons, the thing a follower joins will be called a *proto-coalition*. Precisely a proto-coalition is any subset of $I$, when $I$ is partitioned into three or more disjoint subsets such that no subset has the weight of $m$. The extreme cases are partitions into: (a) one-person subsets of $I$ and (b) multi-person subsets of $I$ such that only one proto-coali-

tion, $P$, has the weight: $w(P) = \frac{1}{2} \sum_{i=1}^{n} w_i$.

Proto-coalitions change size as the result of *moves*, which are all acts of joining or resigning from proto-coalitions. Both individual members and multi-member proto-coalitions may make moves. Although moves are typically actions by one member or one proto-coalition, they may also be simultaneous and previously agreed upon actions by two or more members or proto-coalitions. In this latter circumstance, they will be referred to as *simultaneous moves*.

Each move has the effect of changing the internal structure of the body so that after each move strategic considerations are somewhat different from what they were before it occurred. In order to discuss these considerations, the interrelationships of proto-coalitions just before (or after) a move will be defined as a *stage* in the process of building a coalition. (In terms of a more abstract theory of perception which I have previously developed a move is an *event* while a stage is a *situation,* that is, the abstract and instantaneous-eternal boundary of events.[1]) The first stage is that situation in which there are $n$ single-member proto-coalitions. The second stage is that situation in which there are one two-member proto-coalition and $(n-2)$ single-member proto-coalitions, that is, $(n-1)$ proto-coalitions in all. The last stage, $r$, exists when there is a winning coalition or two blocking ones. The $(r-1)^{th}$ stage is that in which some one winning coalition can be and immediately subsequently is created by the union of two proto-coalitions. Of course, the participants usually do not know whether or not they are in the $(r-1)^{th}$ stage because they cannot foresee the outcome with absolute assurance. But they do know when they are in the first or $r^{th}$ stage. When the $r^{th}$ stage is reached, participants and observers can, if they care to do so, number the stages.

The dynamics of the growth of proto-coalitions depends on the action of leaders in attracting followers. The means by which leaders do so is the offer of what is called in the (perhaps unnecessarily) vivid language of the theory *side-payments*. While in common usage this phrase refers to payments of money, it should be emphasized that it is intended to cover all artifacts and sentences (such as promises on policy) that can conceivably have value for the members of the body. While the classification of side-payments and the calculation of their value will be deferred to a later section, here it must be assumed that every leader has some fund of valuable things which he can use

1. Riker, "Events and Situations," *Journal of Philosophy, 54,* 57–70; and William H. Riker, "Causes of Events," *Journal of Philosophy, 56* (1959), 281–91.

to attract followers. Sometimes this fund is actually in the leader's hands when he begins negotiation so that what he dispenses (money, promises, etc.) is actually a kind of working capital which will, presumably, be replenished out of the gains of the anticipated winning coalition. On the other hand, and possibly more typically, the leader operates on credit, promising rewards with the understanding that he will honor his promises only if he is successful.

It should be emphasized that the side-payments are valuable, regardless of whether they are such material things as money or such intangible things as promises on policy. To say they have value is to say that some people want them badly enough to give up something else to obtain them. (Indeed, one common definition of *value* is a relation between a person and an object, tangible or intangible, such that the person will trade some other object for it.) One of the main properties of the relation of value is scarcity. In the case of material resources the relation between value and scarcity is obvious: Potential users of resources compete for them by bidding up the price. In the case of less definite things like promises, the connection is not so clear, but it nevertheless can be appreciated when one realizes that policy changes are valuable only when they are controversial, only when they involve the satisfaction of one interest at the expense of another. In a sense, the value of a policy is a function of a kind of scarcity, namely, a scarcity of beneficiaries.

The fact of scarcity imposes a form on the process of making coalitions in a number of quite direct ways. In the first place, it limits the number of members whom a leader can ask to be followers. If he is using something of value (i.e. scarce) for side-payments, typically he cannot afford to pay everybody and indeed would not wish to do so if he could. Hence, some persons must be left out of any beginning proto-coalition. The notion of the value (or scarcity) of side-payments is probably the dual of the size principle. Excess members of a winning coalition both cost something to acquire and lessen its gains. And this is to say that the scarcity of side-payments prohibits their use in an extravagant fashion.

In the second place, and as a consequence of the fact that some are left out, the attempt to form a coalition generates opposition. Those who are left out are, of course, aware of the prospect they face in a zero-sum situation, to wit, that they will lose something of value. The loss can be averted only by forming another and competing proto-coalition which is in the end successful. Hence, as a kind of reflex to the first leader's initiation of a proto-coalition, other leader(s) form other proto-coalition(s).

Up to this point several stages and several roles have been distinguished reasonably clearly. The first stage is the original situation of $n$ one-member proto-coalitions. The second stage is the result of forming one two-member proto-coalition. After the second stage, there is some $i^{th}$ stage (possibly the third) in which at least two multi-member proto-coalitions exist. Finally there are the $r^{th}$ and the $(r-1)^{th}$ stages between which some proto-coalition is transformed into a coalition. Similarly some of the roles have been fairly clearly specified: *leaders* and *followers* who are differentiated according to whether they offer or receive side-payments.

This much of the model is intuitively fairly clear for it is just an abstract statement of key points of a process we constantly observe. But beyond the key points it is difficult to specify abstractly and intuitively what occurs. The model itself is at this point quite vague simply because we cannot easily abstract a pattern from the rich complexity of events in the growth of proto-coalitions. It may be regarded as the main task of a dynamic theory of coalitions to specify the pattern of growth and the strategic considerations involved in the process by which a proto-coalition passes from the $i^{th}$ to $r^{th}$ stages; that is, from the key stages already described, one wishes to infer the nature of the transition from the stage of competing proto-coalitions to the final stage when some coalition enforces a decision. An attempt to construct such a theory is reported in the next chapter.

## THE NATURE OF SIDE-PAYMENTS

Before undertaking an analysis of strategy, however, it is necessary to make some observations about the currency leaders use for side-payments. Unlike the data of economics, in which transactions occur in money and are therefore subject to direct numerical analysis, the data of politics are non-numerical in character. The earliest appearance of the compound word "side-payments" in the literature of game theory is in heuristic discussions for which the obvious concrete references are the gaming table and the modern commercial market place. Unfortunately, therefore, the word "side-payments" with its underlying reference to money obscures the reality of politics, where transactions are almost wholly in a primitive form of barter and where the things exchanged are often unexpressible in money (and even in some instances unexpressible in utiles). Since the side-payments of political coalition-formation include such diverse things as money and promises on policy and even such indefinable things as flattery and love, the comparability of the various sorts of political currency must be demonstrated before we can in good conscience use a portmanteau word like side-payments.

Among the various kinds of side-payments in politics are:

1. *The threat of reprisal:* At one extreme a leader may so manipulate events that he is able to threaten members of the body with reprisals if they do not join his proto-coalition. The side-payment then consists of a promise not to carry out the threat and the gain of the follower is simply escape from prospective misfortune. Thus crudely described, this kind of side-payment seems to belong only to dictatorial societies or police states in which coalition-building is not the main kind of decision-making. And, indeed, the whole apparatus of secret police and the denial of conventional civil liberties (especially of that logically and historically primary one, the freedom of members of a governing body from arrest) does fall into this category of side-payments. But even in thoroughly democratic societies where the conventional civil liberties are well protected, this kind of side-payment is frequently offered and accepted. For example, in all bodies in which party discipline is tight, its tightness partially depends on the ability of leaders to threaten potentially rebellious members with expulsion from the party. And if in turn expulsion from the party means the probable loss of office, then the threat of reprisal is an effective side-payment. (And it is actually so used in such diverse decision-making bodies as the House of Commons, some American city councils, and management-controlled boards of directors of business corporations.) Even when a leader cannot threaten members with so dire a punishment as expulsion, however, he sometimes can, by clever manipulation of events, force fellow members to a position in which they must accept this kind of side-payment. In the United States Congress this happens frequently as, for example, when the manager of a bill is able, by successful rhetoric, to define an issue in such a way that opposition will entail popular disapproval. The late Senator Joseph McCarthy was, until his own exposure to popular disapproval via the

television screen, a master of this sort of rhetorical distortion for he was able to transform simple opposition to his methods into what appeared to be a kind of treason. On a more mundane level of congressional transaction, the extension of social security coverage in recent years has always been accomplished by presenting the proposal for extension in such a way that mere opposition to extension appeared to be opposition to the principle of social security.

2. *Payments of objects the value of which can be reckoned in money:* A quite different kind of side-payment appears under this rubric. Money payments are the most obvious example of this kind of side-payment and, indeed, this latter term undoubtedly originated with pecuniary transactions in mind. When we discuss coalition-formation in governments, reference to this kind of payment offends the democratic conscience. But in other institutional settings, direct payments in money are wholly legal and ethically neutral. In a corporate proxy fight in which a set of potential directors attempts to wrest control from the present ones, the purchase of proxies is a common practice. (One not uncommon practice is for the solicitor of proxies to buy a portion of the shareholder's stock at a higher than market price, in return for which the shareholder votes his remaining shares as the solicitor wishes. A particularly involved kind of deferred payment in money has occurred when labor unions, holding corporate shares in trust funds, have voted these shares for the management in proxy fights in return for a promise of subsequent concessions in collective bargaining.) In public institutions, however, payments in money are in our society both legally and ethically improper, although of course they do occur in an indeterminate degree. In American society they are probably considerably less frequent now than they were two or three generations ago. But though

payments in money are frowned upon, other kinds of valuable goods can sometimes be legally used in payment, and,
more rarely, be ethically approved. Offices in the bureaucracy have a value which can be reckoned in money. A job
is a property the value of which can be computed simply
by multiplying the annual income times the years of the
appointment. If the office carries much prestige then such
a calculation probably does not reveal its value; but for
relatively routine jobs, such as postmasterships or assistant
district attorneyships, the calculation results in a fairly
accurate appraisal of its worth. The fact that jobs were so
obviously used as quasi-pecuniary payments in nineteenth-
century politics in England and America was used by civil
service reformers to equate patronage with bribery and
thereby to discredit the former. But now that civil service
reform has in many places eliminated one of the main
kinds of political currency, some morally unimpeachable
political scientists have come to lament its loss and have
pointed out how much the loss increases the difficulty of
leaders' tasks in building coalitions. And in this back-
handed way patronage (that is, money payments for support) has been supplied with a kind of ethical (or at least
*raison d'état*) approval.

3. *Promises on policy:* Only slightly different from tangible or quasi-pecuniary side-payments are promises on
policy, which are the stock in trade of leaders of proto-
coalitions in most public and private decision-making
bodies. Typically, a prospective leader starts with a proposed decision (e.g. a bill in a legislature). Typically, also,
a number of like-minded members join him immediately
in support of it and thereby become his followers. For
these initial followers, the payment will be the achievement of the proposed decision. And this payment is sufficient regardless of the followers' motives for desiring it.
But, unless the initial followers are a winning coalition,

this payment is not enough to win the decision. Assuming that no more followers can be attracted to the proposal as it stands, the leader can, nevertheless, still attract more followers with the same kind of currency by the technique of modifying the proposal. Such action, however, involves him in a dilemma. One horn is the fact that, if he does not modify, he cannot add to his proto-coalition. The other horn is the fact that, if he does modify, he risks alienating his original followers. But though this kind of dilemma really exists, leaders who are persuasive in rhetoric and artistic in political contrivance can easily slip between the horns. Indeed, this kind of payment by modification and reinterpretation of promises is one of the commonest features of democratic government, so common in fact that democracy is often spoken of as "government by compromise." [2] And it is not inappropriate to single out this feature to characterize democracy for "compromise," which sounds so easy and unimportant when verbalized in one sibilant word, seems far more difficult and magical when viewed as what it really means for a leader to tax his old friends (i.e. by revoking his promises) in order to buy new friends (i.e. by uttering partially conflicting promises).

4. *Promises about subsequent decisions:* Not only may a leader pay followers with promises about the content of the immediate decision for which the proto-coalition is formed, but also he may pay with promises about the content of future decisions. If a leader of a proto-coalition on one decision can reasonably be expected to play the same

2. For detailed examples of the process of compromise on specific points in the content of legislation, see Stephen K. Bailey, *Congress Makes a Law* (New York, Columbia University Press, 1950), passim. For examination of a pattern of compromise in a specific area of legislation, compromise lasting over a generation, see William H. Riker, *Soldiers of the States: The Role of the National Guard in American Democracy* (Washington, Public Affairs Press, 1957), pp. 67–103.

role in many future decisions, then his stock of political currency is greatly expanded. By promises to seek or not to seek, to modify or not to modify some prospective decision (perhaps totally unrelated to the issue at hand), leaders can buy additional members of a proto-coalition, often without the necessity of modifying the current proposal. It is this fact about his position that renders an institutional leader so much more influential than the occasional leader in bodies like the U. S. Congress.[3] The institutional leader (e.g. the majority leader), who is expected to lead in the future, can believably offer promises about anticipated decisions, while the occasional leader usually cannot. In one way, however, even the occasional leader can promise future action to purchase current allegiance. This is the technique of log-rolling. That is, a leader of one proto-coalition buys the allegiance of a follower in it with the payment of a promise to become himself a follower when his follower becomes a leader. Although possibly less common than direct promises on policy, this kind of payment is in wide use, so much so that one recent and perceptive account of decision-making in democratic bodies places it at the very center of the process.[4]

5. *Payments of emotional satisfaction:* The kinds of payments included under this rubric are quite different from the previous ones. By emotional satisfaction I mean something more than the mere rhetoric of persuasion. It is true that leaders often attract followers by forcefully arguing that a particular proposed decision is appropriate in light of some culturally agreed-upon norm, such as "reason," religion, patriotism, party standards, ideology, or any other notion commonly used to evaluate behavior. But such persuasion I have already categorized under the third

3. For an elaboration of this distinction, see William H. Riker, *Democracy in the United States* (New York, Macmillan, 1953), chap. 5.

4. Buchanan and Tullock, *The Calculus of Consent,* esp. chap. 10.

rubric when I mentioned that the leader's original followers are "like-minded." Often they have become such by reason of his rhetoric. Rather what I mean by emotional satisfaction is something more magical and far less patent to rational understanding. Freud described leadership as a kind of love affair between each follower and the leader. Max Weber, struggling to deal with what I suspect is the same phenomenon, secularized the word "charisma" to describe that feature of a leader's personality which seems to followers to be the grace of God or at least a more-than-human instinct for right action. Whether this kind of leadership is some obscure sort of sexual attraction or whether it is a rhetoric of magic that persuades the observers of the magician's superhuman powers, I do not now feel called upon to decide. But I am sure that something describable by either of these theories exists. And this is what I mean by payment in emotional satisfaction. If a follower believes that anything a leader proposes is good and right simply because *he* has proposed it, then the full payment for the follower's allegiance lies in the leader's act of starting the proto-coalition. The content of proposals on policy and promises of subsequent rewards are both totally irrelevant. Only *he* counts. And when only *he* counts, any action, any proposal, any decision is its own reward, provided *he* initiates it. This is, I grant, a curious kind of thing to call a payment, yet if the model is to encompass all of the values leaders distribute to followers, then this too must be included. Note, however, that this currency is relevant to the model only when the followers who accept this payment have less weight than $m$. If they have more weight than $m$, then the system changes from decision-making by coalition-formation to dictatorship. But when they are less than $m$, they can only provide the leader with his initial followers and he must negotiate for more in the usual fashion of coalition-formation.

## THE COST AND VALUE OF SIDE-PAYMENTS

The foregoing list of side-payments was not made simply out of an Aristotelian compulsion to categorize phenomena; it was made primarily to facilitate the calculation and comparison of costs and benefits.

From the point of view of a leader, the costs of the payments made to form any particular proto-coalition can be viewed in one of these aspects:

1. Those payments which he can make out of the prospective gains from the decision at hand. For convenience, these will be called *contingent payments out of profits*.
2. Those payments which he can make by the expenditure of present skills and possessions. These will be called *payments out of working capital*.
3. Those payments which he can make only when he has put his whole career, even his life, into the decision at hand. These will be called *payments out of fixed assets*.

*Contingent payments out of profits* include such things as promises of patronage and promises on the content of policy when the content is wholly controlled by the outcome of the immediate decision (e.g., when a leader in a legislature modifies a bill to gain adherents or when a candidate for administrative office promises to follow a particular policy in administration). On the surface, these payments appear to be costless, except for the expenditure of energy in concluding bargains and this should properly be classified as a payment out of working capital. But the costlessness is more apparent than real. The leader who promises a job to one man cannot promise it to another. The cost is thus a limit on his freedom of action. The leader who modifies his bill both sacrifices some of his own goal and runs the risk of losing some of his adherents. The leader who promises to follow a particular policy thereby runs the risk of alienating more persons than he attracts. Etc. Hence, it cannot be said that these payments are costless. Nevertheless, they do have a limit. The sum of the costs cannot total more than the profits when this kind of payment is used exclusively. Hence, there is here a kind of base point for calculation. In some fashion, however rough, the leader can cast up accounts, subtracting payments from profits in order to calculate his own gain.

*Payments out of working capital* are a somewhat different matter. These include the expenditure of energy on bargaining and planning tactics, payments of promises on subsequent decisions, and payments of valuable objects (such as jobs and money) now in the leader's possession. The rationale for all such expenditures and payments is, of course, that the leader hopes to recoup them out of the gains of subsequent victory. There is no question that all these payments are costly to him. Expenditures of energy have an obvious cost as does the paying out of valuable objects. Promises on subsequent decisions have a cost also, although it may not be immediately apparent. Every act of log-rolling, for example, costs a legislator something. Consider, as an imaginary instance, two legislators, $A$ and $B$, and two decisions, 1 and 2, where 1 temporally precedes 2. Suppose that $A$ now leads a proto-coalition about 1, while $B$ anticipates leading a proto-coalition about 2. In order to have an incident at all, we must also suppose that $B$ is unwilling to join $A$'s proto-coalition without some payment. Finally, suppose that $A$ approaches $B$ with the offer that, if $B$ will join his proto-coalition now, he will subsequently join $B$'s proto-coalition around 2. What conditions are necessary for $B$ to accept $A$'s offer? Clearly $B$ will not accept it unless he believes that $A$ would not join

*B*'s own coalition without some payment. That is, *B* must believe that *A* is hostile to *B*'s position on decision 2. Of course, *B* may be either right or wrong in his belief. But in a continuing decision-making body, it is, typically, difficult for *A* to hoodwink *B* about *A*'s true position. And if *B* accepts *A*'s offer and is correct in his belief, then *A*'s offer to join *B* on decision 2 genuinely involves, for *A*, a sacrifice of some possible future gain or the acceptance of a positive future loss. If so, then *A*'s bargain of logrolling is not costless. He has won something, *B*'s support on 1, but he must pay for it with his own support of *B* on 2.

Furthermore, unlike contingent payments out of profits, payments out of working capital are absolutely certain costs. They are laid out before the decision is taken and cannot be recalled or canceled if the leader's coalition fails. Promises made about future decisions must be honored whether or not the promiser is successful. Even if *A*'s proto-coalition ends up a losing coalition, *A* must still support *B* on decision 2. When a leader pours forth much energy in the management of a bill or an election campaign, the energy has been expended and is not recoverable regardless of whether he wins or loses. There is thus a certain absoluteness of cost about payments out of working capital which is in sharp contrast to the contingency of payments out of profits.

There is another notable difference between those categories of costs. While contingent payments out of profits are limited and thus in a certain rough sense calculable, payments out of working capital are not so easily subjected to analysis even by the man who pays them out. Suppose a leader building a proto-coalition pays out his own energy, his own money, and some promises on future decisions. How is he to add up these quite disparate things? The economist, of course, has an answer to this question.

He assumes that each of these things have a value measured in utiles and utiles like money can be summed to arrive at the total amount of utility expended. But, unfortunately, utiles are just a convention for theorizing, not an actual measure which real persons can use. The imaginary persons of the model we are now discussing have no more ability in the analysis of their own values than do real people in the situations the model is supposed to fit. And, hence, our imaginary leaders are as unequal to the task of measuring the value of disparate things as are leaders in the natural world. All one can say about the comparability of the costs of these payments is that at some point in the process of paying them out the leader decides that he has paid out all that winning is worth to him (or perhaps all that the avoidance of loss is worth to him). Only in that extremely rough sense can it be said that this type of payment is calculable.

Turning now to the category of *payments out of fixed assets,* I observe that the calculation of costs is here even more hazardous. These payments involve the leader's whole life and career in every decision. He who pays his followers with love or with the satisfaction of deferring to the grace of God, as well as he who operates by the methods of the police state, must win on every decision in which charisma or the threat of reprisal is brought into play. Threats that do not coerce must be followed by the actual reprisal threatened and, if the reprisal itself fails, then the effectiveness of all future threats is diminished or destroyed. So it is with charisma. The leader who calls charisma into play must win or else be exposed as something of a fraud.[5] So also with love. The leader whose love

5. The cautious realism with which the mystic Gandhi used the political technique of the fast is a case in point. All his fasts of course brought his charisma into play for they depended for success on the fact that the persons whom he sought to influence dared not allow a saint to die. It is instructive to note, therefore, that the vast majority of his fasts were di-

is once discovered to be tainted with self-interest or in-difference has lost the love forever. Now if, in even the most trivial decisions a leader's whole career and life may be at stake, how is he to calculate the cost of each indi-vidual payment? In a sense, he pays his whole life over and over and with each decision risks it. I conclude, therefore, that payments in this category are truly incalculable, al-though it is also clearly apparent that payments are a genuine cost.

The foregoing analysis of the costs to leaders may be summarized thus: Let $v(P) = v$, where $P$ is a winning coalition. Then $v$ represents the objective value of a win-ning coalition. Only conventionally is this a number, how-ever, for it seems difficult to add up numerically the ob-jective values of something like victory in war. But it will nevertheless be assumed that there is some magical market measurement of things not ordinarily bought and sold and that the price in this magical market is the value of what-ever is won: war, elections, motions, etc. Thus $v$ may be regarded as a number, but not a directly calculable one. Let $v_1$ be the subjective value of winning as it appears to leaders of the proto-coalition that may become $P$, the winning one. Again $v_1$ is a conventional number and we assume that, where $v_1(P)$ and $v_1(Q)$ are a leader's estimate

---

rected against caste Hindus, that is, they could be ended only if Hindus either performed some action he desired or desisted from some action he disapproved. Caste Hindus were, of course, those persons most likely to be convinced of his saintliness and therefore the persons most likely to feel the force of this weapon. Some of his fasts were even directed against persons in his immediate entourage. Only four of his fasts were directed against the British, although these are the ones most widely publicized. And these four, it should be observed, were undertaken when all of Hindu India was aflame and when the British were for one reason or another compelled by political circumstances to show greater-than-usual deference to Indian and world public opinion. The inference I draw from a survey of Gandhi's political fasting is that, with a realism somewhat un-expected in a mystic, he fasted only when he could win. Never once did he expose his charisma to the humiliation of abandoning a fast in failure.

of the respective values of winning in alternative ways a leader is able to say that, for him, $v_1(P) > v_1(Q)$, or vice versa.

In summary, when contingent payments out of profits are used, then $\sum_{i \varepsilon P} \alpha_i = v$. When payments out of working capital are used, $\sum_{i \varepsilon P} \alpha_i = v_1$. But no such limit is observable when payments out of fixed assets are used, simply because no limit, relative to a particular decision, can be calculated, even roughly. All that can be said about such payments is that $v_1 > v$ invariably and, since the leader is part of the winning coalition, $\sum_{i \varepsilon P} \alpha_i > v$.

## THE EXCHANGE OF SIDE-PAYMENTS

Just as a leader's perception of the value of a winning coalition may be quite different from the imaginary objective value, so also a follower's perception of this value, which perception we will call $v_2$, may be quite different from either $v$ or $v_1$. In this confusion of values, how can exchange occur? Yet it does. And this fact must be incorporated into the model. One possibility is to assume that all values are measured in units of utility or utiles and that these are the basis of agreement in exchange. But such an assumption involves us in the interpersonal comparison of preferences, on which utility is based, and preference is defined in a wholly subjective and non-interpersonally-comparable fashion. And so, although "transferable utility" has been a common notion in the theory of games, it will be avoided here. Rather, I shall describe the barter of political currency in terms unique to each transaction so that no general interpretation is necessary.

Consider what happens in, e.g., an exchange over the provisions of a bill in a legislature. Let us assume that there is a proto-coalition, $P$, supporting a bill and that it can attract no more supporters without some sort of payments, of which the easiest and most immediately available are changes in the content of the bill. For the leader of $P$, the first question is whether or not to attempt to use this kind of currency. In deciding this question, $P$'s leader must consider (a) the availability of other kinds of currency and the probable amount needed for victory and (b) the probable expectations of payment by other proto-coalitions, $Q$, $R$, and $S$. Assuming that other kinds of currency are either not available or potentially more costly (in terms of the preference of $P$'s leader) and assuming that at least one of $Q$, $R$, or $S$ can possibly be bought with a change not so extreme as to make the final bill distasteful to $P$, then $P$'s leader decides to use this kind of payment. Once having so decided, $P$ must compare the kinds of changes that probably will be required to win the support of the several other proto-coalitions. If there is a difference, $P$'s leader makes an offer of change to that proto-coalition, let us say $S$, who will ask, so he believes, the least distasteful changes. Hence $P$'s decision to make the offer depends not on an interpersonal comparison of utility, but rather on $P$'s perception of available alternatives and of its own perception of other proto-coalition's estimates of value.

As for $S$, the recipient of the offer, its decision about whether or not to accept is based on these considerations: (a) the degree to which the bill, as it is proposed to be amended, satisfies its own ambitions for public policy, (b) the degree to which it is possible for $S$ to ally with $Q$ or $R$ to obtain a decision more to its liking than that offered by $P$, and (c) the degree to which $S$ runs the risk, if it rejects $P$'s offer, of $P$ successfully allying with $Q$ or $R$

to bring about a decision distasteful to $S$. Assuming that the possibility is remote that either $S$ or $P$ ally with $Q$ or $R$, then $S$'s considerations boil down to the attractiveness of $P$'s offer. If what $P$ offers is, for $S$, worth having and, furthermore, if it seems about the best $S$ can do considering its own and $P$'s alternatives, then $S$ decides to accept. Note that it does so, however, only by comparing the offer tendered with its own preferences and its subjective estimation of the state of $P$'s preferences and alternatives. Again no interpersonal comparisons need be assumed.

If $S$ rejects $P$'s offer, then the whole process of successive decisions must be reiterated. But if $S$ accepts, then the bargain is complete. Yet both parties to the bargain have at no point based their decision on a consideration of $v$. The leader of $P$ has based his decision on $v_1$, although, when using this kind of currency $v$ is some sort of maximum limit for $v_1$. Similarly, $S$ has consulted only its subjective estimate of value, $v_2$. And at no point has it been necessary to assume that either $v_1$ or $v_2$ is the same as $v$.

The rub comes when one asks then what $v$ means. The answer is that $v$ stands for a particular winning, an election, a bill, etc., which is conventionally assumed to have a market value. But if this is so, what can it mean to say that $v$ is equal to the payments to the members of the winning coalition? If these payments have been calculated with respect to $v_1$ and $v_2$, what possible connection can these have with $v$? At this point the utility theorist would of necessity say that the utility of the payment to $P$ plus the utility of the payment to $S$ equals $v$. But it is precisely this assertion that we wish to avoid. And in avoiding it, one naturally questions if $v$ has any meaning at all. Nevertheless, we shall say here that $v$ is simply a shorthand notation for a particular victory which is objectively the same for winners and losers (thus satisfying the zero-sum condition) without necessarily suggesting that the utility of the loss and gain is subjectively identical. With respect to a particular winning coalition $(P \cup S)$, we will assume that $v$ is such that payments can be made to $P$ and $S$ to satisfy each of them, without suggesting that the utility to $P$ and $S$ equals $v$. In the next chapter, where the relative satisfaction of $v = v(P \cup S)$ and $v' = v(P \cup R)$ are discussed, it is assumed only that, if $v > v'$, payments can be made to $P$ and $S$ that are mutually more satisfactory than payments to $P$ and $R$. With this set of assumptions about the process, it seems possible to talk about $v$ in a quite meaningful fashion without involving interpersonal comparisons of utility.

## CHAPTER 6

# Strategy in Coalition-building

In this chapter and in more detail in Appendix II the general strategic considerations governing the growth of coalitions will be analyzed. In the literary tradition of political studies it is usually assumed that the crucial events in this growth are wholly unique and therefore not susceptible to generalization. And indeed it is true that unique considerations of personality, tradition, style, and chance loom far larger in the written history of the formation of any particular coalition than do general strategic considerations. Here it is assumed, however, that such general considerations do exist and that their absence from history writing is due to the fact that they have not heretofore been formulated. It is the task of this chapter to begin the formulation.

The starting point is the dynamic model set forth in the previous chapter and the size principle drawn from the static analysis in the first four chapters. It is assumed that the participants in a decision-system in stage $(r-1)$ and earlier stages are guided in their moves by their expectations of the kind of situation they will find themselves in at the $r^{th}$ or final stage. Hence the problem is: How does knowledge about alternative outcomes in the $r^{th}$ stage affect the moves occurring between the $(r-1)^{th}$ and $r^{th}$ stages? How does knowledge about alternatives in the $r^{th}$ and $(r-1)^{th}$ stages affect action occurring between the $(r-2)^{th}$ and $(r-1)^{th}$ stages?

What the leaders of proto-coalitions in stages $(r-1)$, $(r-2)$, . . . are especially concerned about is their chance of belonging to a winning coalition in the $r^{th}$ stage. Shapley has devised a value for $n$-person games which at first glance seems the appropriate device by which to analyze such expectations. It is, in effect, a calculation of the chance each player has under the rules to occupy a *pivotal* position in the formation of a coalition. The *pivotal* position is defined as that occupied by the last-added member of a minimal winning coalition, where a minimal winning coalition is one which ceases to be winning if one member is subtracted.[1] Unfortunately, Shapley's value is only intended to allow players to calculate prospects of outcomes before the play is begun. Shapley remarks: "the value is best regarded as an *a priori* assessment of the situation, based on either ignorance or disregard of the social organization of the players."[2] Hence it does not incorporate information acquired during the play, which involves, of course, the development of social organization. But it is exactly this information which is crucial as the process approaches an end. Shapley's value is an excellent technique for evaluating a constitution or set of rules of a game in order to

1. L. S. Shapley, "A Value for *N*-Person Games," *Annals of Mathematics Study No. 28* (Princeton, Princeton University Press, 1953), pp. 307–17; L. S. Shapley and Martin Shubik, "A Method of Evaluating the Distribution of Power in a Committee System," *American Political Science Review,* 48 (1954), 787–92; John G. Kemeny, J. Laurie Snell, and Gerald L. Thompson, *Introduction to Finite Mathematics* (Englewood Cliffs, N.J., Prentice-Hall, 1957), pp. 74–77, 108–10.

2. Shapley, p. 316.

decide initially whether or not to join a society or play a game. But it is not particularly relevant to a calculus of expectations during the course of the formation of a particular coalition, which is a frequently repeated process occurring after one has joined a society or decided to play a game.

In order to evaluate their prospects at a given (non-initial) point in the play, leaders want to know, not their chance of pivoting, but rather their chance of winning given the immediate state of arrangements into proto-coalitions. The chance of winning may be almost entirely dependent on unique events occurring during the course of the play (e.g. animosities aroused or friendships culti-vated); or it may depend greatly on the traditions of a particular decision-making body. But in part, at least, the chance of winning may depend on general considerations inherent in the game model. Particularly in world politics, and even in national politics, where the influences of one personality or one tradition are not so likely to be con-trolling as they are in smaller bodies, these general con-siderations may be dominant in determining the outcome.

One such general consideration is the size principle, which may place severe restrictions on admissible coali-tions and thereby greatly influence the chance that a particular proto-coalition will become a part of a winning coalition. For example, if there are two almost winning proto-coalitions and several quite small ones, the size principle suggests that the two large ones do not combine, for the resulting coalition would be so large as to be nearly worthless. In some bodies, this general considera-tion is translated into a fairly specific local tradition which renders coalitions of the two main parties inadmissible. This particular illustration is an instance of a general consideration of strategy which follows from the size principle: If at some $j^{th}$ stage, which is, potentially, the $(r-1)^{th}$ stage, some proto-coalitions can form a minimal winning coalition and others cannot, those that can may have a strategic advantage. This advantage consists simply in the fact that those who can form a minimal winning coalition may be able to agree on a more profitable arrangement of payoffs. Among rational players, this advantage is sufficient to guarantee that any coalition so situated in the $(r-1)^{th}$ stage will belong to a winning coalition in the $r^{th}$ stage.

Assuming, as I shall throughout this chapter, that all characteristic functions slope downward and to the right (that is, assuming none are parallel to the abscissa except at zero) and given the influence of the size principle on coalition-building, what leaders of proto-coalitions need is a specification of the situations in which such advantages exist. In order to formalize this specification, I shall use the notions of (1) *uniquely preferable winning coalitions,* (2) *uniquely favored proto-coalitions,* (3) *uniquely essential proto-coalitions,* (4) *unique coalitions,* and (5) *strategically weak proto-coalitions.* The effort of this chapter, then, is to specify the situations in which uniquely situated coalitions and proto-coalitions exist.

## UNIQUELY SITUATED PROTO-COALITIONS

The notion of a uniquely preferable winning coalition is in some respects stronger, and in some weaker, than Von Neumann and Morgenstern's notion of a solution. For them a solution is a set of imputations such that (1) no imputation in the set dominates (i.e. is better for a majority of the players) any other imputation in the set and (2) some imputation in the set dominates any given imputation outside the set. In the essential three-person game, which they discuss at great length, the solution is the set of imputations (in normalized form): (½, ½, −1), (½, −1, ½), (−1, ½, ½). Thus the solution specifies the possible payoffs, but does not determine the winning coalition for, labeling the players "1," "2," and "3," the coalitions (1,2), (1,3), and (2,3) are equally feasible. In many other games there is no solution in the Von Neumann-Morgenstern sense so that the winning coalition is similarly undetermined. The notion of a uniquely preferable winning coalition, on the other hand, involves the specification of a determined winning coalition, while the imputation may be, within, of course, a determined range, undetermined.

In this analysis I shall initially limit the discussion (1) to the $(r-1)^{th}$ stage—a limitation that will subsequently be removed—and (2) to those situations in which there are no more than five proto-coalitions. In most real decision-systems, the number of factions at the penultimate (and even the antepenultimate) stage is in fact seldom likely to exceed five. So this second limitation, while imposed solely for the sake of numerical convenience, still does not involve too great a departure in the model from the conditions of reality.

In order to establish a vocabulary, let us define five proto-coalitions, $P, Q, R, S, T$, as disjoint subsets of $I$. If $I$ is partitioned into three subsets, then $P$, $Q$, and $R$ exist and $S$ and $T$ are undefined. If $I$ is partitioned into four subsets, only $T$ is undefined. Since these are proto-coalitions rather than coalitions $m > w(P), w(Q), w(R), w(S), w(T)$. For convenience of nomenclature $w(P)$ will always be the largest, if there is a uniquely largest, $w(Q)$ will always be the second largest, if there is a uniquely second largest, etc. In general $w(P) \geqq w(Q) \geqq w(R) \geqq w(S) \geqq w(T)$. Since it will be necessary to discuss simultaneously partitions of $I$ into different numbers of subsets, the number of subsets in the partition will be indicated by a superscription to the symbol for the set. Thus $P^3$ is the symbol for the weightiest proto-coalition (or one of the equally weightiest) when $I$ is partitioned into three proto-coalitions.

It is to be understood that these proto-coalitions are, for the purposes of the present analysis, indivisible units even though they may be composed of many individual players. Hence two additional conditions must be imposed: First, followers, once joined to a proto-coalition, may not resign. This is, of course, a highly artificial condition and in the subsequent interpretation it will be abandoned. Second, leaders, once they have purchased the allegiance of a follower with a side-payment, may not lower the payment offered unless the follower agrees. This exception is not as unreasonable as it may initially appear to be, for followers who join a leader early in the process of coalition-formation may be willing to give up some of his initial offer in order to allow him greater freedom in negotiating with a potentially pivotal member of a minimal winning coalition.

The formal definitions of uniquely situated coalitions is reserved for Appendix II, but in this chapter the definitions can be verbally summarized.

An *initial expectation* for a proto-coalition, $X^k$, in the $(r-1)^{th}$ stage is an imputation for $\Gamma$, when a minimal winning coalition containing $X^k$ forms, such that the imputation contains a payoff to $X^k$ equal to the maximum of the values of all nonminimal winning coalitions that $X^k$ might belong to. Put otherwise, an initial expectation for $X^k$ in his bargaining to enter a minimal winning coalition is an amount equal to the best it can do in the best alternative nonminimal winning coalition.

A *uniquely preferable winning coalition* is a coalition such that (1) it has a greater value than any other one possible, given the particular partition in the $(r-1)^{th}$

stage, and (2) it is one in which all the participating proto-coalitions can satisfy their initial expectations.

A *uniquely favored proto-coalition, $X^k$*, is (1) a proto-coalition such that any winning coalition containing $X^k$ is more valuable than one not containing it and (2) if more than one proto-coalition satisfies condition 1, then there is at least one winning coalition containing $X^k$ and none of the others that satisfy condition 1.

A *uniquely essential proto-coalition* is one which appears in all winning coalitions when no other proto-coalition is so favored.

A *unique coalition* is a winning coalition in the $r^{th}$ stage such that only one combination of proto-coalitions in the $(r-1)^{th}$ stage can produce a winning coalition. (For a three-set partition of $I$ in the $(r-1)^{th}$ stage unique coalitions and uniquely essential proto-coalitions can be defined only if extraordinary majorities are required.)

A *strategically weak proto-coalition* is one that cannot, by reason of a given partition in a putative $(r-1)^{th}$ stage, become a part of the most valuable winning coalition.


### *THE $(r-1)^{th}$ STAGE*

With the definitions supplied by the foregoing section, it is possible to consider some of the behavior in the $(r-1)^{th}$ stage in the model. For the sake of the readers' convenience the discussion here is limited to one special case. Other cases are considered systematically in Appendix II.

Let us suppose that in the $(r-1)^{th}$ stage the set $I$ is partitioned into three proto-coalitions, $P^3$, $Q^3$, and $R^3$, such that $w(P^3) > w(Q^3) > w(R^3)$. If $m = (n+1)/2$ or if $m = (n/2) + 1$, the winning coalitions possible in the $r^{th}$ stage are: $(Q^3 \cup R^3)$, $(P^3 \cup R^3)$, and $(P^3 \cup Q^3)$. By reason of the size principle, the values of these coalitions are related thus:

$$\text{If} \begin{cases} v(Q^3 \cup R^3) = a = -v(P^3) \\ v(P^3 \cup R^3) = b = -v(Q^3) \\ v(P^3 \cup Q^3) = c = -v(R^3) \end{cases}, \text{ then } a > b > c.$$

What we wish to know is: Does a uniquely preferable winning coalition exist? That is, we wish to know:

1. Does some coalition have greater value than any other?
2. Can the members of that coalition satisfy their initial expectations?

Since $a > b > c$, it is clear that the first question is answered affirmatively, for $v(Q^3 \cup R^3)$ is greater than the value of any other coalition. But can both $Q^3$ and $R^3$ satisfy their initial expectations? For $Q^3$ the initial expectation is calculated thus: If $Q^3$ joins $P^3$ in a coalition and $P^3$ gets none of the value of $(P^3 \cup Q^3)$, then $Q^3$ can obtain $c$. Considering an alliance of $Q^3$ and $R^3$, the imputation would then be: $\alpha_{P3} = -a$, $\alpha_{Q3} = c$, $\alpha_{R3} = (a - c)$, or, more simply, $(-a, c, a - c)$. For $R^3$ the initial expectation is calculated similarly: If $R^3$ joins $P^3$ and if $P^3$ receives none of the value of $(P^3 \cup R^3)$, then $R^3$ can obtain $b$. In alliance with $Q^3$, then, $R^3$ can initially expect $(-a, a - b, b)$. The crucial consideration, then, is the relative size of $a$, $b$, and $c$, which is, of course, determined by the shape of the curve of the characteristic function. Let us suppose $c < a - b$. In this case it is clear that both $R^3$ and $Q^3$ can obtain the payoff each desires in its initial expectation. Observe that, if $c < a - b$, then $b > a - c$. Hence, if $R^3$ receives its initial expected payoff of $b$, then there is still the amount $a - b$ out of which to pay $Q^3$. And $Q^3$ does not expect as much as $a - b$. So both $R^3$ and $Q^3$ can satisfy their initial expectations, which is to say that both can do better than if either one joined $P^3$. Since $(Q^3 \cup R^3)$ has a greater value than any other coalition and since both $Q^3$ and $R^3$ can satisfy their initial expectations in it, $(Q^3 \cup R^3)$ is a uniquely preferable coalition. We can suppose it will be formed. Of course, either $Q^3$ or $R^3$ might conceivably join $P^3$ and receive at least its initial expectation, which is, however, less than either could expect in $(Q^3 \cup R^3)$. Since it is assumed that the players in the model are rational, it then follows that only $(Q^3 \cup R^3)$ will be formed, which is the reason for seeking to identify uniquely preferable winning coalitions.

By a similar analysis, all possible relations of weights of proto-coalitions and curves of characteristic functions of coalitions can be examined for the case when $I$ is partitioned into three proto-coalitions. It is then possible to specify all situations in which any kind of uniqueness appears. These cases are analyzed in Appendix II and the results are set forth in Table 1. Similarly, it is possible, but more tedious, to examine the possible instances of uniqueness in four-set and five-set partitions of $I$. This has been done in part (though not reported in detail) and the results are set forth in Tables 2 and 3. Note that these tables are the analogues of only columns one and two of Table 1. Exactly what these tables mean is also explained in Appendix II.

## STRATEGY IN THE $(r-1)^{th}$ STAGE

The foregoing analysis of the relative position of proto-coalitions in three-, four-, and five-set partitions permits some general observations on the strategy of coalition-building.

The most obvious and perhaps most important conclusion to be drawn is that remarks on strategy can be uttered at all. As long as proto-coalitions are differently situated—

and the whole effect of this analysis has been to show that they often are—then for each one there are better and worse ways of acting, and it is the task of a theory of strategy to distinguish the better from the worse. Unfortunately, it has, I believe, been generally assumed by game theorists that the theory did not offer much basis for the discussion of strategy in $n$-person, zero-sum games. And, indeed, the inferences on strategy to be drawn from Von Neumann and Morgenstern's exhaustive analysis of the essential three-person game are relatively few and unimpressive: that the winning coalition is unpredictable on theoretical grounds, that the equilibrium payoff is an equal division between the partners in a winning coalition, and that departures from the equilibrium are invitations to disaster. The analysis here adds nothing to these conclusions, for the analogue in this analysis of the essential three-person game is the three-set partition in which the weights of all sets are equal and that analogue occupies the bottom row of Table 1 where it is indicated that no proto-coalition has an advantage. What this analysis does add, however, is the observation that the essential three-person game is a rather special case, probably infrequent in nature. Three-set partitions where the partitions have unequal weights are probably far more common in nature and, what is more, are often characterized by the existence of special advantages. Around these advantages it is possible to build a theory of strategy.

If coalitions are not of equal weight—and I have suggested in Appendix II reasons for believing that they seldom are—then it is often possible that near the end of the process of coalition-building one or more proto-coalitions will find themselves in some sort of uniquely advantageous position. For those who do not have the advantage, the possession of it by others is, of course, a severe disadvantage. These advantages I have described as uniquely favored, uniquely preferable, uniquely essential, and unique. The unifying feature of all these definitions is the possession of some advantage in bargaining, some increment in the chance of winning. On this basis, the general

TABLE 1    *Uniqueness of position of proto-coalitions in three-set partitions of* 1

| | Col. 1 | Col. 2 | Col. 3 | Col. 4 |
|---|---|---|---|---|
| | $w(P^3 \cup Q^3) \geqq w(P^3 \cup R^3) \geqq$ $w(Q^3 \cup R^3) \geqq m$ | | $m > w(Q^3 \cup R^3)$ or $w(P^3 \cup R^3)$ | |
| | $c \leqq a - b$ or $b \leqq a/2$ | $c > a - b$ or $b > a/2$ | $w(P^3 \cup R^3) \geqq m$ | $m > w(P^3 \cup R^3)$ |
| **Row 1** $w(P^3) > w(Q^3) > w(R^3)$ | $\widehat{R^3}$ $Q^3_{\,3.A.1-2}$ | $\widehat{R^3}$ ${}_{3.A.3}$ | $\boxed{P^3}$ $R^3$ ${}_{3.E.1}$ | $\boxed{P^3}$ $\boxed{Q^3}$ ${}_{3.E.2}$ |
| **Row 2** $w(P^3) > w(Q^3) = w(R^3)$ | $R^3$ $Q^3_{\,3.B.1-2}$ | ——— ${}_{3.B.3}$ | $\boxed{P^3}$ ${}_{3.E.1}$ | //// |
| **Row 3** $w(P^3) = w(Q^3) > w(R^3)$ | $\widehat{R^3}$ ${}_{3.C}$ | | //// | //// |
| **Row 4** $w(P^3) = w(Q^3) = w(R^3)$ | ——— ${}_{3.D}$ | | //// | //// |

*Key:* $\widehat{P^3}$    indicates a uniquely favored proto-coalition.

     $P^3 Q^3$    indicates a uniquely preferable winning coalition.

     $\underline{P^3 Q^3}$    indicates a unique coalition.

     $\boxed{P^3}$    indicates a uniquely essential proto-coalition.

     ——— indicates that no sort of uniqueness occurs in the given conditions.

     //// indicates that the combination of conditions is impossible.

## TABLE 1 (continued)

*Note:* The typology of coalitions offered here may be compared with the typology offered by Caplow.[3] He offers eight categories of weights for proto-coalitions, $A$, $B$, and $C$:

1. $w(A) = w(B) = w(C)$
2. $w(A) > w(B); w(B) = w(C)$
3. $w(A) < w(B); w(B) = w(C)$
4. $w(A) > w(B \cup C); w(B) = w(C)$
5. $w(A) > w(B) > w(C); w(A) < w(B \cup C)$
6. $w(A) > w(B) > w(C); w(A) > w(B \cup C)$
7. $w(A) > w(B) > w(C); w(A) = w(B \cup C)$
8. $w(A) = w(B \cup C); w(B) = w(C)$

Types 4 and 6 are irrelevant to our concerns if $m = (n+1)/2$ or $m = (n/2) + 1$, for then $P^3$ is a dictator. If $m > (n+1)/2$ or $m > (n/2) + 1$, then types 4 and 6 are equivalent to row 1, column 3 or 4, or rows 1 and 2, column 3, of Table 1. Again if $m$ is a bare majority, types 7 and 8 are cases of blocking coalitions and are irrelevant to our concerns. If, however, $m$ is larger than a bare majority, then types 7 and 8 are equivalent respectively to row 1, columns 3 and 4, and row 2, column 3. This leaves types 1, 2, 3, and 5 which are equivalent to the positions in Table 1 as follows:

> Type 1 is equivalent to row 4.
> Type 2 is equivalent to row 2, columns 1 and 2.
> Type 3 is equivalent to row 3.
> Type 5 is equivalent to row 1, columns 1 and 2.

Caplow's predictions are the same as the ones offered here, except for his type 5, which is, as is shown in Appendix II, by far the most important case. By reason of his failure to differentiate among payoffs, he does not distinguish between columns 1 and 2. Hence he regards $(Q^3 \cup R^3)$ and $(P^3 \cup R^3)$ as equally likely. Furthermore, he fails to observe the unique position of $R^3$. Gamson has tried to improve on Caplow's categories.[4] But his types do not differ significantly from Caplow's. Gamson predicts for type 5 or case 3A a definitive victory for $(Q^3 \cup R^3)$, which again fails to note the special position of $R^3$.

3. Theodore Caplow, "A Theory of Coalitions in the Triad," *American Sociological Review*, 21, 489–93; and Theodore Caplow, "Further Development of a Theory of Coalitions in the Triad," *American Journal of Sociology*, 64 (1959), 488–93.

4. William A. Gamson, "A Theory of Coalition-Formation," *American Sociological Review*, 26 (1961), 373–82, and "An Experimental Test of a Theory of Coalition-Formation," *American Sociological Review*, 26 (1961), 565–73.

TABLE 2  *Uniqueness of position of proto-coalitions in four-set partitions of* I

| | $z \geq y \geq x \geq m > v; w' \geq m > v$ | | | | | | | | $z \geq y \geq m > x; w' \geq m > v$ | | | | | | | |
|---|---|---|---|---|---|---|---|---|---|---|---|---|---|---|---|---|
| | $w' > x$ | | | | | $w' = x$ | $w' < x$ | $y > w'$ | $y = w'$ | $y < w'$ | | | rotated | rotated | rotated | rotated |
| | $w' > z$ | $w' = z$ | $w' > y$ | $w' = y$ | $w' < y$ | | | | | $z > w'$ | $z = w'$ | $z < w'$ | $z \leq m \leq y; u \leq m < x$ | $z < r \leq w' \leq m$ | $v' \geq m, m'; r < z$ | $v' \geq m \leq m', w' \leq m \leq u; y \leq r \leq m \leq z, r < m$ |
| **Row 1**  $w(P^4) > w(Q^4) > w(R^4) > w(S^4)$ | Ⓟ$^4$ S$^4$ | P$^4$ S$^4$ | P$^4$ S$^4$ | P$^4$ S$^4$ | Ⓟ$^4$ | Ⓢ$^4$ | Q$^4$ R$^4$ / Ⓢ$^4$ | Q$^4$ R$^4$ / Ⓢ$^4$ | — | P$^4$ Ⓡ$^4$ | P$^4$ R$^4$ | Ⓟ$^4$ R$^4$ | Ⓠ$^4$ | (hatched) | (hatched) | (hatched) |
| **Row 2**  $w(P^4) > w(Q^4) > w(R^4) = w(S^4)$ | Ⓟ$^4$ | — | — | (hatched) | (hatched) | — | Q$^4$ R$^4$ / S$^4$ | (hatched) | — | (hatched) | (hatched) | Ⓟ$^4$ | Q$^4$ R$^4$ | (hatched) | P$^4$ Q$^4$ | (hatched) |
| **Row 3**  $w(P^4) > w(Q^4) = w(R^4) > w(S^4)$ | Ⓟ$^4$ S$^4$ | P$^4$ | (hatched) | P$^4$ S$^4$ | P$^4$ Ⓢ$^4$ | Ⓢ$^4$ | Q$^4$ R$^4$ / Ⓢ$^4$ | Q$^4$ R$^4$ / Ⓢ$^4$ | (hatched) | (hatched) | (hatched) | Ⓟ$^4$ | Q$^4$ R$^4$ | (hatched) | — | (hatched) |
| **Row 4**  $w(P^4) > w(Q^4) = w(R^4) = w(S^4)$ | Ⓟ$^4$ | (hatched) | (hatched) | — | (hatched) | — | Q$^4$ R$^4$ / S$^4$ | (hatched) | (hatched) | (hatched) | (hatched) | (hatched) | Ⓡ$^4$ | (hatched) | (hatched) | — |
| **Column Number** | 1 | 2 | 3 | 4 | 5 | 6 | 7 | 8 | 9 | 10 | 11 | 12 | 13 | 14 | 15 | 16 |

Row 5  $w(P^4) = w(Q^4) > w(R^4) > w(S^4)$

Row 6  $w(P^4) = w(Q^4) > w(R^4) = w(S^4)$

Row 7  $w(P^4) = w(Q^4) = w(R^4) > w(S^4)$

Row 8  $w(P^4) = w(Q^4) = w(R^4) = w(S^4)$

*Key:*  For symbols in cells, see Table 1.

$w(P^4 \cup S^4) = x$    $w(Q^4 \cup R^4 \cup S^4) = w'$

$w(P^4 \cup R^4) = y$    $w(P^4 \cup Q^4 \cup R^4) = q$

$w(P^4 \cup Q^4) = z$    $w(P^4 \cup Q^4 \cup S^4) = r$

$w(Q^4 \cup R^4) = v$    $w(P^4 \cup R^4 \cup S^4) = v'$

$m$ = minimal winning weight

**TABLE 3** *Uniqueness of position of proto-coalitions in five-set partitions of 1*

| | $z \geq y \geq x \geq x \geq w \geq m > v$; $s' \geq m > w$; $z \geq y \geq x \geq x \geq m > w$; $w' \geq m > x$ | | | | | | | |
|---|---|---|---|---|---|---|---|---|
| | $s' > w$ | | $s' = w$ | $s' < w$ | $w' > x$ | | $w' = x$ | $w' < x$ |
| Row number | $s' > z$ | $s' \leq z$ | | | $w' > z$ | $w' \leq z$ | | |
| 1  $w(P^S) > w(Q^S) > w(R^S) > w(S^S) > w(T^S)$ | $(P^S)\ T^S$ | $P^S\ T^S$ | $(T^S)$ | $Q^S\ R^S$ $S^S\ (T^S)$ | $(P^S)\ S^S$ | $P^S\ S^S$ | $(S^S)$ | $Q^S\ R^S$ $(S^S)$ |
| 2  $w(P^S) > w(Q^S) > w(R^S) > w(S^S) = w(T^S)$ | $(P^S)$ | — | — | $Q^S\ R^S$ $S^S\ T^S$ | $(P^S)$ | ////// | ////// | $Q^S\ R^S$ $(S^S)$ |
| 3  $w(P^S) > w(Q^S) > w(R^S) = w(S^S) > w(T^S)$ | $(P^S)\ T^S$ | $P^S\ T^S$ | $(T^S)$ | $Q^S\ R^S$ $S^S\ (T^S)$ | $(P^S)$ | ////// | ////// | $Q^S\ R^S$ $(S^S)$ |
| 4  $w(P^S) > w(Q^S) = w(R^S) > w(S^S) > w(T^S)$ | $(P^S)$ | — | — | $Q^S\ R^S$ $S^S\ (T^S)$ | $(P^S)$ | ////// | ////// | $Q^S\ R^S$ $(S^S)$ |
| 5  $w(P^S) > w(Q^S) > w(R^S) = w(S^S) = w(T^S)$ | $(P^S)\ T^S$ | $P^S\ T^S$ | $(T^S)$ | $Q^S\ R^S$ $S^S\ (T^S)$ | $(P^S)\ S^S$ | $P^S\ S^S$ | $S^S$ | $Q^S\ R^S$ $S^S$ |
| 6  $w(P^S) > w(Q^S) = w(R^S) > w(S^S) = w(T^S)$ | $(P^S)$ | — | — | $Q^S\ R^S$ $S^S\ T^S$ | $(P^S)$ | ////// | ////// | $Q^S\ R^S$ $S^S$ |
| 7  $w(P^S) > w(Q^S) = w(R^S) = w(S^S) > w(T^S)$ | $(P^S)\ T^S$ | $P^S\ T^S$ | $(T^S)$ | $Q^S\ R^S$ $S^S\ T^S$ | $(P^S)$ | ////// | ////// | $Q^S\ R^S$ $S^S$ |
| 8  $w(P^S) > w(Q^S) = w(R^S) = w(S^S) = w(T^S)$ | $P^S$ | — | — | $Q^S\ R^S$ $S^S\ T^S$ | ////// | ////// | — | ////// |
| Column number | 1 | 2 | 3 | 4 | 5 | 6 | 7 | 8 |

*Key:* See Table 1 for symbols in cells.

$w(P^S \cup T^S) = w$; $w(Q^S \cup R^S \cup S^S) = w'$; $w(P^S \cup R^S) = y$; $w(Q^S \cup S^S \cup T^S) = y'$;
$w(P^S \cup S^S) = x$; $w(Q^S \cup R^S \cup T^S) = x'$; $w(Q^S \cup T^S) = t$; $w(P^S \cup R^S \cup S^S) = t'$;
$w(P^S \cup S^S) = x$; $w(R^S \cup U S^S \cup T^S) = z$; $w(Q^S \cup U S^S) = u$; $w(P^S \cup R^S \cup T^S) = u'$;
$w(Q^S \cup R^S) = v$; $w(P^S \cup S^S \cup T^S) = v'$; $w(P^S) = s$; $w(Q^S \cup R^S \cup S^S \cup T^S) = s'$

TABLE 3 (continued)

$z \geq y \geq m > x;\ w' \geq x' \geq m > y';\ v' \geq m > v$

| Row number | 9: $y \geq \cdots \geq w', \cdots$ | 10: $y > x, w' \geq v', \cdots$ | 11: $y = v > x, w', \cdots$ | 12: $y = v = x, w', \cdots$ | 13: $v > x, y > y', \cdots$ | 14: $v > x, y = y', \cdots$ | 15: $v > x', \cdots, y', \cdots$ | 16: $v'' = x', \cdots$ | 17: $x > v > \cdots$ | 18: $x > \cdots > v, \cdots$ | 19: $x > \cdots > w', y', \cdots$ | 20: $x = y > v', \cdots$ | 21: $x = m > y', \cdots$ or $x = m > y, \cdots$ | 22: $x = m' > \cdots u \geq v, \cdots$ |
|---|---|---|---|---|---|---|---|---|---|---|---|---|---|---|
| 1  $w(P^s) > w(Q^s) > w(R^s) > w(S^s) > w(T^s)$ | $P^s R^s$ | $P^s R^s$ | — | — | $\dfrac{P^s S^s}{T^s}$ | $\dfrac{P^s S^s}{T^s}$ | $\dfrac{P^s S^s}{\boxed{T^s}}$ | $\boxed{T^s}$ | $\dfrac{Q^s R^s}{\boxed{T^s}}$ | $\dfrac{Q^s \boxed{R^s}}{T^s}$ | $\dfrac{Q^s R^s}{T^s}$ | — | $\boxed{R^s}$ | ▨ |
| 2  $w(P^s) > w(Q^s) > w(R^s) > w(S^s) = w(T^s)$ | $P^s R^s$ | $P^s R^s$ | — | — | $\dfrac{P^s S^s}{T^s}$ | $\dfrac{P^s S^s}{T^s}$ | $\dfrac{P^s S^s}{T^s}$ | ▨ | ▨ | ▨ | ▨ | ▨ | $\boxed{R^s}$ | — |
| 3  $w(P^s) > w(Q^s) > w(R^s) = w(S^s) > w(T^s)$ | ▨ | ▨ | ▨ | ▨ | ▨ | ▨ | ▨ | ▨ | ▨ | ▨ | ▨ | ▨ | ▨ | ▨ |
| 4  $w(P^s) > w(Q^s) = w(R^s) > w(S^s) > w(T^s)$ | ▨ | ▨ | ▨ | ▨ | ▨ | ▨ | ▨ | ▨ | ▨ | ▨ | ▨ | ▨ | ▨ | ▨ |
| 5  $w(P^s) > w(Q^s) > w(R^s) = w(S^s) = w(T^s)$ | $\boxed{P^s}$ | — | $\boxed{P^s}$ | — | $\dfrac{\boxed{P^s} S^s}{T^s}$ | $\dfrac{P^s S^s}{T^s}$ | $\dfrac{P^s S^s}{\boxed{T^s}}$ | $\boxed{T^s}$ | $\dfrac{Q^s R^s}{\boxed{T^s}}$ | $\dfrac{Q^s \boxed{R^s}}{T^s}$ | $\dfrac{Q^s R^s}{T^s}$ | — | — | ▨ |
| 6  $w(P^s) > w(Q^s) = w(R^s) = w(S^s) > w(T^s)$ | $\boxed{P^s}$ | — | $\boxed{P^s}$ | — | $\dfrac{\boxed{P^s} S^s}{T^s}$ | $\dfrac{P^s S^s}{T^s}$ | $\dfrac{P^s S^s}{T^s}$ | ▨ | ▨ | ▨ | ▨ | ▨ | — | — |
| 7  $w(P^s) > w(Q^s) = w(R^s) = w(S^s) = w(T^s)$ | ▨ | ▨ | ▨ | ▨ | ▨ | ▨ | ▨ | ▨ | ▨ | ▨ | ▨ | ▨ | ▨ | ▨ |
| 8  $w(P^s) = w(Q^s) = w(R^s) = w(S^s) = w(T^s)$ | ▨ | ▨ | ▨ | ▨ | ▨ | ▨ | ▨ | ▨ | ▨ | ▨ | ▨ | ▨ | ▨ | ▨ |
| Column number | 9 | 10 | 11 | 12 | 13 | 14 | 15 | 16 | 17 | 18 | 19 | 20 | 21 | 22 |

# TABLE 3 (concluded)

$z \geq m > y$; $w \geq x \geq y \geq m$; $u \geq v \geq m$

| Row number | $z < y < v'$ | | $z = y < v'$ | | $y < z < v'$ | | $y < v' \leq z$ | $z < y = v'$ | $z = y = v'$ | $y = v' < z$ | $z \geq y \geq m$ <br> $v \geq m$ | |
|---|---|---|---|---|---|---|---|---|---|---|---|---|
| | $v' \leq x', w'$ | $w', x' < v'$ | $v' \leq x', w'$ | $x', w' < v'$ | $x', w' < v'$ | $v' \leq x', w'$ | $y < v' \leq z$ | $z < y = v' $ | $z = y = v'$ | $y = v' < z$ | $z \geq y \geq m$ | $w \leq m$ ... |
| 1  $w(P^s) > w(Q^s) > w(R^s) > w(S^s) > w(T^s)$ | $P^s Q^s$ | $(Q^s)$ | — | $(Q^s)$ | $(Q^s)\,S^s/T^s$ | $Q^s S^s/T^s$ | $Q^s S^s/T^s$ | $P^s Q^s$ | — | — | $Q^s\,(R^s)$ | $R^s S^s/T^s$ |
| 2  $w(P^s) > w(Q^s) > w(R^s) > w(S^s) = w(T^s)$ | $P^s Q^s$ | $(Q^s)$ | — | $(Q^s)$ | $(Q^s)\,S^s/T^s$ | $Q^s S^s/T^s$ | $Q^s S^s/T^s$ | $P^s Q^s$ | — | — | $Q^s\,(R^s)$ | $R^s S^s/T^s$ |
| 3  $w(P^s) > w(Q^s) > w(R^s) = w(S^s) > w(T^s)$ | $P^s Q^s$ | $(Q^s)$ | — | $(Q^s)$ | $(Q^s)\,S^s/T^s$ | $Q^s S^s/T^s$ | $Q^s S^s/T^s$ | $P^s Q^s$ | — | — | //// | $R^s S^s/T^s$ |
| 4  $w(P^s) > w(Q^s) = w(R^s) > w(S^s) > w(T^s)$ | $P^s Q^s$ | $(Q^s)$ | — | $(Q^s)$ | $(Q^s)\,S^s/T^s$ | //// | //// | $P^s Q^s$ | — | — | //// | $R^s S^s/T^s$ |
| 5  $w(P^s) > w(Q^s) > w(R^s) = w(S^s) = w(T^s)$ | //// | //// | //// | //// | //// | //// | //// | //// | //// | //// | $Q^s R^s$ | //// |
| 6  $w(P^s) > w(Q^s) = w(R^s) > w(S^s) = w(T^s)$ | //// | //// | //// | //// | //// | //// | //// | //// | //// | //// | //// | //// |
| 7  $w(P^s) > w(Q^s) = w(R^s) = w(S^s) > w(T^s)$ | //// | //// | //// | //// | //// | //// | //// | //// | //// | //// | //// | //// |
| 8  $w(P^s) > w(Q^s) = w(R^s) = w(S^s) = w(T^s)$ | //// | //// | //// | //// | //// | //// | //// | //// | //// | //// | //// | //// |
| Column number | 23 | 24 | 25 | 26 | 27 | 28 | 29 | 30 | 31 | 32 | 33 | 34 |

| Row number | 30 | 31 | 32 | 33 | 34 |
|---|---|---|---|---|---|
| 9   $w(P^s) = w(Q^s) > w(R^s) > w(S^s) > w(T^s)$ | $P^s Q^s$ | — | — | $R^s$ | $R^s S^s/T^s$ |
| 10  $w(P^s) = w(Q^s) > w(R^s) > w(S^s) = w(T^s)$ | $P^s Q^s$ | — | — | $R^s$ | $R^s S^s/T^s$ |
| 11  $w(P^s) = w(Q^s) > w(R^s) = w(S^s) > w(T^s)$ | $P^s Q^s$ | — | — | //// | $R^s S^s/T^s$ |
| 12  $w(P^s) = w(Q^s) > w(R^s) = w(S^s) > w(T^s)$ | $P^s Q^s$ | — | — | //// | $R^s S^s/T^s$ |
| 13  $w(P^s) = w(Q^s) = w(R^s) > w(S^s) > w(T^s)$ | //// | //// | //// | //// | — |
| 14  $w(P^s) = w(Q^s) = w(R^s) > w(S^s) = w(T^s)$ | //// | //// | //// | //// | — |
| 15  $w(P^s) = w(Q^s) = w(R^s) = w(S^s) > w(T^s)$ | //// | //// | //// | //// | — |
| 16  $w(P^s) = w(Q^s) = w(R^s) = w(S^s) = w(T^s)$ | //// | //// | //// | //// | — |

features of a theory of strategy in the end-play can now be formulated:

1. For those proto-coalitions in some kind of uniquely advantageous position, the main task is to exploit the advantage.
2. For those proto-coalitions lacking an advantageous position when others have it, the main task is to minimize or eliminate the advantage of others.

These statements are not of much practical use, however, so I shall in the following paragraphs attempt to elaborate on them with reference to the actual positions of proto-coalitions in the model.

In three-set partitions of $I$, the most striking fact is, it seems to me, the relative absence of advantage for the largest or weightiest proto-coalition, $P^3$. This fact is in sharp contradiction with the common sense of politics where it is assumed that the strongest has the best chance of winning. It is true, as Table 1 indicates, that the strongest does have an advantage when the value of $m$ is increased to the point that all coalitions not including $P^3$ are turned from winning into blocking ones. (See the two right-hand columns in Table 1.) Then $P^3$ becomes uniquely essential. While such situations are undoubtedly common in natural decision-making bodies, they are not situations of very great interest inasmuch as the winner can be predicted with confidence. In those much more interesting situations in which the outcome is really in doubt, that is, in those situations defined in the two left-hand columns in Table 1, it is apparent that $P^3$ never has an advantage. While $P^3$ may be a part of some winning coalition, $P^2$, in the situations of the second column of Table 1, it may never be expected to win much when $R^3$ is uniquely favored. In the cells (1,1) and (2,1), $P^3$ is an almost certain loser. For the situations encountered on the left-hand side of Table 1, the best advice to $P^3$ on strategy is:

1. When some decision is inevitable and when $P^3$ has any chance at all of winning, minimize losses by accepting a minimal payoff in coalition with $R^3$ or $Q^3$.

2. When some decision is inevitable and the situation in cells (1,1) and (2,1) exists, change the situation, if possible, by moving to a four- or five-set partition.

The former strategy is clear enough and, as a practical matter, only involves the (psychologically difficult) operation of $P^3$ disabusing itself of the common-sense notion that the weightiest player "deserves" the largest payoff.

The latter strategy is, however, somewhat complex and deserves some explication. Heretofore, we have assumed (with the promise that the assumption would ultimately be discarded) that proto-coalitions were indissoluble. In a dynamic world, this is, of course, absurd; and so to analyze a dynamic situation we now discard the assumption. It is, of course, appropriate to use the strategy of dissolving a three-set partition only when $P^3$ seems certain to lose—i.e., when the situations of cells (1,1) and (2,1) exist; and it involves the fission of $P^3$, which in most real political systems is a drastic process. This strategy may be initiated in one of two ways: (a) a majority of $P^3$ may expel some members, or (b) a minority of $P^3$ may resign. The strategic possibilities of the two kinds of action are quite different and will be considered separately.

Suppose a majority of $P^3$ decides to improve its position by expulsion of a minority (or, what is the same thing, by refusing to meet demands of a minority and allowing them to resign). Since this majority may become any one of $P^4$,

$Q^4$, or $R^4$, it may at first seem a relatively easy task for it to pick some uniquely preferable position in a four-set partition and force itself into that position by appropriate pruning. Actually, however, relatively few of the uniquely preferable positions can be reached by a majority of $P^3$ by this route. If it seeks to transform itself (that is, if $P^3$ becomes $P^4$ and $S^4$, or $P^4$ and $R^4$, or $P^4$ and $Q^4$, or $Q^4$ and $R^4$, or $Q^4$ and $S^4$, or $R^4$ and $S^4$), only four (quite restricted) forms of these transformations renders a majority of $P^3$ either a member of a uniquely preferable winning coalition or a uniquely favored proto-coalition.[5] These four transformations are (a) when $P^3$ goes into $Q^4$ and $S^4$ in such a way that the conditions of column 13 of Table 2 are satisfied and (b) when $P^3$ goes into $R^4$ and $S^4$ in such a way that the conditions of columns 11, 12, or 13 of Table

5. The full extent of the difficulty facing the majority of $P^3$ can be appreciated by a survey of the possibilities:

(1) To become $P^4$ and $Q^4$, it must be that $w(P^3) = w(Q^4 \cup R^4)$, that is, the situation of column 4 on Table 1 must prevail. Even if $P^3$ becomes $P^4$ and $Q^4$, it can do so only by establishing the situation of cell (8,16) of Table 2, in which no proto-coalition has an advantage.

(2) To become $P^4$ and $S^4$, presumably to achieve an advantageous position for $P^4$ in columns 10–12 of Table 2, is impossible for $Q^3$ becomes $Q^4$ and $R^3$ becomes $R^4$. Since in these columns one of the conditions is that $w(Q^4 \cup R^4) < m$ and since $w(Q^3 \cup R^3) = w(Q^4 \cup R^4) \geqq m$, the majority of $P^3$ cannot carry through this maneuver.

(3) To become $P^4$ and $R^4$, presumably to achieve an advantageous position for $P^4$ in columns 1–5 of Table 2, is also impossible. In these columns $w(P^4 \cup R^4) \geqq m$, which means that $P^3 \geqq m$, which is impossible under the conditions of Table 1.

(4) To become $Q^4$ and $R^4$, presumably to achieve as $Q^4$ an advantageous position in columns 7 and 8, is impossible. If $P^3$ goes into $Q^4$ and $R^4$, $Q^3$ must go into $P^4$ and $R^3$ into $S^4$. To achieve the advantageous position of column 7, $w' < x$, that is $w(P^3 \cup R^3) = w(Q^4 \cup R^4 \cup S^4) < w(P^4 \cup S^4) = w(Q^3 \cup R^3)$. But $w(P^3 \cup R^3) < w(Q^3 \cup R^3)$ is not possible under the conditions in Table 1. Likewise, it is impossible to achieve an advantageous position in column 8 in which it is prohibited that $w(P^4 \cup S^4) \geqq m$; yet $P^4$ is $Q^3$ and $S^4$ is $R^3$ and $w(Q^3 \cup R^3) \geqq m$. Finally to obtain an advantageous position in column 13, in which $w(Q^4 \cup R^4) \geqq m$ is impossible for them $w(P^3) \geqq m$ which contradicts the assumptions of Table 1.

2 are satisfied. Note that each of these fissions of $P^3$ involve the majority of that set foregoing its superficially "leading" or weightiest position, an action which in the traditional common sense of politics is undoubted folly. Note also that each of these transformations can be undertaken only in some circumstances and not in others. Suppose the majority of $P^3$ goes into $Q^3$. Then the best it can hope is to achieve the position of cell (1,13), in which its partner in a uniquely preferable coalition is itself uniquely favored. And this is hardly a great achievement. Furthermore, if $w(Q^4) = qw(P^3)$, where $q \geqq \frac{1}{2}$, then the range of $w(S^4) = (1 - q) \; w(P^3)$ is quite restricted: $(w(P^3) -w(Q^3)) \leqq w(S^4) < w(R^3)$. Thus, an only moderately better position can be achieved and then only with quite re-

---

(5) To become $Q^4$ and $S^4$, presumably to obtain as $Q^4$ the advantageous position of columns 7–8 or 13. Of course $P^3$ goes into $Q^4$ and $S^4$, while $Q^3$ goes into $P^4$ and $R^3$ into $R^4$. To achieve for $Q^4$ a position in column 7, it must be that $w(P^3 \cup R^3) = w(Q^4 \cup R^4 \cup S^4) < w(P^4 \cup S^4) = w(Q^3 \cup S^4)$. But $w(P^3) \geqq w(Q^3)$ and $w(R^3 = w(R^4) > w(S^4)$. Hence, $w(P^3 \cup R^3) > w(Q^3 \cup S^4)$, which violates the conditions of column 7. To achieve the position of $Q^4$ of column 8, it must be that $w(Q^3 \cup R^3) = w(P^4 \cup R^4) > w(Q^4 \cup R^4 \cup S^4) = w(P^3 \cup R^3)$, which is impossible, for in Table 1, $w(Q^3 \cup R^3) > w(P^3 \cup R^3)$. It is possible for the majority of $P^3$ to achieve the position of $Q^4$ in column 13 and that possibility is discussed in the text.

(6) To become $R^4$ and $S^4$, presumably to obtain for $R^4$ one of the positions in columns 7, 8, 10–12, or 13. Of course, $P^3$ goes into $R^4$ and $S^4$, while $Q^3$ goes into $P^4$ and $R^3$ into $Q^4$. To achieve for $R^4$ the position of column 7, it must be that $w(P^3 \cup R^3) = w(Q^4 \cup R^4 \cup S^4) < w(P^4 \cup S^4) = w(Q^3 \cup S^4)$. But since $w(P^3) \geqq w(Q^3)$ and $w(R^3) = w(Q^3) \geqq w(S^4)$, it cannot be that $w(P^3 \cup R^3) < w(Q^3 \cup S^4)$. To achieve the position of column 8 for $R^4$, it must be that $w(Q^3 \cup R^3) = w(P^4 \cup R^4) > w(Q^4 \cup R^4 \cup S^4) = w(P^3 \cup R^3)$. Since however, $w(P^3) \geqq w(Q^3)$ and $w(R^3) = w(Q^4) \geqq w(R^4)$, this also is impossible. To achieve the position of column 10 for $R^4$ superficially appears to be possible for column 10 is partially the opposite of column 8. But here it must be that $w(Q^3 \cup R^3) = w(P^4 \cup Q^4) > w(Q^4 \cup R^4 \cup S^4) = w(P^3 \cup R^3)$; yet $w(P^3) \geqq w(Q^3)$ and of course $w(R^3) = w(R^4)$ so it is impossible for $w(Q^3 \cup R^3) > w(P^3 \cup R^3)$. But the failure of $R^4$ to satisfy the conditions of column 10 means that it can satisfy the conditions of columns 11 and 12. It can also satisfy the conditions of column 13. These cases are discussed in the text.

stricted selections of $S^4$. Suppose, on the other hand, $P^3$ goes into $R^4$ and $S^4$ so that $R^4$ can achieve some position in columns 11, 12 or 13. These are, of course, only feasible if $w(R^3) > qw(P^3)$, where $q \geqq \frac{1}{2}$, which fact severely limits the possibility of these transformations. Furthermore, to achieve the only really desirable one of these positions, column 13, it must be that $(w(R^3) + qw(P^3)) \geqq m$. These conditions together mean that $P^3$, $Q^3$, and $R^3$ must approach an even division. Deliberately to split the largest proto-coalition in such a circumstance requires action sharply at variance with received common sense. Perhaps this is why few instances are available of the majority of the weightiest proto-coalition deliberately casting off members. Indeed, it is psychologically difficult for large *winning* coalitions to lose excess weight, although a number of examples of such loss are recorded in Chapter 3. How much more difficult it is, then, for simply a leading *proto*-coalition to lose weight. Furthermore, common sense, when it is based on caution rather than simply on uncritical admiration of size, is far from wrong. What is the abstractly correct strategy for a situation analogous to cells (1,1), (2,1), and (3,1) of Table 1 may be a very dangerous practical strategy given the unpredictability of the future. In view of the deterring mythology and the uncertainty of the future, it is not surprising the majorities of disadvantaged $P^3$-type coalitions seldom follow this abstractly rational strategy.

It is quite otherwise with minorities. For a minority of $P^3$, the advantageous positions of $S^4$ are readily obtainable, subject only to the (easily met) conditions that, for columns 1–7 of Table 2, $w(S^4) > (w(P^3) - w(Q^3))$, and, for column 8, $w(S^4) < (w(P^3) - w(Q^3))$. These conditions of course mean that a minority of the disadvantaged leading coalition is able, in almost any instance of a three-set partition, to obtain an advantageous position in a four-set partition. This minority can put itself in a really strong position (column 6 of Table 2) only if it shapes itself so that $w(S^4) = (w(P^3) + w(R^3) - w(Q^3))$. Though considerable artistry may be required to achieve this in practice, there is no doubt that a resigning minority of $P^3$ can almost always improve its position, provided it is large enough to avoid the conditions of column 13 on Table 2. Hence, the resignation of a minority of a leading proto-coalition is a common maneuver in real political situations. One instance comes to mind immediately, although it arises in a nine- to twelve-set partition of $I$: After its great victory in the elections of 1951, the Gaulliste party in the French National Assembly was the leading proto-coalition. Within two years, by several successive resignations, there were three proto-coalitions larger than it. Although the resignations were said to be based on ideological grounds, it is quite possible (especially considering the atmosphere of real-politik in coalition-building in the Assembly) that the resignations were also based on rational calculations of advantage similar to the calculations set forth here.[6]

To complete the analysis of three-set partitions, we now turn briefly to the positions of $Q^3$ and $R^3$. Possessed, as they often are, of great advantages, their main strategic problem is to recognize and exploit them. For both, the main cell to be avoided is (2,2) and each, by the (psychologically difficult) process of revising its initial expectations, is able to do so.

Turning now to the strategy in four-set partitions, the elementary (and possibly most interesting) observation is, as with Table 1, that so many of the cells in Table 2 record that some proto-coalitions possess some kinds of unique advantages. Table 2 differs from the first column of Table 1 (to which the former is strictly comparable) in that every

6. William H. Riker, "A Test of the Adequacy of the Power Index," *Behavioral Science, 4* (1959), 120–31.

proto-coalition appears in at least one column. Hence, unlike the situation with three-set partitions, no proto-coalition is necessarily disadvantaged by very existence of this partition.

The strategic situation is also markedly different in the four-set partition from that in the three-set. In the latter, the only available courses of action are:

> 1. $X^3$ unites with $Y^3$ to form $P^2$.
> 2. $X^3$ dissolves to form $X^4$ and $Y^4$.

In the four-set partition, however, these actions are available, although not simultaneously to all proto-coalitions:

> 1. $X^4$, $Y^4$, and perhaps $Z^4$ unite to form $P^2$.
> 2. $X^4$ and $Y^4$ unite to form $Z^3$.
> 3. $X^4$ dissolves to unite with $Y^4$ and form $Z^4$.
> 4. $X^4$ dissolves to form $Y^5$ and $Z^5$.

The extension of choices often complicates the strategic considerations.

Let us consider the situation of a disadvantaged proto-coalition in the four-set partition, for example, the situation of $R^4$ in cell (1,5) of Table 2. Given the appropriate division of weights, $R^4$, or some portion of it, may extricate itself in at least the following ways:

> 1. A majority of $R^4$, that is $qw(R^4)$, can expel enough members to become $S^5$ of cells (1,5), (1,6), or (1,7) of Table 3, provided $w(S^4) > qw(R^4) > (1 - q) w(R^4)$.
> 2. A minority of $R^4$, that is, $(1 - q) w(R^4)$, can resign to become the $T^5$ of cells (1,2), (1,3), or (1,4) of Table 3, provided that $(1 - q) w(R^4) < w(S^4)$.
> 3. The proto-coalition $R^4$ can as a whole join $Q^4$ to form the $Q^3$ of cells (1,1), or (2,1) of Table 1, provided that $(w(Q^4) + w(R^4)) < w(P^4)$, a fact which

is almost guaranteed by the circumstances of cell (1,5) of Table 2.

4. A majority of $R^4$, that is, $qw(R^4)$, can join $Q^4$ so that $(1 - q) w(R^4)$ becomes $S^4$ and the former $S^4$ becomes $R^4$. This rather contrived action requires, of course, that the members of $Q^4$ be sufficiently reconciled to certain loss to accept additional members, who may increase their loss, but who will also share it and who do not otherwise affect their position. It requires also, presumably, that the members of the minority of $R^4$, that is, those who become the new $S^4$, recompense their old comrades now in $Q^4$ for this sacrifice. This is, of course, highly contrived action and I know of no instance of it in actual decision-making bodies.

As against this wide range of available action for $R^4$ in cell (1,5), not all proto-coalitions in four-set partitions have so many alternatives. For example, $Q^4$ in cell (1,10) can escape (partially) only if a minority forms $S^5$. Or again, $S^4$ in cell (1,12) can only achieve cell (1,11) or (1,12) of Table 3, in which at best it is not strategically weak. Nonetheless, the four-set partition is, on the whole, more fecund of possibilities for extricating the disadvantaged than is the three-set partition.

Presumably, although I have not set up a table of uniqueness of position of proto-coalitions in a six-set partition and although such a table is necessary for systematic comparison, still a five-set partition probably contains more alternatives of action for the strategically weak than does a four-set one. And this presumption leads to another interesting observation about the end-play: As proto-coalitions approach the three- or four- or five-set partition, those likely to be strategically weak in the end-play ought to revise their ambitions (and perhaps their membership) so that in the actual $(r-1)^{th}$ stage they are in an advantageous position. This observation applies especially to proto-coalitions likely to reach the $(r-1)^{th}$ stage as $P^3$ of Table 1, or as $S^4$ of cells (1,10) through (1,13) of Table 2, or $Q^4$ or $R^4$ of cells (1,1) through (1,6) of Table 2. By rational action at an earlier point, they may be able to avoid at least these positions and possibly reach the $(r-1)^{th}$ stage in an actually advantageous position.

## SUMMARY AND INTERPRETATION

This chapter started out with the suggestion that there are in fact abstract considerations of strategy in the growth of proto-coalitions. It was suggested that action in the earlier stages of the process might be affected by anticipations about the necessary strategy in the penultimate stage. Therefore, a fairly exhaustive analysis of the relative positions in the end-play was undertaken to discover differences in the situation of proto-coalitions (distinguished by their relative weights). The main tool of discovery was the size principle in the somewhat restricted form that requires all characteristic functions to slope downward and to the right. The completed analysis did reveal differences of position in the end-play, differences that might well affect strategy at earlier stages. These differences of position were some sort of advantage possessed uniquely by one proto-coalition or by one prospective coalition. The most startling of the advantages was the observation that, in general, the smaller proto-coalitions more frequently had uniquely advantageous positions than did the larger or weightier ones.

The fact that one coalition or proto-coalition often has an advantage suggests that this model has a bias toward decision. Indeed it lacks any kind of equilibrium. The notion of equilibrium is that of a relationship of forces arranged so that deviation from some point of balance results in a (possibly automatic) correction back to balance. And this is precisely what this model does not have because of the existence of unique advantages. Its dynamic is toward the upsetting of any balance that might temporarily exist. The relationship of forces maintains pressure toward a decision. And once a decision is taken, its dynamic is to encourage the repetition of the process.

The notion of an equilibrium has played so important a part in contemporary social theory partly because an equilibrium is felt to be desirable in fact. Equilibrium in society is a kind of stability despite change. And to say that this model lacks equilibrium is to say that the social processes it purports to describe are also unstable—that the political society itself is in fact unstable. This conclusion is hardly startling to the observer of politics, who must necessarily take a rather Heraclitan view of the universe. But it is doubtless disappointing to those who seek for peace and order. And for their sake, therefore, we will in later chapters examine the significance and meaning of instability in the model and in the social processes it represents.

CHAPTER 7

# An Interlude and Illustration from American Politics

The foregoing analysis of the strategic possibilities of the end-play in the model may have seemed to some readers rather arid and lifeless. Many students of politics and history are accustomed to explications of events in terms of personality or ideology or custom so that the abstract considerations of real-politik are perhaps felt to be wholly unreal. In order that some sense of immediate reality may be imported into the analysis, therefore, this brief chapter will be devoted to an interpretation of one event in terms of the model of Chapter 5 and the inferences from it in Chapter 6.

The so-called corrupt bargain of 1825 is a good example for our purpose. Since it concerned politics at the highest national level, one can expect motivations of real-politik in at least some of the participants. Since it occurred in the end-play of a process that had been going on for about five years, the proto-coalitions had been reduced to a manageable number: four. And since the weight of each participant was fixed by the constitution at each of the final stages in the process, one can speak rather confidently of the weights, at least in the end-play.

The era of good feeling that produced Monroe's nearly unanimous election in 1820 resulted (as has been recounted and accounted for earlier) in an almost immediate breakup of the Republican party into numerous factions. Among the major factions were those centered around the candidacy for President in 1824 of John Quincy Adams, then Secretary of State and the favorite of the ex-Federalists; William H. Crawford, Secretary of the Treasury and the favorite of that alliance between Virginia and New York which had produced the succession of Presidents from Virginia and Vice Presidents from New York; John C. Calhoun, then Secretary of War and the favorite of South Carolina and himself; Andrew Jackson, governor of Florida territory and later senator from Tennessee during the long maneuvering; and Henry Clay, representative from Kentucky and unofficial leader of the opposition in the House. Jackson and Clay were the favorites of the West, but Jackson as a national hero was also favored by those states disenchanted both with ex-Federalists and the alliance of Virginia and New York.

Initially Crawford had, perhaps, the greatest strength, but he was incapacitated by a stroke in 1823 and was for that reason substantially out of the running. Calhoun wisely settled for the Vice Presidency and thereby removed himself. Thus Adams, Jackson, and Clay were left. Adams had the advantage of being Secretary of State, an office which by then had come to be regarded as preparation for the Presidency. Jackson and Clay were both romantic figures of great popular appeal, although Jackson was, of course, by far the better known of the two. And, of course, there were a few die-hard supporters of Crawford. The result of this four-way contest in the canvass of 1824 was that no candidate could obtain the absolute majority necessary for election in the electoral college. The standings were:

| Jackson: | 99 votes and a majority in 11 states |
| Adams: | 84 " " " " " 7 " |
| Crawford: | 41 " " " " " 3 " |
| Clay: | 37 " " " " " 3 " |

$$261 \div 2 = 130\frac{1}{2} \qquad\qquad 24 \div 2 = 12$$

As a result of this contretemps, the election went to the House where, by the Twelfth Amendment, a maximum of three candidates might be considered. Clay was thereby institutionally forced to transfer his votes. Had this rule not operated in this particular way, Clay might have remained in the running somewhat longer, perhaps outlasting Crawford. One main feature of the event may thus appear to be the result of a concrete local institution rather than a result of the abstract considerations of the end-play. On the other hand, considering Clay's temperament, his romantic devotion to cabal, his skill in and fascination with bargaining, it seems quite possible to me that the local rule merely facilitated a result that Clay's calculations would have led him to anyway.

In the House, voting is, in this circumstance, by states. That is, each state has one vote which is cast as decided by a plurality of its representatives. And, furthermore, electors and representatives must be different persons. Again, therefore, local institutions facilitated a result dictated by the inferences from the model. After the returns were in (December 1824), the weights of the proto-coalitions were:

$$w(P^4) = 11 \quad \text{(Jackson)}$$
$$w(Q^4) = 7 \quad \text{(Adams)}$$
$$w(R^4) = 3 \quad \text{(Crawford)}$$
$$w(S^4) = 3 \quad \text{(Clay)}.$$

This is the situation in cell (2,7) of Table 2 in which $Q^4$, $R^4$, and $S^4$ are members of a uniquely preferred winning coalition and $P^4$ is strategically weak. The appropriate strategy for some of the members of $P^4$ is, therefore, to desert, especially if time is available for extensive bargaining prior to the decision. This is, of course, precisely what happened. Jackson's support dissolved away. It might not have dissolved so easily had electors and representatives been the same persons, of course, but dissolve it did. Despite intense Jacksonian pressure on the wavering representative from Illinois, he deserted to Adams. Maryland also went to Adams. North Carolina went to Crawford. Louisiana went to Clay. (Louisiana could not, of course, vote for Clay. What its representatives did was put themselves in Clay's hands for bargaining purposes.) In short, Jackson lost four, Adams gained two, and each of the others gained one. Interestingly and appropriately (in terms of the theory), Jackson gained none. Even Missouri, where the Benton influence counted heavily for Jackson, remained undecided. Its representative would not change from Clay to Jackson.[1]

As the session of Congress opened, the standings were:

$$w(P^4) = 9 \quad \text{(Adams)}$$
$$w(Q^4) = 7 \quad \text{(Jackson)}$$
$$w(R^4) = 4 \quad \text{(Crawford)}$$
$$w(S^4) = 4 \quad \text{(Clay)}.$$

Note that the assignment of weights is made on the assumption that New York remained firmly for Adams, for so it seemed until one vote began to waver. As again can be readily observed from Table 2, this is the situation of cell (2,3), where no proto-coalition has a unique advantage, but where either $(P^4 \cup R^4)$ or $(P^4 \cup S^4)$ is a *minimal*

1. J. S. Bassett, *Life of Andrew Jackson* (rev. ed. New York, Macmillan, 1925), pp. 350 ff., 363.

winning coalition. Hence, one can expect desperate bargaining, with Clay and Adams as natural allies. Note that it is Clay and Adams rather than Crawford and Adams, not only because Clay was formally excluded but also because, a principal in Washington rather than in a Georgian sickbed, he was able to maneuver more effectively. Furthermore, as Clay gradually lost Missouri to Adams, whether by his own design or by a small-scale "corrupt bargain" between Adams' managers and the representative from Missouri, the situation hardened: [2]

$$w(P^4) = 10 \quad \text{(Adams)}$$
$$w(Q^4) = 7 \quad \text{(Jackson)}$$
$$w(R^4) = 4 \quad \text{(Crawford)}$$
$$w(S^4) = 3 \quad \text{(Clay)}.$$

This is the situation of cell (1,4), where $P^4$ and $S^4$ are members of a uniquely preferred winning coalition. The alliance of Adams and Clay is the only possible minimal winning coalition. Its creation is, therefore, indicated and this is precisely what occurred. Clay had to throw his support somewhere. The Kentucky legislature had instructed its representatives to vote for Jackson when Clay was out of the running; but the congressmen in Washington proved to be far more loyal to Clay in Washington than to a legislature in Lexington, which, moreover, had no authoritative control over them anyway. Had Clay followed instructions, the result would have been:

$$w(P^3) = 10 \quad \text{(Adams)}$$
$$w(Q^3) = 10 \quad \text{(Jackson)}$$
$$w(R^3) = 4 \quad \text{(Crawford)}.$$

And, of course, the supporters of Crawford would have been uniquely favored, able thus to drive a very hard bargain. Naturally, Clay had no reason to wish for this out-

2. Ibid., p. 363.

come. Again, had Clay joined Crawford, the result would have been:

$$w(P^3) = 10 \quad \text{(Adams)}$$
$$w(Q^3) = 7 \quad \text{(Jackson)}$$
$$w(R^3) = 7 \quad \text{(Crawford)}.$$

And thereby he would have lost every advantage he might otherwise have had. It is true that $Q^3$ and $R^3$ are members of a uniquely preferred winning coalition, but the gains accruing to this coalition must be split three ways. So not unreasonably Clay could unhesitatingly reject this possibility.

This left for Clay only one reasonable course of action: alliance with Adams. This was the corrupt bargain, for Clay's price was the office of Secretary of State, which presumably put him next in succession. Adams apparently had no hesitation in paying it.[3]

Once Clay had made his decision, great pressure to defect was put by Crawford's managers on several of Adams' supporters. Had they been able, as they hoped, to swing New York and Maryland into the Crawford column, the result would have been:

$$w(P^3) = 11 \quad \text{(Adams)}$$
$$w(Q^3) = 7 \quad \text{(Jackson)}$$
$$w(R^3) = 6 \quad \text{(Crawford)}.$$

Then, of course, a Jackson-Crawford alliance would have been the only minimal winning coalition. But this was a last-minute maneuver with little hope of success. Why should men break up a minimal winning coalition in order to form a proto-coalition which is at best a member of a uniquely preferred winning coalition? Certainly Maryland had no reason to shift back to Jackson in this roundabout way when it had already shifted to Adams for

3. Ibid., p. 352.

a reward. And if Maryland was unlikely to move, so was New York. If the Crawford managers had had two months, they might well have shaken up the winning coalition. But March 4 was near and the winning coalition stuck together, probably because it was winning. Looked at exclusively from the point of view of New York at the last moment, the weights were:

$$w(P^4) = 12 \text{ (Adams)}$$
$$w(Q^4) = 7 \text{ (Jackson)}$$
$$w(R^4) = 4 \text{ (Crawford)}$$
$$w(S^4) = 1 \text{ (New York).}$$

If New York abstained or did not vote, no candidate would have a majority and the election would be delayed. But then what? In this arrangement $P^4$ is uniquely essential (owing to the fact of a requirement of an absolute majority with an even number of participants). Hence, New York must perforce go with Adams anyway in the end. So Adams was elected sooner rather than later—indeed on the first ballot.

This incident is especially interesting in that it displays at least three features of the strategy of the end-play. In the first place, just as the theory from the model dictates, Jackson lost support. It is true that this loss was facilitated by the fact that electors and representatives were different people. But nonetheless the loss occurred despite great political pressures. In the second place, and again just as the theory from the model dictates, Clay joined Adams. Again it is true that the corrupt bargain was facilitated by the fact that Clay was not eligible himself. But nevertheless the bargain was consummated with Adams, *not* Jackson. In the third place, and possibly the most interesting of all, the *minimal* winning coalition of Adams and Clay suffered no desertions once it was formed. Van Buren tells a fascinating story on this last point. As a Crawford man, he was eager to delay decision by producing a tie in the New York delegation. This he might do if Stephen Van Rensselaer, an ex-Federalist and brother-in-law of Alexander Hamilton, were to vote for Crawford. While this would be an ideologically absurd result—for Crawford had the best claim to the Jeffersonian mantle—still it was not personally absurd inasmuch as the old man found it difficult to vote for the son of John Adams, who had broken Hamilton's power. Both Clay and Van Buren labored mightily with the Patroon and placed him in a real quandary. When he entered the House Chamber on the day of the vote, he was, so Van Buren said, about decided on Crawford out of family and personal pique. But, in Van Buren's words, "he dropped his head upon the edge of his desk and made a brief appeal to his Maker for his guidance in the matter—a practice he frequently observed on great emergencies—and when he removed his hand from his eyes he saw on the floor directly below him a ticket bearing the name of John Quincy Adams. This occurrence, at a moment of great excitement and anxiety, he was led to regard as an answer to his appeal, and taking up the ticket he put it in the box. In this way it was that Mr. Adams was made President." [4] Van Buren did not tell this story for twenty-five years, apparently out of deference to the childlike piety of a good old man. And when he did tell it, his story makes a kind of cynically literal instance of Selden's remark: "They talk . . . that the Holy Ghost is President of their . . . Councils, when the truth is, the odd man is still the Holy Ghost." [5] From another point of view, however, it is simply remarkable that what the Patroon regarded as divine guidance happened to coincide

4. Martin Van Buren, *Autobiography*, ed. by J. C. Fitzpatrick, *Annual Report of the American Historical Association, 1918* (Washington, Government Printing Office, 1920), p. 152.
5. John Selden, *Table Talk*, "Councils."

with the advice of most of his friends, with the general principles of his ideology, and most of all with the dictates of real-politik. This is a fact that no fair-minded observer can fail to note. We are, of course, forever in doubt as to whether it was God or the Patroon's own quite clear (though mystically expressed) perception of self-interest that guided his hand to the Adams ballot. If his indecision represented familial guilt about an intention to vote for Adams, then the effect of prayer was to reinforce a decision he had already made but not fully acknowledged. All we know for certain, however, is that he voted his present preferences against his ancient loyalties.

In the case of all three of these crucial actions (i.e., Jackson's loss, Clay's choice, and Van Rensselaer's loyalty) there are local institutional or personalistic reasons available to explain the adoption of a rational strategy. Yet in each action the rational strategy *was* adopted. And this fact leads me to believe that it was not so much custom or prayer that determined conduct as it was the intuitive perception of the abstractly "best" strategy as here calculated from the model. It is not, of course, that the participants made calculations such as these but rather that in the concrete problems they perceived the concrete advantages of minimal winning coalitions and acted accordingly. At least the consistent agreement between custom and prayer on one side and the adoption of rational strategy on the other is a striking isomorphism.

The historians' usual explanation of the corrupt bargain are all on a fairly personal level, although, as far as I can discover, only Van Buren himself took the story about the Patroon really seriously. Some deny that a corrupt bargain was made, asserting simply that Adams chose the "best" man. This is the story of late nineteenth-century Republican historians and is too naïve to be taken seriously. Others rather cynically accept the notion of the bargain and justify it as a typical feature of democracy. Still others, those of the pure Jacksonian faith, denounce it in Randolph of Roanoke's words as the alliance of "puritan and blackleg, of Blifil and Black George." None have, however, interpreted the bargain as a rationally best choice by those who deserted Jackson, by those who followed Clay, and by those who resisted the seductions of the Crawford men. It was, I suggest, not just a simple bargain, whether corrupt or no. As a simple bargain, it was presumably rational, but beyond that the setting for it was rational desertion, the agreement on it was rational combination, and the maintenance of it was rational loyalty. This latter, more extensive interpretation is what is added here.

# CHAPTER 8

# The Stability of the Model

At the end of Chapter 6 it was suggested that the model there analyzed was essentially and inherently unstable in the sense that it contained forces favoring decision rather than indecision. Differentials in weight coupled with the size principle tend, it was assumed, to encourage participants to conclude alliances and thereby to make decisions. While decisions themselves are no more necessarily disequilibriating than are transactions in an economic system, still in political decisions the stakes may be so high as to change the structure of the body or system and this is, of course, what renders the body or system unstable.

## THE SIGNIFICANCE OF INSTABILITY

The presumably inevitable instability of the model is of considerable concern not only for understanding society but for operating it and living in it. If the model is at all an adequate representation of reality, then the instability of the model simply mirrors an instability in society. Since the model concerns only events commonly perceived as zero-sum, this possible reflection does not mean that the entire structure of society is unstable. But it does mean that the zero-sum events are themselves unstable and that the instability inherent in them may react on the larger society destroying the bonds of common interest, loyalty, and love that hold any society together.

To say that rational behavior in zero-sum situations is a disequilibrating force in social life is to deny the assertion, made repeatedly since the eighteenth century, that there is some kind of inner, hidden stability in the rational conduct of politics. This assertion is the theory of the balance of power. While this theory does not deny the occurrence of decisions, it does assert that the decisions are so bounded by the internal logic of the decision-making process that no member of the system is eliminated or destroyed. The game may be zero-sum, but the stakes are never, it is said, so high that the loser loses everything. Thus there is supposed to be a kind of higher equilibrium that admits of change (i.e., decision) within the limits of stability (i.e. change which does not really change anything). As against this theory, the argument from the model asserts that minimal winning coalitions are preferred because they win more, that a tendency toward such coalitions and immediate decision is encouraged by differentials in the weight of members and by the size principle, and that no necessary restriction is placed on the size of the stakes. And so we are faced with a direct conflict between the traditional theory of a balance and the inferences from the model. The question for this chapter is, then: Does any sort of equilibrium exist in the model or in the society it supposedly mirrors?

## THE BALANCE OF POWER THEORY

To answer this question we need to know, first, precisely what the theories in conflict are. Since the model has been fairly thoroughly examined, this leaves the balance of power theory for elucidation. For that purpose we are fortunate to have at hand Kaplan's work in which the rules of a system in balance are precisely specified.[1] These rules apply to a body in which the members (or actors) are nations, or, more precisely, the official(s) who are the recognized authoritative voice of the government of nations. In terms of the model, nations are proto-coalitions of fixed membership which can combine with others to form larger proto-coalitions or winning coalitions. While Kaplan's rules are for an international balance, they can with an appropriate modification of the names of actors, fit any theory of balance. For a balance of power to exist, nations must, so Kaplan asserts, obey the following rules:

1. "Act to increase capabilities, but negotiate rather than fight." That is, get as much as one can of what is to be gained in maneuvers in the system, but avoid if possible "the costs entailed by war and . . . the possible disequilibriating consequences war may have . . ."

2. "Fight rather than pass up an opportunity to increase capabilities." Presumably, this rule is to be read in light of the previous one lest a self-evident contradiction between them occur.

3. "Stop fighting rather than eliminate an essential national actor." "Essential national actor" is undefined but substantially equivalent to the phrase "great power" in common political usage.

4. "Act to oppose any coalition or single actor which tends to assume a position of predominance with respect to the rest of the system."

5. "Act to constrain actors who subscribe to supranational organizing principles." Later, p. 24,

1. Kaplan, *System and Process*, p. 23.

Kaplan remarks: "The fourth and fifth rules are merely rational rules necessary to maintain the international action system. A predominant coalition . . . would constitute a threat to the interests of those who do not belong to the coalition. Moreover, if a coalition were to succeed in establishing hegemony . . . the dominant member(s) of the coalition would then also dominate the lesser members of the coalition. Coalitions therefore tend to be counterbalanced by opposing coalitions when they become threatening to non-members and to become fragile when they threaten the interests of some of their own members. In the last instance, threatened members find it advantageous either to withdraw into neutrality or to join the opposed coalition." Although some of the sentences in this quotation are in the language of description, it seems clear from the context that they are meant prescriptively, that is, as the necessary strategies of a system of balanced powers. The descriptive sentences mean that the described tendencies occur when nations follow the rules.

6. "Permit defeated or constrained essential national actors to re-enter the system as acceptable role partners or act to bring some previously inessential actor within the essential actor classification. Treat all essential actors as acceptable role partners." "Acceptable role partners," while undefined, is substantially equivalent to my specification of leaders and followers in Chapter 5.

These precise rules deserve some commentary and explication. The rest of this section is, therefore, devoted to an elaboration of the meaning of Kaplan's system.

Kaplan's first two rules are, it seems to me, extensions

in the particular system he is prescribing of the assumption of rationality made in this book. Hence they need little reinterpretation except to note that all actors, not merely the winners as I have occasionally assumed, are in Kaplan's system required to be rational. This in itself is a very strong assumption—often likely to be absent in fact. The likelihood of absence is thus an important component of disequilibrium. Indeed, when Kaplan turns to a discussion of instability in the balance (p. 27), all the conditions for instability turn out to be matters of irrationality or lack of information or violations of the fifth rule. One can, of course, render Kaplan's rules somewhat more conducive to equilibrium by relaxing the first two rules so that only some of the actors must be rational. In a fairly large system, where relatively few actors occupy marginal positions at any one moment, it is only the marginal ones who must be presumed to be severely rational. Of course, as the number of actors is reduced to the point that all of them are in one way or another marginal, then my assumptions are identical with Kaplan's.

Turning now to the remaining rules, it should be noted that these are the unique features of a balance of power system. Many political systems must impose the rules of rationality (rules 1 and 2) but only the balance of power system must impose both the rules on maintaining the number of actors (rules 3 and 6) and the rules on minimizing preponderant coalitions (rules 4 and 5). That these latter four rules are the essentials of a system of balance has been recognized by many other writers on the subject. Liska, for example, writes: [2]

> the idea of a balance of power becomes realistic only
> if there is a factor ensuring actual or potential pre-
> ponderance on the side devoted to the protection of

2. George Liska, *International Equilibrium* (Cambridge, Mass., Harvard University Press, 1957), p. 36.

legitimate rights. An intangible element is a moral climate favorable to an enlarged conception of the national interest as one served by the general equilibrium. . . . the tangible component is the existence of the balancer.

His task is difficult. A balancer is expected to be partial to no single national subject of the balance of power system but to direct his own mobile weight in such a way as to ensure the international object of an equipoise of power. . . .

For a long time, the position of balancer was held by Great Britain.

Liska's notion of an actor who directs "his own mobile weight . . . to ensure . . . an equipoise of power" is, it seems to me, substantially equivalent to Kaplan's fourth rule "to oppose any coalition or single actor which tends to assume a position of predominance." Again, Liska's reference to the intangible element of a moral climate favorable to the general equilibrium is, I believe, an oblique mention of rules 3 and 6. Since Liska's formulation is heavily dependent on the recent tradition of writers on the balance, one may infer that his statement in some way carries forward an older tradition.[3] From an entirely different tradition, Fredrik Barth has also set forth the essentials of a balancing system and his formulations also turn out to be very similar to Kaplan's last four rules.[4] The Pathans will, he concludes his theoretical discussion of the dynamics of political events in northwestern Pakistan, achieve a balance of power in practice only if in some obscure way they recognize the theoretical principles he

3. Carl J. Friedrich, *Foreign Policy in the Making: The Search for a New Balance of Power* (New York, Norton, 1938), passim.
4. Fredrik Barth, "Segmentary Opposition and the Theory of Games: A Study of Pathan Organization," *Journal of the Royal Anthropological Institute, 89* (1959), 5–22.

has formulated out of a brief analysis of the theory of
$n$-person games. In practice, they must, he argues, realize
two strategic principles: "(1) the advantage of joining the
*weaker* bloc [emphasis in the original], so victory is won
with a narrow margin but the value of the victory maxi-
mized, and (2) the importance from the point of view of
the chief of restricting the intensity of opposition between
the blocs." The first of these strategies is substantially the
same as Kaplan's fourth rule. Note that the rationale of
it is a version of the size principle, which indicates Barth's
belief that the operation of the size principle reinforces
obedience to the rule. (The justification for this belief
will be considered in detail at a later point in this chapter.) Barth's second strategy is an immediate version (out
of Pathan data) of Kaplan's third and sixth rules. On the
basis of this evidence from other sources, we can, I believe,
feel some confidence in Kaplan's precise statement of the
rules of the system. Furthermore, we can be fairly certain that rules 4 through 6 are the essential features of
a balance.

The third and sixth rules are, of course, the really
definitive features. An equilibrium must preserve something and here the thing preserved is the participants in
the system or body. The main purpose of these rules is,
then, to express the main equilibrium in the system.
These rules do have an incidental purpose, however, and
that is to maintain the number of actors or members
above a stated minimum. Precisely what this minimum is,
however, cannot be specified with certainty. Kaplan requires that the essential actors number at least five, but
does not explain why.[5] In a more recent essay, Kaplan,
Burns, and Quandt argue that three is too small a number

5. Morton A. Kaplan, "Balance of Power, Bipolarity, and Other Models
of International Systems," *American Political Science Review*, 51 (1957),
684–95; and Kaplan, *System and Process*, p. 22.

simply because two victorious allies might not see the
need of restoring a defeated third.[6] Beyond this point the
authors do not agree, for Quandt apparently believes four
is an admissible minimum while Kaplan and Burns believe at least five are necessary. Burns believes five is also
maximal, for a larger number requires too great sophisti-
cation in the calculations for decision-making. Having
several times gone through the labor of constructing Table
3 in Chapter 6 only to discover that some possibilities
were omitted (and indeed may still be), I am on emotional grounds inclined to agree with Burns. But it is
also, I believe, clear from Tables 1, 2, and 3 that there
is a great increase in possibilities of coalitions, so I am
for that reason inclined to agree with Kaplan that "the
gain from potential coalition partners is still great enough
above the number five to justify some additional number
of nations." [7]

The controversy about size is not quite clear to me,
however. Since the very notion of a balance requires that
coalitions be formed and dissolved, it is, of course, necessary that three actors or proto-coalitions exist. Beyond
this point I see no reason to place a restriction on the
minimal number. The argument offered for rejecting a
minimum of three is, it seems to me, irrelevant. This
argument (that two victorious allies might not restore a
defeated third) is pointless as long as the third or sixth
rule is obeyed. In effect, this argument is not a reason
for requiring more than three actors but rather a reason
for believing that, when there are only three, some may
be tempted to ignore the third rule. While I wholly agree
that the temptation is very great to eliminate some members in a three-partition division, still I see no reason to

6. Morton A. Kaplan, Arthur Burns, and Richard Quandt, "Theoretical
Analysis of 'Balance of Power,'" *Behavioral Science, 5* (1960), 240–52.
7. Ibid., p. 245.

exclude a system of balance among three actors when the third and sixth rules are inserted precisely to prohibit the temptation.

As for the maximum number of actors in a system of balance, it occurs to me that no actor should be regarded as essential (in Kaplan's terms) unless it can, in alliance with no more than two others, become part of a winning coalition. In most instances this rule would limit the number of essential actors to no more than eight, although extreme instances can be imagined in which the number would be much larger.

While the third and sixth rules express the fundamental equilibriating feature of a balance of power system (since they express the very preservation of the system itself), the fourth and fifth rules direct the operation of its main mechanism. These are, Kaplan asserts, "merely rational rules necessary to maintain the international action system. A predominant coalition . . . would constitute a threat to . . . the national actors who did not belong. . . . Moreover, if a coalition were to succeed in establishing hegemony . . . the dominant member(s) of the coalition would then also dominate the lesser members of the coalition." [8] As stated, however, the fourth and fifth rules are rather general and cover a wide variety of specific actions. In order to clarify their meaning, therefore, I have made the following list of some of the actions they direct. This list is based in part on Kaplan's discussion and in part on my inferences from it:

1. When one proto-coalition forms, nonmembers must form an opposing one.
2. When one proto-coalition is close to victory, neutral actors must join the weaker of the two strongest proto-coalitions.

8. Kaplan, *System and Process*, p. 24.

3. When one proto-coalition is close to victory and neutrals either do not exist or do not take the requisite action, some members of the leading proto-coalition must resign and join the weaker of the two strongest proto-coalitions.

When stated this way, the contradictions between rules 4 and 5 and the traditional common sense of politics is immediately apparent.

### THE STABILITY OF A SYSTEM OF BALANCE

Given these rules, the first question one asks is: Are they sufficient to maintain a balance of power such that no fundamental change (e.g., elimination of members) is made in the system? Naturally one might expect the balance to falter if any one of the rules were violated. If governors behave irrationally or on the basis of such incomplete information that uninformed action is equivalent to irrational action, then the balance may very possibly be upset. Or if victorious actors eliminate defeated ones and do not allow replacement, then also the balance may almost certainly be upset. So we must expect disequilibrium if the rules are disobeyed. This kind of imbalance we will call *practical disequilibrium*. The crucial question, however, is not about disobedience but about obedience itself. Can one expect balance if all the rules are obeyed? This, in effect, is the question of whether or not the rules are internally consistent. If obedience to one rule never necessarily involves disobedience of another, then the rules are indeed internally consistent and one may provisionally expect a balance in fact. But if obedience to one rule necessarily involves disobedience to another, then the system is unstable in a much deeper sense. This we will call *inherent disequilibrium*.

It seems to me apparent that the probability of practical

disequilibrium varies with the historical circumstances: this probability is much greater, for example, when there are three actors or proto-coalitions than when there are five. Inherent disequilibrium, on the other hand, is not a function of circumstances but of the rules themselves. If one should find disequilibrium in the rules, then, no matter how propitious the circumstances, the system itself is unstable.

In Kaplan's discussion of the balance, the possibility of practical disequilibrum is exhaustively considered. But the possibility of inherent disequilibrium is ignored. As against this, I suggest that there is in fact an inherent disequilibrium in the rules adumbrated by Kaplan. Since these rules are more carefully considered than any others previously formulated, I conclude (provisionally) that no rules of balance can be formulated for $n$-person, zero-sum games. To support this inference, it is necessary to examine the internal consistency of these rules, using, of course, the notions developed in Chapter 6.

At the outset I point out the primary inconsistency. Kaplan's fourth rule requires that members oppose proto-coalitions which tend to become predominant. But as Tables 1, 2, and 3 of Chapter 6 indicate, such opposition is not always rational. That is, $P^4$ appears in some of the cells of row 1 of Table 2 and $P^5$ appears in some of the cells of row 1 of Table 3. Hence, there follows a direct conflict between rule 4 and the requirements of rationality (rules 1 and 2). In a three-partition division of the system, it is true that, when all possible coalitions of proto-coalitions are permitted (columns 1 and 2 of Table 1), then the smallest proto-coalition has a rational preference for alliance with the weaker of the two larger proto-coalitions. This is precisely what the fourth rule requires. But if $m$ is large enough to prohibit some coalitions that would be admissible were $m$ at a minimum, then alliance with the weaker of the two stronger may be an irrational strategy for the weakest. That is, when only $(P^3 \cup Q^3)$ and $(P^3 \cup R^3)$ are winning coalitions, $R^3$ would be mad to ally with $Q^3$ when it might ally with $P^3$. Of course, a defender of Kaplan's rules might argue that in such circumstances $R^3$ is not really an "essential national actor" and that, for this reason, the minimum number of actors necessary for a balance does not exist. Since "essential national actor" is not defined by Kaplan, one would be compelled to accept this defense, while feeling a certain uneasiness about just what "essential" meant.

Turning to a four-partition division of the system, however, it is apparent that there are a number of occasions in which it is irrational for the marginal proto-coalition to join the weaker of the two leading coalitions. There are, it will be observed in Table 2, a number of cells in which $(P^4 \cup S^4)$ is indicated as the uniquely preferred (i.e. rationally chosen) winning coalition. In short, there are circumstances in which the weakest ought not oppose the strongest. Indeed there are even circumstances in which the weakest should join the strongest. That such circumstances exist not only in theory but in fact is demonstrated by the history of the event recounted in Chapter 7 in which Clay joined Adams after Jackson's support had partially evaporated and New York remained loyal to Adams even though his was the leading proto-coalition. The event there described was a four-partition case. But when one turns to the five-partition case the point is made even more emphatically. Then there are even more occasions on which the weakest should join, not the second strongest, but the strongest. In both the four-partition and five-partition cases, it is, of course, true that in the more common circumstances the neutral and weaker proto-coalitions should join, not the strongest, but the weaker of the two stronger proto-coalitions. Still, there exist circumstances in which the weakest should join the strongest in the application of rule 1 and in direct controvention of rule 4. Thus there is an inherent contradiction in Kaplan's rules.

The question now is: Does this inherent contradiction result, as I have hitherto assumed, in an inherent disequilibrium?

Kaplan, Burns, and Quandt distinguish two versions of the balance of power theory. The first they call the "hidden hand" theory because it involves the assertion that the system is self-maintaining, or, more precisely, that the operation of rules 4 and 5 enforces obedience of rules 3 and 6. This is the version of the theory to which Kaplan seems to adhere in *System and Process in International Politics*. So also does Barth in the essay already mentioned. The second they describe as one in which players follow a "conserving or legitimist code." This theory might well be called the "moral restraint" theory. In this second version, rules 3 and 6 are not enforced by rules 4 and 5 but rather are independent constraints on the operation of the system.

I think it is quite apparent that the existence of an inherent contradiction in the rules is sufficient to demolish the claims of the hidden hand theory. If, in obedience to rules 1 and 2, members of the system violate rule 4, then it is quite possible that the stakes at the time of violation will be high enough to break rule 3 also. This is, however, not the conclusion arrived at by Barth in his game-theoretic examination of politics among the Yusufzai Pathans of the Northwest Frontier Province of Pakistan. Pointing out that the leaders of proto-coalitions, the chiefs of Pathan society, obtain some value out of the very fact of chieftainship, Barth suggests that this reward, which accrues even to the leader of the losers, has a moderating effect on factional strife. This reward tends to make him content with his loss. Only when the stakes are so high that his loss "considerably exceeds" the value he places on his chieftainship will the leader of the losers offer a high enough price to the pivotal member of the winning coalition to seduce him to change sides. From this deductively arrived at conclusion, he infers further that the leaders of winning coalitions must exhibit a tendency to moderate the stakes so that losing leaders will not be tempted to seduce some of the winning leader's followers. Furthermore, he adduces observational evidence in support of this final inference (e.g., British political agents' observation that chiefs have a greater interest in peace than young warrior hotheads). While I have no doubt that in recent years the Pathan system has worked in the fashion Barth describes, I am far from convinced that this argument and example support a general "hidden hand" theory of balance (and indeed Barth at no point suggests that it does for he is not interested in developing such a general theory—I hope he will forgive my use of his explication out of context to discuss a theory he was not attempting to develop in its most general form). For one thing, Barth's model is that of a three-person game and any general theory of balance must at least encompass four-person and five-person games as well. Even without Barth's argument from imputations, a simple argument from the size principle (e.g., the analysis leading to Table 1 in Chapter 6) supports Barth's conclusions in the three-partition case. But in the four- or five-partition case the argument from size may contradict Barth's argument from imputations. In short, the tendency of behavior following rule 1 to enforce a behavior following rule 4 and in turn following rule 3, that is, the tendency for rationally behaving persons to follow rules 3 and 4 simultaneously, is certain enough when the system is partitioned into three subsets of different weights but not at all certain when it is partitioned into four or five or more. The fact that Barth's argument is based exclusively on the three-partition case renders it irrelevant for the four- or five-partition cases.

While the hidden hand theory of the balance is thus demolished by the revelation of the inherent contradiction in the rules, it may be that the moral restraint version can stand. If the rule about preserving actors is an independent constraint on the size of the stakes, and need not be enforced by the operation of the sometimes irrational rule about siding with the weaker, then the defect in the fourth rule may not render the system as a whole unstable. The question then is, do rules 3 and 6 (about preserving actors) conflict with any other rule in the system? The answer is, of course, that they may. Specifically they may conflict with the first rule about increasing capabilities. There may be occasions in which it is impossible to increase capabilities without eliminating actors, in which case there is again an inherent contradiction in the rules and hence an inherent disequilibrium in the system.

In no way, therefore, may a balance of power system of the sort defined by Kaplan *guarantee* stability. At some point the participants are necessarily faced with a conflict of rules, in which circumstance they must decide to follow one rule rather than another. There is no constraint in the system that forces them to follow the equilibriating rule as against the nonequilibriating one. This discovery of this instability, a discovery made possible by the similarity of the model set forth in Chapters 5 and 6 to the model of the balance of power system, is of great significance, I believe, for life in the real world. It points up sharply the contrast between economic activity, most of the models for which are self-equilibriating or assume some kind of "dynamic" equilibrium, and political activity, where a fundamental instability seems inherent and ineradicable. I suspect that the essential reason for this is the fact that most economic activity is viewed as non-zero-sum while the most important political activity is often viewed as zero-sum.[9] For life in the real world, a truly vital question is, then: How can one moderate the effects of perception of zero-sum situations in order to import some stability into political life?

## THE MODERATION OF INSTABILITY

### Moral Restraint

There seem to be two general ways of moderating instability, and only two, for every natural method I have been able to observe seems to be a variant of the two general ones. The first method of moderating is that of rendering Kaplan's third and sixth rules absolutely inviolable, even if thereby all the other rules are necessarily broken. This we will call the *method of moral restraint*. The second method of moderating is to transform the system of balance into what Kaplan calls a bipolar system. Alternatively, in the terminology of game theory, this

9. This difference between political and economic decisions has been observed by other recent writers on political theory. Duncan Black, for example, noting the similarity between the notion in economics that price is a function of demand and supply and his notion that a winning motion is a function of its marginal position in the preference curves of voters, observes, however, that the similarity is only in the form of the theories and not in the materials to which they relate. He concludes: "This is one of the several grand harmonies running through the material of economic life, a harmony by which no one who understands it can fail to be impressed—and by which the economists of the last generation were perhaps over-impressed. In the material of committee decisions (or of political phenomena in general), on the other hand, no such grand harmony exists. The possibility of the persistence of disharmony and discord is as striking in the one case as is the certainty of harmony in the other." Duncan Black, *The Theory of Committees and Elections* (Cambridge, Cambridge University Press, 1958), p. 19.

method is the creation of two quasi-permanent blocking coalitions or two quasi-permanent almost blocking proto-coalitions. If the coalitions are actually blocking, the *n*-person game has been transformed into a two-person game; and if the proto-coalitions are almost blocking, the *n*-person game has been transformed into something like a three- or four-person game. This method of transforming the very nature of the system we will call the *method of institutional restraint*. The two methods are similar in the sense that both involve some sort of universal agreement not to eliminate losers. They differ, however, in the fact that the first imposes this agreement by means of an internalized morality, while the second imposes it by means of inducements in the structure of the system.

The method of moral restraint of course requires for its effectiveness that all participants be aware of the possibilities and effects of disequilibrium. Beyond that, however, they must all be agreed that disequilibrium is itself undesirable. When these conditions exist, as in fact they often have, then a system of balance of power may be sustained for a very long time. Several examples of a balance long sustained by this method spring immediately to mind. The system of European politics from the end of the Napoleonic Wars to the First World War was undoubtedly of this sort. Again, the long sustained multi-factionalism within the Democratic party in many Southern states is probably of this sort also. In both these natural situations the participants apparently recognized and feared the effects of disequilibrium. And, owing to this fear, they maintained the structure of the system without any institutional device to enforce the rules.

In the long-sustained European balance, the key feature seems to me to have been that conservatism which engendered the Concert of Europe and which the Concert itself articulated so effectively that governments continued to abide by it long after the Concert was disbanded. In this system the ideal of the status quo was so powerful that wars were restricted to a fairly local sort. Throughout the nineteenth century the neutrals (and even the winners) always helped revive the losers. No essential national actor was eliminated although two new ones (Germany and Italy) were created when one principality gobbled up a number of smaller ones. But in the twentieth century this conservative ideal disappeared. After the First World War, two of the losers were thoroughly dismembered and, after the Second World War, the main loser was dismembered (temporarily, it was said, but this temporary structure seems to have become permanent). The effect of the disappearance of the restraint of the conservative ideal was simply that the members of the system might make moves that led surely to the kind of war in which dismemberment was envisaged. This effect appears most clearly in the moves just preceding the outbreak of the Second World War, i.e., Germany's attack on Poland, the alliance of Germany and the Soviet Union, and the defense of Poland by England and France. While these moves can be interpreted as thoughtless gambles by irrational men, it seems more likely that their probable consequences were carefully calculated before they were made. If so, then the actors were either indifferent to rule 3 or sought to disobey it deliberately. Considering first the attack on Poland, it may be that Hitler absolutely believed that England and France would no more fight to defend Poland than they had to defend Czechoslovakia. If he did so believe, then he simply miscalculated. But if he gambled, that is, if he allowed for the possibility of general war, then very probably he deliberately violated rule 3. His obsessive and continually more far-fetched reinterpretation of the history of the First World War and the Versailles Treaty must surely have instilled in him the understanding that some essential national actors had been eliminated at that time. Certainly he must have expected the same in a war that he provoked. Certainly also his own intentions as announced in *Mein Kampf* included some dismemberment of empires. Hence, if he allowed for the possibility of a general war which, in his own expectations, would involve the elimination of some national actors, then clearly he deliberately violated rule 3.

Almost the same interpretation can be given of his offer of alliance to Stalin, an act which was directly and causally connected with the attack on Poland. Furthermore, Stalin's acceptance can also be interpreted in almost these same terms. If Stalin absolutely believed that England and France would not fight, then of course his action was simply a maneuver within the system of balance. But if he too gambled and thereby admitted the possibility of general war, then he too deliberately violated rule 3. Assuming that he took seriously the Marxist theory of that day, namely, that the prospective general war was the death throes of a decadent capitalism, then clearly any step he took toward war was also a step toward the elimination of a number of actors.

Of course no historian can ever say whether or not Hitler and Stalin gambled on war, a gamble that necessarily involved the conditional violation of the third rule. But they can surely say that the cabinets of England and France, acting in compliance with rule 2 (i.e., "Fight rather than pass up an opportunity to increase capabilities"), deliberately choose to violate rule 3. The members of these cabinets approached the war with an obvious reluctance and vacillation, from which I infer that in the beginning they knew it was not just a minor punitive engagement but a war to exhaustion. They may not have stated an aim of unconditional surrender until much later, but they clearly felt it the day the war began. And a war with this goal is a patent violation of rule 3.

These three instances of the violation of the third rule are satisfactory evidence that the system of balance cannot be maintained without it. To obtain a balance, then, this rule must be inviolable. In the nineteenth century it was—owing to an agreement on the conservative ideal of the status quo. But in the twentieth century no agreement existed and the balance could not be maintained, all of which demonstrates the weakness of the moral restraint method of ensuring stability when there is no agreement on the essentials of morality.

But when there is such an agreement, the system of balance can be maintained indefinitely. Indeed, in the United States today we have immediately at hand such a system in operation in several of the Southern states. These are the states in which a persistent multi-factionalism exists within the Democratic party. It will be recalled that in Chapter 4 an explanation, in terms of the size principle, was given for the persistence of a two-faction system in several state Democratic parties. This explanation was, for the states with significant Republican minorities, that the size principle led to a reduction in the size of the winning coalition in the Democratic party. What this explanation does not explain is the existence or non-existence of dual factionalism in the Democratic party in states without significant Republican minorities. We have at hand now, however, a sufficient theory to discriminate between these two categories of states. Assuming that, as the Democratic dominance developed from the 1870s and 1880s on to the present, the appropriate model of politics in those states without traditional Republican minorities was that set forth in Chapters 5 and 6, then our present question is: Why have some state Democratic parties at some time developed a two-faction system and why have others not done so? The fundamental element of the answer is, of course, the fact that a peculiar double sort of game is played there: One is a game for control of society as a whole; the other is a game for control of the government. In the former and more important game the key feature is the fact that Negroes have been excluded entirely from the political system. That is, by means of a systematic and almost complete agreement among whites, Negroes are excluded from participation in the game for control of government. The exigencies of the game for control of society, which most Southern politicians regard as the more important, are what determine the structural features of the game for control of government. What is absolutely essential in the latter game is that, if any actors are eliminated (i.e., if any become more or less permanent losers in a two-faction system), they must not ally with Negroes to upset the white victory in the game for control of society. Hence the players in the game for control of government have their own unwritten version of Kaplan's third rule, to wit, that no faction may be allowed to be a quasi-permanent loser if there is any likelihood that it will attempt to escape this position by bringing Negroes into the political system. In most of the state parties most of the time since the 1890s, this rule has in practice meant that no issue may be raised that is so divisive in the white society that two permanent factions may be built around it. Occasionally agrarian radicals have evaded this rule and actually created a two-faction system in the game for the control of government (e.g., Tillman, Talmadge, Long, et al.), but in almost every instance they have done so only by identifying themselves as the most virulent of Negro-haters. In effect they have given assurance that the creation of a two-faction system will not, from their side at least, involve the re-entry of Negroes into Southern politics. The only agrarian radicals in a two-faction Southern Democratic party who have not also been white supremacy extremists were the Longs of Louisiana. It seems likely that they were able to operate without giving this assurance chiefly because white supremacy was so well established that no one suspected that they might coalesce with Negroes. Indeed, in the particular structure of Louisiana politics, it was usually their opponents who might more easily be suspected of racial treason rather than they. It is also interesting to note that the fall of Earl Long was occasioned by an action that seemed to violate the agreement. Immediately after his rejection and death, Louisiana developed a new balance of power system.

As can be seen from these examples of the maintenance and collapse of a system of balance equilibriated by the method of moral restraint, the essential feature of the operation is the almost universal acceptance of some moral standard that prohibits extremely high stakes (e.g., elimination of a nation, substantial redistribution of income, class warfare, etc.). Although I cannot show that it is generally true, I suspect that the adoption of such a moral standard by the participants depends upon the existence of an intense fear that the breakup of the equilibrium may occasion results which every participant would regard as devastating. In the nineteenth-century European balance, all rulers feared the spread of republican ideas. The ghost of Robespierre haunted every European privy council, frightening them into a certain moderation. But particular ghosts are forgotten, especially when rationalist devotees of real-politik become privy councilors. So one might say that Bismarck exorcized the ghost of Robespierre and thus removed the moral restraint maintaining the balance. To some degree the ghost of Lenin sustained a new balance after the First World War.

The difference in the twentieth century, however, was that Lenin's flesh and blood successor was the cunning head of a major power, not a café revolutionary like Saint-Simon or Louis Blanc. So the ghost was not sufficient to maintain the balance. The Southern politicians have their ghosts too, but they are phantoms of the future, not the past. They envisage mulatto grandchildren, and then moderate their politics. They have admitted the really high stakes of agrarian radicalism only when the radicals have proved that the phantom was unreal.

If, as I have suggested, only universal terror of the possible consequences of high stakes can force men voluntarily to obey the third rule of the balance of power system, then it seems to me that there is hope today for a long-sustained international balance of power equilibriated by the method of moral restraint. Such a system seems to be developing as more and more substantial proto-coalitions appear on the world scene, as a bloc of Afro-Asian nations develops, as China pulls away from the Soviet Union, and as Western Europe and Latin America pull away from the United States. It is easy to imagine a world in which at least one leading nation in each of nine or ten fairly permanent proto-coalitions (e.g., U.S. and allies, Latin America, British Commonwealth, Western Europe, U.S.S.R. and allies, Arab nations, African nations, Southeast Asian neutralists, China and allies) possess accurate intercontinental missiles with nuclear warheads. In such a system, there may truly be a balance of terror. Not the least of the terrors is that in some place some man of authority may not be terrified. And it is the possibility that the last terror may be justified that renders the system of balance by moral restraint an unsatisfactory protection, even though it may be the only one really available.

*Institutional Restraint*

The method of institutional restraint consists of the
transformation of an $n$-person system into a two-person
system by the creation of a set of quasi-permanent blocking coalitions. There is a powerful tendency in the dynamic model set forth in Chapters 5 and 6 for such a transformation to occur. The nature of the side-payments, the
zero-sum feature, and the size principle are the essential
structural features that encourage this tendency. If on
each decision there clearly exist winners and losers and if
the participants have a clear preference for a minimal
winning coalition, then the existence of one winning coalition is assured for at least one decision. The nature of
the side-payments used to construct it encourages its continuation for subsequent decision. If the side-payments
are release from the threat of physical force, the accumu-
lation of force for one decision stands readily available
for a later one. Similarly, the development of a charismatic appeal by a leader is the process of a lifetime, not to
be dissipated by one decision alone. Those who acknowledge the charisma for one act will acknowledge it for
subsequent ones. Hence, a quasi-permanent proto-coalition necessarily results. If the side-payments involve promises about future policy, future payoffs, etc., then a coalition on one decision necessarily involves the expectation
of some permanence. When the payments are related only
to the decision in question, however, they need not carry
an implication of permanence. Nevertheless, since any one
of the several kinds of payments may be used and since
most actual decisions are made by coalitions constructed
by a blend of these several, it follows that the existence
of a winning coalition on one decision implies that something very like it will win on the next. This argument

from the nature of side-payments concludes, then, with the assertion that the system tends to guarantee the existence of at least one quasi-permanent coalition. Now, if one is guaranteed, there is, I suggest, a strong tendency toward the creation of at least one and only one more. Those outside the winning coalition, that is, the losers, are, of course, free to try to avert continual and repeated loss. The only way they can do this is by drawing together into one group and, in addition, by attracting some dissatisfied members of the already existent coalition. Since this coalition must be held together by some blend of the several kinds of payments, it too has some tendency toward quasi-permanence. Hence, in a majority system such as that set forth in Chapter 5 and 6, the tendency toward a quasi-permanent two-faction system is very strong. Indeed, one may say that the system will inevitably develop into such unless there is a commitment to some moral restraints (like Kaplan's third and fourth rules) that prohibit permanent losers and enjoin alliance with the weaker side.

The same structural guidelines that encourage quasi-permanent two-factionalism in a majoritarian system also encourage it in a system in which a plurality wins. (This is the voting system typical of most Anglo-American countries.) Here, however, the zero-sum feature and the kinds of side-payments guarantee the existence only of a quasi-permanent largest coalition (which may of course be less than a majority) opposed by more than one other. But the existence of a larger coalition is itself sufficient to encourage its opponents (if they are more than one) to ally against it in one way or another. Hence, a plurality system can be expected to turn into a majority system with two quasi-permanent blocking coalitions.[10]

10. This assertion is equivalent to the "sociological law," stated by Duverger, that single-member districts maintain and even encourage the

In a system of quasi-permanent dual factionalism there are two moderating considerations forever present in the calculations of leaders. One is the consciousness of the danger, from the point of view of a winning coalition that expects to continue to win, that it may kill the goose that lays golden eggs. If a winning coalition of this sort sets the stakes too high, then it faces the likelihood that it will have no losers in the future, in which case it may be forced to turn in on itself to find losers, thereby doubly

two-party system (Maurice Duverger, *Political Parties,* trans. by Barbara and Robert North (New York, John Wiley, 1955), p. 217). Single-member districts are, of course, a feature of plurality or majority voting. (The contrast is multi-member districts in which, possibly, losers—those having less than a plurality—win. Quite obviously proportional representation systems are non-zero-sum at the electoral level, since losers as well as winners are elected. But at the parliamentary level, even these systems become zero-sum.) Hence Duverger's assertion about single-member districts is strictly equivalent to my assertion that, in a majority or plurality system, the structure within which a dynamic decision-making process occurs favors a two-party system. The difference between Duverger's formulation and mine is simply that his is a low-level generalization which does not fit into any known sociological or political theory, while the formulation given here is a deduction from a quite general theory. I conclude with several unrelated observations about the parallelism recorded in this marginal note:

(1) Since Duverger's assertion, though demonstrably true for Western Europe and the Anglo-American parliamentary systems, seems at first reading to be a mere overemphasis of a trivial feature of constitutional structure (and seemed even more so when first set forth by Ferdinand A. Hermens, *Democracy or Anarchy: A Study of Proportional Representation* [South Bend, University of Notre Dame Press, 1941], passim), students of politics generally have been reluctant to recognize the considerable significance this assertion has. Entirely aside from its intrinsic importance in the interpretation of constitutions, it is important for the science of politics as such because it is one of the few generalizations that has been fully verified for a wide variety of political systems. If the reformulation of it to fit into a more general theory of politics can render it intuitively more acceptable, then the fact of parallelism between Duverger's statement and my deduction from a model should help to clarify an important proposition.

(2) The parallelism permits us to use the extensive evidence adduced by Duverger and Hermens for verifying the dynamic model and the size

upsetting the balance in an unpredictable way. Since the eventual outcome is unpredictable, any leader of a regularly winning coalition who sets the stakes very high runs a great risk that he himself will be among the losers after the goose is killed. In such circumstances rational men moderate their expectations. The second moderating consideration is the consciousness of the danger, from the point of view of winners who are uncertain about their future status, that by setting high stakes on this decision

principle and might well be added to the evidence mentioned in Chapters 3 and 4.

(3) The advantage of a general theory over *ad hoc* or "inductive" theories is especially evident here. *Ad hoc* theories are proven false if a contrary instance can be found. More general theories, which account for exceptions, permit us to deal with a greater variety of experience in relatively simple terms. As it happens, Duverger's assertion was proven false soon after he uttered it by the history of the following decade in India, where rigid single-member districts were, for the most part, imposed, and where no observable tendencies toward a two-party system could be discerned. No sooner had Duverger written than the next political system to satisfy his antecedent failed to satisfy his consequent—thereby making it easy to disprove his *ad hoc* theory. The more general formulation offered here can, however, account for this apparent exception and indeed account for some of the delays of the "district effect" in the European systems that Duverger examined. In a plurality system, one can expect two factions to develop only if all the losers combine against the winner, who is the largest coalition but not a winning coalition in the majoritarian sense. But if the plurality winner occupies an ideological position that prevents the coalescence of the losers, then one may expect that a two-party system will not develop until the winner has been in some way dislodged from its ideological position. In the Indian experience the Congress party has, ever since independence, occupied a central position on a unidimensional scale so that the socialists and communists at one end find it difficult to combine with the liberals, independents, and religionists at the other. The new formulation offered here allows us to explain the failure of Duverger's assertion by saying that a two-party system is to be expected only if the distribution of proto-coalitions in a plurality electoral body (i.e., a single-member district electoral body) is such that the winner is near one end of a scale of ideology. In the Indian instance, one may expect a two-party system only when (presumably after the retirement of Nehru) the Congress party is forced out of the center and toward one or the other end of the ideological continuum.

they may encourage retaliation by the present losers when the latter are transformed into winners. Excessively high stakes on the one "we" win imply the retribution of excessively high stakes on the later decision "they" win. Again, in such touchy circumstances, rational men moderate their present expectations in order to avoid future loss.

The effect of both these moderating considerations on leaders in a two-party system is to render them reluctant to eliminate losers, or, more generally, to set the stakes too high. Thus it is that a two-party system moderates instability.

As against the method of moral restraint, which operates by an internalized and presumably absolute morality, the method of institutional restraint operates by an externalized and presumably instrumental morality. Which of these two methods is the most effective in moderating instability is not immediately clear. Both techniques can fail. I have already cited the failure of the method of moral restraint in the international system of the first half of the twentieth century. To this I should add the instances in the history of American politics in which the two-party system (an institutional restraint) has failed to maintain an equilibrium (e.g., the Civil War and, perhaps, the disappearance of the Federalist and Whig parties). Still, which method fails most easily I cannot say, although intuitively I am inclined to believe that the method of institutional restraint is more effective.

The considerations raised in the last two sections lead me to reiterate the conclusion of the sixth chapter: that in a dynamic model politics are fundamentally and inherently unstable. Insofar as the structure of the model reflects the structure of the real world, its politics too are fundamentally and inherently unstable. To a generation that knows the danger of nuclear warfare, the assertion that disequilibrium is a probably ineradicable feature of politics is certainly disquieting. Yet if we are to live at all in this world, it is better, I think, to obtain as logically defensible a general theory as we can, even though it may not superficially suit our optimistic bias in favor of living.

# CHAPTER 9

# Components of Disequilibrium

The main import of the previous chapter is that one general equilibrium theory for a model of coalition-making contains internal inconsistencies. Consequently, this theory, which has often been thought to be a proof of stability, in no way denies the conclusion of Chapter 6 that the model is unstable. What remains to be considered in this chapter is, then, the occasion for disequilibrium.

As a preliminary, suppose a body or system is in perfect equilibrium, a condition that might occur because of

1. The existence of two quasi-permanent blocking coalitions,
2. The existence of two large and fairly evenly matched proto-coalitions along with one or more smaller proto-coalitions that play the role of balancer if a temporarily winning coalition sets the stakes too high.

How, one asks, might either kind of equilibrium break up? Manifestly, one thing that must happen is that the relative weights of members change. In the first case, a potentially disequilibrating change would be, for example, an increase in the weight of a member of one block-ing coalition at the expense of some member(s) of the other one. Thereby a quasi-permanent blocking coalition would be transformed into a quasi-permanent winning one. In the second case, the same kind of potentially dis-equilibriating change might be an increase in the weight of a member of one proto-coalition (at the expense of members of other ones) to the point that the strengthened proto-coalition becomes a winning coalition without the aid of any of the balancers. In either case, the scene is thus set for disequilibrium. But it need not actually oc-cur unless also the new winner is willing to set the stakes very high. If it is so willing, then, of course, the body or system becomes in fact unbalanced.

Thus two conditions appear to be necessary for disequi-librium:

1. A change in the weight of two or more partici-pants, and
2. A willingness on the part of the winner to set high stakes.

Both conditions together are sufficient. Hence, the cause of disequilibrium is the simultaneous occurrence of the two conditions.

This statement of the cause of disequilibrium is prob-ably clear except, perhaps, for the requirement that at least two participants change their weights. One might rea-sonably inquire why disequilibrium could not occur if only one changed its weight. The answer is, of course, that one participant alone cannot change. Heretofore the no-tion of weight has been left undefined, partly for the reason that weights are seldom defined clearly in the real world—except, perhaps, when they are expressed as votes or some other normalized amount. All that one can say about weight is that it is the sum of all those circumstances that give a participant significance relative to prospective decisions. (In this sense, "weight" is possibly equivalent to "power," an equally slippery term.) Manifestly, the components of weight differ in different situations, according to what is and what is not significant in the real world at the moment. Hence, of weight in general one can assert only this: that the weights of all participants at any moment total one. That is, each participant's weight can be expressed as a fraction of the total weight. The total weight is a fixed sum, i.e., that which may bring about a decision, given any possible coalition. Since weight is thus a function of decision itself rather than an inherent quality of particular members, total weight is a function, not of members, but of the decision at hand. Hence, if one member increases its capacity to influence a decision, then some other member(s) must lose some of its (their) capacity to do the same thing. In this respect weight is quite different from money. An increase in the amount of money one person has does not affect the amount or value of money in the hands of other persons (assuming, of course, a free market). But an increase in the weight of one person necessarily alters the weight of other persons. This is why one can get rich without necessarily impoverishing other people while at the same time to become powerful one necessarily weakens others.

To state the two necessary and jointly sufficient conditions of disequilibrium does not, however, carry us very far in an understanding of events either in the model or the world. These conditions are so far abstracted from even the imaginary events of the model that they do not tell us much about the concrete occasions. Hence, for real understanding, one must investigate all the motives, relations, qualities, and circumstances subsumed under each of the two conditions.

Unfortunately, however, each manifestation of the second condition (i.e., a willingness to set the stakes high) is so deeply imbedded in the particular circumstances of a particular event that the social features of the manifestation can be studied only as history or as a unique event. While the motives for setting high stakes can be generalized about in the same way one generalizes about any human motives, still to ask what brings them into play is to ask what occasions greed, aggressiveness, hatred, vengefulness, etc. Thus, in order to specify the occasions for the second condition, it is necessary to restate almost all the discoveries of social and clinical psychology. I have no intention of doing so here. Instead, I merely call the reader's attention to the relevance of these sciences for understanding the components of disequilibrium.

About the first necessary condition, however, it is possible to generalize somewhat more informatively. This aspect of disequilibrium can be categorized into several component parts, and such categorization is the purpose of this chapter.

Heretofore it has been emphasized that the seeds of disequilibrium lie within the decision-making system itself—in, that is, the preference the system gives to decision and in its lack of effective restriction on the content of decision. Furthermore, all the circumstances and motives of the second necessary condition lie within the system also. Hence it might appear that the generalized decision-making system contains on the one hand an equilibrating force (i.e., the often existent advantage for the weakest proto-coalition to join, not the strongest, but the second strongest proto-coalition) and on the other hand a disequilibriating one (i.e., the preference for decision coupled with indifference about content) so that the system is entirely self-contained and generates both its own breakdowns and its own recoveries. When one turns to an examination of the first necessary condition, however, this neat isolation of the political system disappears. While the system for making political decisions is indeed a universe and is commonly abstracted as such both for analysis and for action, still it exists in and among people and therefore in and among other commonly abstracted universes. It would be strange indeed if such universes did not jolt one another. And, in fact, they do. When one analyzes the first necessary condition (changes in weights), it appears that some of these may be occasioned by events entirely outside the decision-making body or system in which the changes occur. In the categorization of the components of disequilibrium, I have, therefore, distinguished between exogenous and endogenous variations in weight in order to point up the dependence of disequilibrium on what may be essentially accidental conditions. I do not mean thereby to suggest that exogenous influences are the main influences for disequilibrium. Indeed, my subjective impression is quite the contrary. My sole intention in so categorizing is to call attention to the fact that, as against the implication of the analysis hitherto, disequilibrium is not entirely a function of internal events in a decision-making body or system.

## EXOGENOUS VARIATIONS IN WEIGHT

Some of the supposedly extraneous influences on relative weights are mechanical invention and changes in the means of production. That these may have a profound effect on reordering national and international politics no one of this nation or generation could deny. Not only have we seen the effect of the discovery of atomic fission on international politics, but also we have been taught to read history at least partly through the eyes of Marx. Even if we did not have a quasi-Marxian rendition of modern history written into most of our schoolbooks, we would still have the example of our own Civil War, around which our politics are still partly bifurcated. This war, even in its own day, was generally interpreted as a conflict between two contradictory systems of production. Moreover, few men in 1865 doubted that the outcome was largely determined by the fact that one system produced more weapons and more men than the other. In the colonial era, both North and South produced by means of yeoman agriculture. In the North, this remained and was supplemented with a rudimentary capitalism. In the South, however, yeoman agriculture was subordinated to plantation agriculture. And these divergent changes are what occasioned and decided the war. With that observation always in our national consciousness, we of this nation cannot doubt that invention influences the weight of players and has thereby profoundly disequilibriating effects.

The question, therefore, does not concern whether invention is influential. On that point there can hardly be disagreement (especially since this kind of explanation of disequilibrium is at least as ancient as Aristotle's attribution of the rise of the Athenian demos to the development of a kind of naval warfare that required numerous oarsmen). Instead, the question is whether or not invention is an exogenous variable. Is it an accidental occurrence outside decision-making systems but fraught with significance for what happens inside? Or is it a part of the system itself, one tactic of maneuver in the preparation of new coalitions?

On this question, we cannot utter a certain answer. Indeed, even the theories to account for invention are themselves somewhat ambiguous. In the Marxian analysis, for example, it is asserted, on the one hand, that the capitalist mode of production itself generates the mechanical and organizational changes that in turn are expected to destroy capitalism. In this phase, therefore, invention is inside the system so that the system itself generates its own disequilibrium. On the other hand, in the pre-capitalist systems of production (feudal, classical, oriental) nothing in the systems themselves generate the inventions appropriate to induce capitalism. In the pre-capitalist phases, therefore, invention is essentially exogenous. Such accidental things as the flow of gold from America and the intellectual renaissance with its emphasis on natural science were the impetus for changing the feudal world—yet presumably nothing in this world necessitated their occurrence.

While the Marxian analysis is thus thoroughly ambiguous, one might expect that the history of science—a relatively new academic discipline inspired partly by Marxism and partly by the obvious significance of science in our own era—would provide a less ambiguous theory. Unfortunately it has not. Some writers in this field argue that science has a wholly self-contained history, building on its own past but not influenced by events in the larger world. In such theories, the motive for invention is a combination of the two motives identified by Veblen as "the instinct of workmanship" and "idle curiosity." But in other theories of the history of science, scientific advance is perceived as a response to social needs. Such theories are, of course, an elaboration of the old saying that necessity is the mother of invention. They emphasize such facts as that Newton's laws were discovered in an age that desperately needed to improve navigation and that Maxwell's and Einstein's laws were discovered in an age that desperately needed to improve its source of energy. Without demonstrating that Newton was interested in commerce or that Maxwell and Einstein were interested in industrial production, it is possible to assert, in such theories, that the questions presented for these thinkers to answer were questions vitally important to the technology (and warfare) of the era.

As between these two kinds of theories, one of which suggests that mechanical invention is independent of the struggle for power and the other of which suggests that it is wholly dependent on it, we have insufficient evidence to make a choice. By temperament, I am inclined to believe that the latter theory is more persuasive and I emphasize to myself the close connection, for example, between viniculture and Pasteur's discovery of the relevance of germs to disease. But at the same time I must admit that the theory of natural selection, which has turned out to have tremendously significant commercial applications in, especially, the technology of agriculture, had for its creators no technological significance whatsoever. Indeed, it is difficult even to assert that Darwin's question was presented to him as a social necessity. Perhaps its very impact was owing to its unnecessary character. So I retain for myself the same degree of ambivalence I attribute to historians of science. And I conclude: Invention, especially invention directly instigated by questions of the wealth and weight of nations, is usually a function of the internal struggles in the system. But counterexamples may be found which suggest that invention is an exogenous variable.

Another variable, often believed to be exogenous, is the internal organization of the player, whether he be a person, a faction, or a nation. That this feature of social life changes weights in the decision-making system can hardly be doubted by a generation that has witnessed, for example, the remarkable rise of the Soviet Union in international politics, a rise that must in great part be attributed to its internal reorganization after 1917. But granted that this internal change, and others like it elsewhere, have overwhelming effects on relative weights in the decision-making system, the important question is whether or not such change is exogenous. Are changes in the internal organization of players in the game occasioned by the desire and chance to increase the players' weights or by some wholly extraneous desires and chances? Again, the answer must be ambiguous. In one circumstance, however, motives outside the system appear to be dominant.

To state a concrete instance of the former, the change in the weight of Germany after 1933 may be said to have resulted from a motive generated by the system itself. While Hitler and his cohorts had of course a variety of private and evil motives and while the motives of those who accepted him (Hindenburg et al.) were also mixed, still the justification of nazism that probably satisfied most Germans was the assertion that Hitler reorganized Germany to recover what it had lost in 1919.

Although in this instance the motive for the reorganization of a player seems fairly clearly to lie within the international system itself, it is not so clear when one looks at an American instance of a disequilibriating reorganization. The reorganization of the losing party in American politics in the 1850s involved the abandonment of a party based on a national appeal (the Whig) for a party based on a sectional appeal (the Republican). Unquestionably part of the motive for this reorganization lay within the system of national politics. It was simply the desire of losers to find an issue and organization with which they could win. But the issue upon which the losers seized could hardly be said to have been generated by the system itself. The antislavery movement was indeed something which both the main participants in the system had sought to ignore, shushing it as one would shush a boisterous child. So while the motive for the reorganization that adopted this disequilibriating ideology was inside the system, the ideology itself was probably of wholly extraneous origin.

The ambiguity in the origin of a disequilibrating force in this instance can be compared to a reorganization in Russia that probably was motivated by wholly extraneous concerns. Imperial Russia was only by courtesy and tradition regarded as a great power in 1914, although England with its interests in India was annoyed and obscurely frightened by Russian expansion in Asia.

Thirty years later the Soviet Union was the greatest power in Europe and the first or second power in the world. Although some White Russians in exile have argued, with a charming and pathetic myopia, that this would have happened anyway if either Imperial or Kerenskian Russia had survived, few disinterested observers would deny that the main reason for this change of national weight in the international system was the October Revolution and all its consequences. The interesting question for our purposes now is, therefore: Did this revolution derive from the international system? The answer is fairly clear that the motives of the participants certainly did not. While Lenin may have wished for power in Russia in order to remake the world on a Marxist model, it was surely not the revival of the international influence of Russia itself that concerned him. As Carr has shown, Lenin and his successors never hesitated to desert the international communist movement if this collided with Russian national interest,[1] but I see no reason why one cannot fully accept their own rationale that a strong Soviet Union was in the long run the best agency for their professed ideal of world communism. Indeed, events seem to have borne out their contention very well. So if the motives of the revolutionaries of 1917 were not to reorganize

1. Edward Hallett Carr, *The Bolshevik Revolution: 1917–1923* (3 vols. London, Macmillan, 1950–53), *3*, 21 ff.

Russia as a stronger player in the game, but rather to introduce a new game with new rules which, conceivably, would not even include Russia at all, then it could hardly be said that their motives derived from the international system. The fact that the Soviet Union is now so significant a participant in this system is testimony, not to the intent of the revolutionaries, but to the revision of their motives and their successors' motives when it appeared that world revolution was not immediately imminent. In terms of motives, therefore, I conclude that this reorganization was entirely extraneous to international politics, although, of course, fraught with the most unpleasant consequences for it.

In terms of the occasion, however, this reorganization was entirely due to events within the international system. The Imperial government was notably inefficient as modern governments go, but still it was able to place an army of some millions of men in the field. This army was too ill-fed, ill-equipped, and ill-led to win any notable victories, but nonetheless it was able to hold some sort of line against an enemy whose chief war was on another front. Now a government able to put an army of this size in the field is hardly a government about to topple. There is undoubtedly truth in the White Russian argument that the Imperial government was much stronger in 1914 than in 1904. What rendered this inefficient but reasonably viable despotism unfit to resist even a few riots was the drain of the war itself—and that is an event entirely within the international system. The war weakened not only the Imperial government but also Kerensky's government and thereby set the scene in which a few imaginative gamblers could carry through a successful coup d'état. Considering, then, the total situation of both motives and occasion, it appears that this reorganization of a participant was consciously (i.e., from the point of view of motives) wholly outside the system, but unconsciously (i.e., from the point of view of the occasion) inside it.

From these examples, it seems fairly clear that the internal organization of a participant may be, at least partially, exogenous to the body or system itself. Perhaps in an even more general theory than the theory of coalitions here set forth, the variables of invention and reorganization can be fully integrated into the system. But, as I have already suggested, in the present state of theory about society they are only partly in and partly out.

## ENDOGENOUS VARIABLES

### Changes in Rules

Any change in the rules of a game or body or system is, of course, likely to alter the outcome. Indeed, in many parliamentary bodies members are continually preoccupied with inventing plausible reasons for changing rules in a way that is likely to work to their advantage. In the United States Congress during the last generation, for example, there has been much agitation about and some actual shifting of the rules on debate in the Senate and the jurisdiction of the Rules Committee in the House. As against the hitherto considered events that change weights, such changes as these are wholly endogenous. They involve an attempt to win with the weight one has by changing, not weight, but the situation in which weight is applied. Most rewriting of constitutions is of this nature, as, for example, the Parliament Act of 1911 which did not change the formal weight of the Lords but simply ruled that this weight would no longer count for much.

The most common and perhaps most disequilibriating type of rule-changing, however, does involve a change in weights. Changes in the rules specifying membership in the body or system change weights directly inasmuch as the sum of weights can always be normalized to one. Additions or subtractions of members must therefore affect the weight relationships among all the other members in an expanded or contracted body. The intent behind all changes of the rules of membership is, of course, to secure the quasi-permanent ascendancy of a temporarily ascendant coalition. That is, a coalition that is momentarily winning hopes that it may prolong its winning through future decisions by means of the support of new members who will presumably be grateful for admission to those who admitted them. Or, in the opposite maneuver, a coalition that is momentarily winning hopes that it may prolong its winning by expelling members of the losing side so that the losers will not be strong enough to win even if they should be able to seduce a part of the winning coalition. The expansion of the electorate in all democratic countries has almost always been occasioned by transparent motives of this sort. In the case of the United States, for example, the relaxation of property qualifications for voting were maneuvers by Jeffersonian Democrats (or the radical wing of that party) to defeat Federalists or conservative Democrats; the Fifteenth Amendment was a maneuver by Republicans to defeat Democrats by obtaining Negro votes, and the Nineteenth Amendment was a maneuver by reformers to defeat political bosses (on the theory that women would be more hostile than men to political corruption).[2] Or in the case of the first consciously democratic system, the reforms of Cleisthenes in Athens were a maneuver to grant citizenship to persons who would support the radical party that was ultimately led by Pericles.[3] Examples of such expan-

2. For detail on the process and motives of expansion of the electorate, see Riker, *Democracy in the United States*, chap. 2.
3. Aristotle, *Constitution of Athens*, chap. 21.

sion can be multiplied indefinitely from popular governments in ancient medieval and modern times. Indeed I know no instance in which the expansion of an electorate does not have exactly this intention, although (as in the instance of women's suffrage in the United States) the hopes of those who enlarged the electorate are not always justified by later events. Similarly the contraction of electorates in democratic countries is almost always a maneuver by winners to exclude losers who might subsequently contribute to the winners' defeat. Again, in the case of the United States, the exclusion of white Southerners after the Civil War was a maneuver to ensure Republican ascendancy in the South, the later exclusion of black Southerners was a maneuver to secure Democratic victory, and the various literacy tests for voting were, originally, maneuvers in New England by Know-Nothings to ensure their victory by excluding recent immigrants (especially from Ireland) or maneuvers in the West to secure Republican victory by excluding Mexicans or Indians, or maneuvers by Southern whites to secure Democratic victory by excluding Negroes.[4]

Turning from electorates to legislative bodies, here too the expansion and contraction of membership has been a persistent and standardized technique for changing the relative weights of members. In the United States, the regular expansion of the House of Representatives after each decennial census in the nineteenth century was an attempt to minimize the loss of relative weight by old states as new states were added. More to the point, controversies over the admission of new states were regularly fought out in terms of the effect the prospective admission would have on the partisan balance in the legislature. Two types of maneuver have been characteristic of the process: In one, when the balance was very close, an agree-

4. Riker, *Democracy in the United States*, chap. 2.

ment has been made to bring in two states at once, that is, a state on each side. (This is the kind of maneuver involved in, for example, the Missouri compromise of 1820 and the admission of Alaska and Hawaii in 1959.) In the other maneuver, an ascendant party has brought in a state that would vote on its side. (This is the kind of maneuver, for example, to be seen in the admission of Kentucky and Tennessee in the 1790s and Arizona and New Mexico in 1912.) Similar kinds of maneuvers have been apparent in both the world political organizations of this century. Thus, the admission of the Republic of China to the United Nations has occasioned so much debate, not because of the slight readjustment of weights of the Eastern and Western blocs that it would induce in the General Assembly, but rather because of the major readjustment of weights it would induce in the Security Council.

When viewed either in very large or relatively small decision-making bodies, conscious changes in rules on membership are seen to be endogenous variables in the weights of members. Hence also they are endogenous variables in the disequilibrium of political systems.

## The Bankruptcy of Leadership

In Chapter 5 the costs of the payments made by leaders to followers were categorized as:

1. Contingent payments out of profits,
2. Payments out of working capital,
3. Payments out of fixed assets.

It was further pointed out that these kinds of payments were hardly commensurate with each other and only with difficulty commensurate with some imaginary market value of decisions. In the very fact of incommensurability lies, I suggest, an immensely important possibility of disequilibrium. If leaders make mistakes in calculations of the several different kinds of payments, they can seriously overpay or underpay their followers. Overpayment results in the exhaustion of leaders' capacity to pay. Underpayment results in the disillusion and desertion of followers. Either kind of event is thoroughly endogenous to the body or system or game inasmuch as both result simply from the variety of kinds of payments available in a political system.

The possibility of disequilibrium owing to miscalculation in side-payments is enormously increased if one takes into consideration not only payments to followers, but payments to leaders themselves. Necessarily the leaders' share of winnings on any decision must be a part of the total calculation. Hence, a theoretical analysis of a system or body cannot leave out the leaders' share.

The list in Chapter 5 of payments to followers does not fully describe the payments to leaders. Of course, leaders do receive some of the same kinds of payments, e.g., valuable objects, changes in the content of policy, support on subsequent coalitions, etc. But leaders are not ordinarily subject to the threat of reprisal nor can they experience the emotional satisfaction of following. Instead they receive at least the following kinds of additional rewards:

1. *The satisfactions of power:* One can imagine at least two general types of motives for desiring power, which I define, following Dahl, as the ability to make someone else do something he would not otherwise do.[5] One motive is instrumental, the desire for power in order to accomplish some additional goal such as a change in policy or victory in a conflict. The other motive is absolute, the desire for power for its own sake and the emotional satisfaction that

5. Robert A. Dahl, "The Concept of Power," *Behavioral Science, 2* (1957), 201–15.

comes from playing a quasi-divine role. There seems to be some tendency among social theorists to regard the latter motive as psychopathological although it seems rather strange so to interpret a motive frequently displayed in the behavior of "great men." Here, however, I shall regard it as a given and normal human motive and assume that in any real circumstance of leadership both instrumental and absolute desires for power are operating. If this is correct, then one of the rewards of leadership is power itself, regardless of the purpose for which it is desired.

2. *The satisfactions of prestige:* While leaders cannot experience the emotional satisfaction of following, they can, perhaps, experience a complementary satisfaction of being followed. Unfortunately social scientists and psychologists know very little about what these satisfactions are. Not being themselves leaders, they have no intuitive perception of leaders' motives which can serve as heuristic in the formulation of hypotheses. Furthermore and typically, they have not been able to study intimately and objectively important people in the world of affairs. Hence, most discussions (e.g., Freud, Weber) of the emotional features of the leadership relation emphasize the motives of the followers rather than of those who are followed. Since these theories are oriented toward the followers, the application of them to leaders—as, for example, the numerous armchair analyses of Hitler—are confusing, contradictory, and far from convincing. Yet in spite of the sad state of theory on this matter, we can, I think, safely assume (without adequate theoretical justification, of course) that leaders do obtain some satisfaction from prestige. Precisely what the satisfactions are, however, we cannot say. Perhaps charismatic leaders are rewarded by a sense of accomplishing a mission. Perhaps they naïvely enjoy the veneration and deference their followers dis-

play. (For example, it has been persuasively argued by George and George that Woodrow Wilson sought victory after victory to prove to himself again and again that the feelings of inadequacy, instilled in him by a dominant father, were not justified.[6]) Perhaps, ignoring all satisfactions which common men might attribute to them and projecting themselves entirely into a mystically perceived reality, their very absorption in a reality of their own creation justifies their existence to themselves. Regardless, however, of whether the satisfactions are accomplishment, deference, commitment, or something else entirely we can assume that there do exist some emotional satisfactions in the act of leadership itself.

3. *The satisfactions of continuation:* The leader who has never paid followers with emotional satisfaction or threats of reprisal need not fear the loss of his role. Upon losing it, he simply reverts to the role of follower, probably, indeed, without trauma of any serious sort. But for the leader who has used either the terrible currency of fear or the magic currency of love, to be deposed is to be destroyed. And when destruction is in prospect, a leader must hang on, simply to continue to live. A small reward, perhaps, but vital. In effect, therefore, the assumption of certain methods of leadership necessitates the maintenance of it—and this very maintenance is an important reward.

A deposed leader who used physical force and the threat of force can reasonably expect that force of some sort will be turned upon him. And, indeed, it is the rare tyrant who escapes tyrannicide when his rebellious subjects have him in their hands. While revolutionaries (other than simple jacquerie) are usually more concerned with reconstruction than with vengeance, still they usually find some time for vengeance too. Their vengeance is, typically, inefficient

6. Alexander L. George and Juliette L. George, *Woodrow Wilson and Colonel House: A Personality Study* (New York, John Day, 1956), passim.

—far less efficient, for example, than the tyranny they punish. But since the vengeance can be expected to fall on the tyrant and his immediate coterie, the tyrant has an urgent motive to avoid retirement.

The leader who is not clearly a tyrant but who has used the authority of office to acquire wealth is, nevertheless, in something of the tyrant's position. That is, if his wealth is a function of his leadership (rather than of some non-political fact, such as economic productivity), then he cannot expect to keep it or very much of it when he loses his leadership. This proposition holds, I believe, for social classes and nations as well as for families and persons. On the personal level, one is struck by the fact that the enormous sums of money acquired by some city bosses in the United States in the late nineteenth and early twentieth centuries did not survive as great personal or family fortunes. Presumably the major portion of these monies was dissipated simply in maintaining a position to receive more. On the class level, one is struck by the fact that, even if a ruling class is not expropriated by revolutionaries (as in the Soviet Union), still, when it ceases to rule it gradually ceases to have great wealth (as the aristocracy in Great Britain). And on the national level, one is struck by the fact that, in the contraction of empires, the elegance and creativity of the imperial center degenerates into stylized and parsimonious living (as in Hellenic Athens or republican Vienna). In short, whenever wealth is partially a function of political leadership— and it almost always is, even in the open society of modern capitalism—then the leader who lets go of leadership jeopardizes all else that he has acquired, and this fact is, of course, a powerful motive to continue to hang on to the leader's role.

A similar kind of trap enmeshes the leader who pays with the currency of love. While he need not fear reprisals from his former followers if he ceases to lead, still in the process of leading he incurs so many obligations to them that he cannot cease. He mixes his life with theirs until he loses an independent existence. He is *their* spokesman, *their* agent, *their* leader and, if he continues long in this role, his life becomes *their* life. To cease to lead, therefore, is for such a man to cease to live in all but the physiological sense of the word. This fact probably explains the extraordinary personal bravery of charismatic leaders on the battlefield (e.g., General Custer), the equanimity with which they face death when captured (e.g., Jeanne d'Arc), and their occasional resort to suicide when their future is destroyed (e.g., Hitler). Leaving aside the speculations of this last sentence, however, it is still apparent that the charismatic or partially charismatic leader does not dare to lose. Hence continuance in the role becomes an end itself just as much for him who rules with the currency of love as for him who rules with the currency of terror. And when charisma and tyranny are combined in the same man, the motive for continuance is probably most urgent of all.

The significance of the existence of these three types of special payments to leaders is twofold. In the first place, it encourages the development of opportunistic leaders. None of these three rewards can be paid out of contingent profits in the decision itself. The payment here lies in winning, not in what is won. Hence, the leader who pays himself exclusively with these special rewards can put all the objective winnings of the coalition into payments to followers. As a consequence, therefore, the leader who pays himself nothing of material or ideological value has a bargaining advantage over the leader who tries to make some profit for himself. Thus the general decision-making model is deeply biased toward the leader who wants nothing but power, prestige, and continuance in his role. And such a leader is in the exact sense of the word opportunistic. If he has an ideology, it is not a deeply felt belief for the realization of which he selflessly struggles. Rather, it is simply a tool in building winning coalitions. If circumstances change so that a conflicting ideology is a more useful tool, then such a leader easily discards the old and takes on the new. Woodrow Wilson, as an example, espoused "democratic" policies as president of Princeton, turned himself into a conservative to get the nomination for governor of New Jersey, and then finally became a progressive in order to win that office and subsequently the Presidency. Or, for another example, Stalin found it easy to adopt almost exactly Trotsky's policy once he had driven him out of office on the ground that his policy was wrong. If a leader pays followers partially in charisma, such maneuvers are disconcerting to the faithful who, unlike the leader, really believe the ideology he has espoused and propagated and abandoned. Hence some of the most amusing political (and theological) literature is that which explains to the faithful that ideological somersaults are great leaps forward. It was a small section of this literature that Orwell satirized in *1984*. This book is a brilliant denunciation of tyranny, but its fatal defect lay in Orwell's inability to see that most leaders, regardless of ideological hue, have the character of a trimmer.

The fact that, in the model, leaders who want power and glory rather than ideological satisfaction are preferred to those who want some share of the actual gain of the victorious coalition means that the model itself tends to guarantee the axiom of rationality on which it is based. The rational political man is, as has already been observed, he who prefers winning to losing. And if anything can be said of the opportunist it is that he wants to win. In that sense, then, the operation of the model jusifies its axioms.

The second significant feature of the existence of the three types of special payments to leaders is that, by reason of their existence, leaders may pay out more to win than a victory is objectively worth. In the heat of competition, leaders of competing proto-coalitions, men intent on the rewards of power and glory and office, may promise to prospective followers not only *all* the objective gains from victory, but also payments out of working capital and fixed assets. To retain leadership for the moment they may be forced to dissipate those very assets on which their continuing leadership is based. Translating from the metaphorical language of the theory to the language of ordinary political life, a leader may use up all the patronage at his command to win on a relatively trivial issue, only to lose because he has nothing left to bargain with when a really great issue comes along. Or a tyranny may exhaust its political police in putting down minor revolts so that when a great revolt occurs it has neither the will nor the terrifying effect it formerly had. (Something like this happened, perhaps, in the February Revolution in Russia in 1917. Trotsky remarked that the revolution crept under the belly of a Cossack's horse. Presumably it did so only because the Cossacks were disillusioned and exhausted.) On the international level, a dominant nation may exhaust its resources in maintaining the imperial status quo and then stand helplessly by while its subjects shake off the yoke. This is what has happened in the last fifteen years to the British and French empires after the metropolitan states were disabled by two world wars aimed at maintaining the status quo.

The retention of leadership is costly under any circumstances. But when the leader's rewards are not reckoned in the same currency paid out to followers, then the retention of leadership may be far more costly than the objective value of what is won in all the coalition's victories.

If so, then the existence of the special rewards to leaders is a persistent temptation to political waste.

Considering together the two features of special rewards to leaders, it is apparent that these rewards are a powerful force toward disequilibrium. If, as I have argued, there is a tendency in the model to favor leaders who value winning for its own sake and if, as I have also argued, there is a tendency for such leaders to spend more on victory than victory is worth, then the very existence of these special rewards to leaders encourages disequilibrium. Overspending is encouraged by the mere fact that the model prefers leaders who overspend. And overspending, of course, exhausts the resources of the coalition or proto-coalition that does so. Thereby weights are redistributed in the body or system and the scene is set for disequilibrium.

At the beginning of this chapter it was shown that there are two necessary and jointly sufficient conditions for disequilibrium. The second condition (i.e., a willingness to set the stakes high) was said to be wholly endogenous to the body or system. But the first condition (i.e., a variation in the weights of participants) was said to have both endogenous and exogenous origins. After an examination of the factors influencing a change in weight, it may be asked what is the relative importance of exogenous and endogenous factors. To this question I can give no certain answer, except to say that my subjective impression is that the endogenous factors count the most. In the fall of leaders, men and nations alike, it seems to me that the miscalculations of leaders themselves, their overspending, their restless search, as Hobbes put it, for power after power, is the primary factor in the change of weights. And if this is so, then the decision-making system is in disequilibrium unavoidably and absolutely.

# CHAPTER 10

# Reflections on Empires: An Epilogue on the United States in World Affairs

So far three main propositions about political coalitions have been developed from the model of $n$-person games:

1. *The size principle.* This is the assertion that, with complete and perfect information, winning coalitions tend toward the minimal winning size. (Chapters 2, 3, and 4.)

2. *The strategic principle.* This is the assertion that, in systems or bodies in which the size principle is operative, participants in the final stages of coalition-formation should and do move toward a minimal winning coalition. (Chapters 5, 6, and 7.)

3. *The disequilibrium principle.* This is the assertion that, in systems or bodies where the size and strategic principles are operative, the systems or bodies are themselves unstable. That is, they contain forces leading toward decision regardless of stakes and hence toward the elimination of participants. (Chapters 8 and 9.)

The first principle was deduced from the model and the latter two were deduced both from the model and the first principle. Some empirical evidence was offered from the size principle, though of course it needs much more detailed verification from less partial hands than mine before it can be generally accepted. Insofar as the size principle is verified, however, its two corollaries are somewhat verified also.

In one sense it is proper to end at this point for the theory from the model has now been carried as far as I am at present prepared to carry it. Nevertheless, the model was constructed in order to study the real world and, because of that purpose, it seems appropriate to conclude by inquiring further into the significance of the principles for reality. Assuming, then, that the three principles are validly deduced and either verified or verifiable empirically, what do they imply about the state of world politics?

## THE DECLINE OF EMPIRES

A speculation which has frequently entranced historians and sociologists with a broad view of their studies is the dynamics of the decline of empires and great coalitions. Few scholars have wondered greatly about the rise of empires for this phenomenon is readily explicable in terms of the rational desire to win and the energy and aggressiveness of particular politicians. But the opposite occurrence, the atrophy of bureaucracies and the dismemberment of viable social systems, has no readily apparent explanation—or at least no readily apparent explanation that men are willing to accept. Just as men generally have often been unwilling to accept the obvious physiological explanation of the death of individual persons and have disguised the unpalatable fact with a variety of probably delusive theories, so scholars have been reluctant to accept simple explanations of the death of societies. Thus, in the last three centuries, scholars have produced a plethora of contrived explanations of the decline of empires. Some have explained the events in terms of a (usually mystical) dissipation of the will to win (e.g. Gibbon, Spengler, Toynbee). Others have explained them in terms of some (equally mystical) death and rebirth process in disguised and probably unconscious analogy to animal life (e.g. Hegel and Marx). Still others, especially those in the Christian tradition, have explained in terms of unresolved conflicts in the human psyche (e.g. Niebuhr) or more simply still in terms of divine retribution and testing (e.g. Berdyaev). None of these have, however, explained in terms of ordinary social processes that are observable on a less grand scale than in the decline of empires.[1] The model developed in the previous chapters, however, suggests interpretations of the decline of empires in terms analogous in their simplicity and lack of mysticism to the explanation of death as a physiological event.

Two processes heretofore mentioned in connection

[1]. I have elsewhere criticized the method of such theorizing about history on the ground that the gross events studied (e.g., the decline of empires) are too unprecise to be generalized about by some sort of inductive process (Riker, "Events and Situations," *Journal of Philosophy*, *54*, 57–70). The criticism here, however, is of a substantive rather than methodological nature for I am asserting that the content of such theories is unrelated to ordinary social processes. Still, the two criticisms are related in the sense that exclusive preoccupation with the grand question of the rise and decline of empires, a question far too complex to approach *de novo*, leads writers to overlook the relevance of considerations apparent in lesser events to the grand questions they are trying to answer. The approach to these questions undertaken here avoids, I hope, both pitfalls. By starting from a simple model for simple events it avoids basing generalizations on wholly ambiguous events. At the same time, the extension of the principles from simple events to complex ones permits an explanation of history in terms of ordinary social processes.

with the model have special relevance for the explanation of the decline of empires and great coalitions. One is the size principle itself and the other is the tendency, mentioned in the last chapter, for leaders to miscalculate side-payments and to pay more for winning than winning is "objectively" worth. By reason of the size principle, leaders with the certain assurance of winning may actually expel some "minor" members whose interests conflict with the interests of some "major" members of the coalition. Even without expulsions, however, such leaders may reduce the size of their coalition simply by neglecting the interests of some members until the neglected ones defect to the other side. By such processes of expulsion and neglect, world-dominating empires can be expected to pare off their excess weight, even to the point at which they are barely capable of winning. At this point the danger of overpayment for victory becomes great indeed. Assuming that an opposing coalition or empire exists and that the ejected or defecting ex-members of winning coalitions join this opponent, then the size principle guarantees the existence of a formidable opponent for the winner. And if such an opponent exists, then it is imperative for the winner to keep on winning. In such circumstances, each decision reallocates relative weights and serves as a harbinger of the eventual outcome. When a previous winner loses on one decision, however minor, the very loss strengthens its opponent and, furthermore, renders the opponent more likely to succeed on future decisions. In this sense the whole of the future of a winning coalition or dominant empire may appear to be—and may actually be—at stake on each decision. This is the setting for overpayment. Decisions with a negligible objective worth are by the positional considerations rendered very important. Thus the expenditure of great amounts of working and fixed capital may appear to be justified even on decisions that cannot possibly result in any substantial repayment to capital resources. Repeated victory on such trivial decisions dissipates the winner's resources until it becomes incapable of winning.

At the end of the nineteenth century there were four world-dominating empires, England, France, Austria-Hungary, and Germany, whose leadership of the world was expressed not only in the force of arms but also in the creativity of scientific and humanistic culture. Today all four have been dismembered; their arms are negligible; and their intellectual creativity is overshadowed by people in other nations. All four are still rather well off financially—better off, for example, than most of their former dependencies. But relative to the rest of the world, they have lost place even in this respect. The decline of Germany and Austria-Hungary is explicable enough by the fact that they lost two major decisions involving dismemberment as a penalty for loss. The decline of England and France, however, is not so easily explained. Were not these the winners? Should not their empires have flourished in victory? But they did not flourish. One can only conclude that, in the exigencies of conflict, they paid more for winning than winning was objectively worth. In the decadence of these nations, in the fact that even their cultural and intellectual leadership has passed to other peoples, one can see the results of overpayment. This is not to say that either of these winners might reasonably have acted other than they did, for the loss they would have sustained as losers would undoubtedly have been far greater than the loss they actually sustained. But nevertheless in the very act of winning they lost most of what had made their leadership worthwhile.

It would be tedious and unrewarding to examine here all instances of notable declines of empires. But the interested reader may, if he chooses, carry through such an examination for himself. If he does so, he will find that the decline of every one of Toynbee's twenty-three past civilizations, as well as the decline of empires within the four existent ones, is fully explicable in terms of the size principle and overpayment to allies and followers, especially by means of military expenditures on Pyrrhic victories. In short, one can explain all declines of empires in terms of bad management rather than in terms of such mystical categories as a loss of will or a drive toward death or divine intervention. Bad management may, of course, be an inherent and inescapable feature of the political system, but it is an ordinary process within the system, not some mystical force outside it.

## THE PLACE OF THE UNITED STATES IN THE WORLD

Since 1945 at least consciously and since 1941 in retrospective consciousness, the United States has been the leader of a world-dominating coalition. It has been challenged, of course, by the Soviet Union, but at least as late as 1957 the challenger acknowledged a subordinate position for itself. In the course of an interview on 24 July 1957 in which Prime Minister Khrushchev was advocating a greater degree of exchange of persons between the U.S. and the U.S.S.R., he spoke quite incidentally of the power relationships between the two countries, calling his own nation "the second greatest power in the world." Considering the incidental and accidental nature of the utterance, this statement probably represented his actual intuitive judgment at the time.[2] Whether the subsequent Soviet

2. For the sake of conveying the full flavor of the judgment a larger quotation from the interview follows:

Even Soviet cooks are not allowed in the United States because the U.S. is afraid they will shake the foundations of its way of life! I met a farmer by the name of Garston who is a specialist on the hybridization of corn. He was very nice and wanted to invite a group of agron-

success in the technology of rockets and missiles has altered his judgment, one cannot say. Yet the tone of his remarks during his visit to the United States in 1960 (e.g., his references to passing the United States in the next decade) indicate, I believe, that he still holds his pre-Sputnik opinion. If the main opponent of United States leadership regards the United States as its superior to be emulated, there can be little doubt, I believe, that this country has, at least from 1945 to 1957 and probably still today, been the leader of a world-dominating coalition.

American citizens have on the whole been loath to recognize and accept this national role. The prevailing isolationist sentiment among politicans of all persuasions during the 1920s and 1930s effectively prevented our as-

omists to the U.S. They were refused entry by your government and when he went to champion their entry he had no luck. How can we improve prospects for peace when we can't even discuss corn.

Question [Mr. Jerome Davis]. We had an exchange of farmers recently, didn't we?

Answer: Yes, but only once, then it stopped. We would like to maintain the exchange. We favor an exchange of engineers since we have ideas of engineering even as you do.

The idea of not letting people into our respective countries is stupid or foolish. I don't know if such words are polite and I don't want to insult but I think so anyway. When people respect or accept a certain idea or system, that depends on their will but you can't ignore the fact that Bulgaria, Roumania, Albania, China, one third of Germany, North Vietnam and Poland exist. When we set up our system we didn't ask Dulles. You hate Communism and we Capitalism but that's not important. We have done wonders in our country and you envy us because *we are the second greatest power in the world* and will, through Communism, soon be the first. We must subdue passion and subordinate it into commonsense. Some politicians are blinded by hate and, like a bull seeing red, they leap forth blindly. Let us exchange scientific information and cooperate with each other.

*Report of the American European Seminar on the USSR Including their Interview with Krushchev in the Kremlin* (West Haven, Conn., Promoting Enduring Peace, Inc., no date, presumably 1957), p. 18, emphasis added.

sumption of the role of world leader in that period, although probably this role was ours for the asking even then. Still today, in the face of the objective fact of our leadership, we are isolationists enough in sentiment to try to close our eyes to our real position. Our national reluctance to play the role of world leader in Korea—a reluctance demonstrated by Eisenhower's overwhelming victory in 1952—was undoubtedly a reflection of this isolationist temper. In short, most Americans would prefer that their government be a follower rather than a leader so that, freed from the responsibilities of leadership, the citizens can go quietly about their business.

This political isolationism has been socially intertwined with a kind of cultural timidity and deference. Despite our cultural chauvinism on a popular level—a chauvinism that may well have had its roots in a repressed sense of inferiority—our intellectuals have generally been accustomed to defer to the taste and intellectual standards of Europeans. We have sent our best students to study painting in France, philosophy in England, medicine in Austria, chemistry in Germany, music in Italy, and mathematics all over Europe. Such action was objectively justified up to the time of the First World War for indeed the world centers of learning were in European cities. Since then, and especially since the Second World War, the export of students has been justifiable only on political or sentimental grounds—not on intellectual grounds, especially since the cream of European scholarship has gradually migrated to the United States. But despite the change, the export of students continues—a kind of intellectual deference that expresses our deep-felt hesitation about the role of world leadership, even on the intellectual level.

As a consequence of our isolationism and our reluctance to lead or to acknowledge leadership even in areas of action quite peripheral to politics, we have been quite unable to formulate a political position appropriate to our role. While many of our international difficulties of the past score of years have been an inescapable function of circumstances beyond our control, part of our difficulty does stem, it seems to me, from our reluctance to recognize the role we actually now play. Hence, one of the first steps toward the construction of an adequate posture in world affairs is the self-recognition of our leadership. The next step is to discover the content and possibilities for action in this role.

### THE CONDITIONS OF LEADERSHIP

Probably the essential fact about the role of leader in a world-dominating coalition is that the actor who once occupies this role cannot resign from it without unpleasant consequences. Many Americans, harking back to a joyful and carefree golden age of national adolescence in the nineteenth century, would perhaps prefer to resign from the role rather than accept its incessant crises, its worrisome calculations, and its perpetual sense of high stakes on a hair trigger. But such sentimental preference for resignation—which is probably the main emotion driving such diverse groups as peace-marchers and McCarthyites, both of whom prefer domestic conflict to combating the external enemy—is almost invariably expressed in ignorance or scorn of the actual consequences of resignation. In order to demonstrate, therefore, how fully committed we are to (some would say "trapped in") the role of leadership, let us consider some of the putative consequences of resigning from the role.

Most Americans fancy that their commanding position has been achieved without forceful mistreatment of other peoples. Compared with other empires of the past, compared even with so liberal and guilt-stricken an empire as the British, American leadership has been milder still. But mild as it has probably been, it does not follow that our dependents have felt kindly toward us. The discovery that Castro expresses the deep hostility of the Cuban— and indeed the Latin American—middle class toward the United States, has been a shock to many North Americans. But we have used force, mostly economic, but occasionally military, to control Latin America. It should be no surprise, therefore, that the persons so controlled have regarded the controller as a tyrant. To the degree that some dependent nations have regarded our leadership as tyrannical, we can expect retribution if we relinquish the leadership role. Initially such retribution might be no more than the seizure of our investment in Latin America and a restriction of trade. (This may or may not be negligible: About one-third of our income from foreign investments and about one-third of our imports originate there. About one-fifth of our exports are destined for there. If one assumes that foreign trade has a multiplier effect, then this loss alone might have serious repercussions on our economy.) But in the course of time surely the effects of the loss of leadership would be greater than this. It is not too fanciful to suggest that the ultimate effects would even include a reopening of the territorial settlement after the Mexican War.

Our leadership elsewhere in the world has involved less use of force than in Latin America and hence the loss of the role would doubtless involve less retribution. But political loss would surely involve also the loss of many commercial advantages and a drastic reduction in foreign trade. It would be an interesting enterprise in economic prediction to calculate the effect of these potential losses on our gross national product. Although I cannot make such a calculation in detail, a reasonable guess seems to me that we would return initially to about the level of our preleadership position, adjusted for the loss of income from Latin America. This would mean an average family income about like that of the early 1930s. Eventually, of course, one would expect the income to slide much lower.

Entirely apart from economic losses, which would undoubtedly be very great were the United States to abandon its leadership, other potential losses seem to me to be greater still. As a function of our leadership we have developed a really large intellectual class, perhaps the largest the world has seen. The mathematicians, physicists, biologists, psychologists, and social scientists necessary to maintain our military position vis-à-vis the Soviet Union are a remarkable collection just now beginning to establish an intellectual tradition which holds great promise of creativity. American intellectual life was once dominated by a kind of utilitarianism or pragmatism that produced much of immediate value but little new knowledge in the absolute sense. The postwar generation of intellectuals is, however, gradually overcoming the pragmatism of its ancestors and hence stands on the threshold of magnificent intellectual achievements. Should the United States abandon its role of leadership, most of this class would no longer be necessary and indeed too expensive to support. The loss of leadership would then mean also a heavy sacrifice of potential intellectual creativity.

It can be expected also that the loss of leadership—even though in our present imaginary examination it would occur by voluntary resignation—would, very probably, also involve a loss of self-confidence in all other areas of life, as well as the intellectual. American self-confidence, which often unfortunately appears to be brashness to other peoples, is, in my opinion, one of the most attractive of our national traits of character. Its replacement with either a chastened humility or a querulous debility would, I believe, be an incalculable personal loss.

Finally, resignation of leadership would involve the systematic betrayal of many peoples who have believed in us. A foretaste of what might happen can be observed in the results of the abortive Hungarian revolution of 1956. That revolution, which was partly predicated on an expectation of American aid, resulted in the slaughter of a large number of people, especially of idealistic and trusting adolescents. They did not understand that the foreign policy of "liberation" was announced by Secretary Dulles mostly for domestic consumption as an incident for the struggle for votes in the era of McCarthyism. Nor did they realize that Radio Free Europe, again inspired by McCarthyism, represented purely the private opinion of persons who would doubtless have liked to make American policy but in fact did not. The United States was culpable, of course, to the degree that it did not indicate that the slogan of "liberation" did not mean what it might appear to mean and that Radio Free Europe did not represent the United States. But to how much greater a degree would it be culpable if it abandoned the smaller nations of NATO, CENTO, and SEATO to Soviet imperialism after binding them into formal defensive alliances. The guilt of betrayal would be almost insurmountable.

In short, the loss of or resignation from leadership would involve, at the very least, unpleasant consequences for economic life, for intellectual creativity, for national character, and for the national conscience. The isolationists of the last generation may well have been wiser than they knew in seeking to avoid the leader's role. But once we are in it, we cannot abandon it without substantial sacrifice. This is indeed a larger sacrifice than most citizens are, I believe, willing to make. Hence, we probably

cannot voluntarily abandon our position of leadership. This is the first and essential fact about our present occupancy of the leader's role.

## THE PRESENT BALANCE OF COALITIONS IN WORLD POLITICS

In 1945 the United States stood at what has turned out to be the apex of its world leadership. Its previous enemies —Germany, Italy, and Japan—had been reduced to insignificance and the way was prepared to bring them back into the world society under the aegis of American leadership. Its most immediate allies—England, France, and China—were so crippled by the war that they had no choice but to look to the United States for leadership. Most of Latin America, while perhaps covertly hostile to the United States (and, in the case of the Peronist Argentine, openly hostile), was nonetheless willing to accept American leadership in affairs outside the hemisphere. The only conceivable threat to world leadership by the United States lay in the Soviet Union which, somewhat like the United States, had been physically strengthened by its very participation in the war. Yet the Soviet Union could not then defend itself against nuclear weapons so that it too had reason to accept American leadership.

Five years later, however, American hegemony was a thing entirely of the past. The United States was opposed by a fairly strong minority coalition which could check many American actions and might even reasonably aspire to defeat it. How did this change come about?

In 1945 and for a few years thereafter, the United States had an opportunity to consolidate its position as world leader and to impose, perhaps, an imperial order on the whole world. There were some among us, indeed, who urged that we do so (e.g., Henry Luce, whose notion of the American century apparently meant an imperial *pax Americana*). But with characteristic reluctance to lead, with characteristic hesitation to tell other people what to do, the United States chose not to maintain the commanding position. (Although it is doubtless immodest for an American to say so, there stands no finer tribute to the essential modesty of the American character than the fact that, during the brief period of our exclusive possession of atomic weapons, the nation as a whole rejected as preposterous the temptation to establish world empire. It does not, I think, detract seriously from the humaneness of this decision that we subsequently executed the traitors Rosenberg who were in some part responsible for removing this temptation from our consciousness.)

Having chosen not to maintain indefinitely the status quo of 1945, something which could have been done only by the imposition of world empire, the United States necessarily also condemned itself to a long (?) period of attrition in which, by the operation of the size principle, the scope of its leadership would be reduced. Since it refused the imperial technique (the only feasible technique) of preventing change and since it was in an almost world-dominating position, its decision to allow change meant that most change that might occur would be to its disadvantage.

This is, of course, what happened. First, without serious opposition the Soviet Union was allowed to solidify its influence in all those nations whose territory it physically occupied in 1945. Presumably the ejection of the Red Army from those places was a task beyond our energy. That is to say, having accepted the international world not as something to govern but as something in which to play an $n$-person (probably zero-sum) game, the United States decided that the allegiance of Poland, Hungary, Bulgaria, Romania, Czechoslovakia, Eastern Germany, and Yugoslavia was not worth expending energy for, inasmuch as it could control the main things it desired to control without them. Put another way, the U.S. decided to rehabilitate Western Europe, but not to go to the expense and trouble of rehabilitating Eastern Europe. Very shortly thereafter, however, the United States decided to expend considerable energy in preventing further Soviet expansion in Greece and Turkey, an action which doubtless informed Tito that when Yugoslavia defected from the Soviet bloc it could count on sympathy from the United States. In Eastern Europe, then, the United States, after initially losing those Soviet satellites which it had initially expected to return to their prewar status of independence, successfully contained its opponent and even weaned partially away one of its opponent's hitherto wholly dependent allies. Almost all American energy was spent on maintaining this portion of its coalition, however. Consequently, elsewhere in the world its opponent was able to make serious inroads on the American coalition.

In concentrating on the rehabilitation of its European allies, the United States in effect decided that it would not pay very much to keep China, which perhaps seemed relatively worthless in military potential and indeed would have been an extremely expensive ally to maintain. It seems fairly clear also that the Soviet Union devoted relatively little energy to winning China, but when, suddenly, the Chinese Communists were successful, naturally the Soviet Union expended considerable energy in helping them consolidate their power. The important point is that here the size principle operated in terms of American policymakers' judgments of where to spend their working capital on side-payments. Having chosen Europe and the Near East, the United States allowed its relatively unsupported ally in the Far East, beset with internal strife, to be taken over by the other side. At the time most Americans did not even regard China as a serious loss.

While the United States chose to expend considerable energy on maintaining its European alliance, it made no effort to maintain its allies' empires. Indeed, for ideological reasons, it usually approved the dismemberment of them, doubtless hoping that if it covertly aided the revolutionaries, they would as leaders of free governments ally themselves with the United States. Unfortunately for the United States, however, it has not always turned out that way. To ally with the United States has often meant that the ex-colonies ally with the ex-colonial powers and this has often been an unpalatable contract. Furthermore, each of the new participants in world affairs (whether ex-colonies or hitherto neglected states) has been the object of courtship by the opposing coalition. In selected instances it has bid the price of alliance up to the point that the United States has believed it not worthwhile, either in terms of the price itself or in terms of internal strains within the coalition led by the United States. Thus, in the case of Egypt, the price has become much military equipment, much purchasing of cotton, and perhaps the financing of the Aswan Dam. But military subsidies are not only costly; they are also deeply offensive to Israel, one of our few firm allies in the Near East. As for cotton, we already have too much of it. And the Aswan Dam is not only extremely expensive and a doubtful financial risk, but also is opposed by the Sudan, which might well turn out to be as valuable an ally as Egypt. And so, in accordance with the size principle, we have not paid for an ally which is not, at the moment at least, necessary for winning interim decisions. Similar considerations have led us to bid only half-heartedly for Afghanistan, which the Soviet Union has successfully integrated into its own economy. Not only is Afghanistan hard to defend, directly exposed as it is to the Soviet Union, but also to arm it is offensive to our firm ally, Pakistan. Furthermore, Afghanistan's oil, which presently the West does not need, is with little expense exported to the Soviet Union, while to export it to the West would require a very large capital investment. And so we have in effect allowed the Soviet Union to integrate the Afghan economy with its own.

In other areas, where substantial economic or military penetration has not been feasible for either side, the curious phenomenon of neutralism has appeared. By judicious management of the neutralist position, numerous Asian and African governments have been able to wring some side-payments from each coalition for temporary support (as on a vote in the United Nations) without firmly committing themselves to either side. In a sense, both Africa south of the Sahara and many states of north Africa and the Near East have managed to avoid both coalitions, thus reducing the significance of each, and to deploy their mobile diplomacy to their own greatest advantage.

Thus, in accordance with the size principle, the coalition led by the United States has been whittled down in size fairly continuously since the end of the Second World War. Where once it controlled most of the world, it now has certain control only of Western Europe, the Americas, some of the maritime portions of Eastern Asia and scattered portions of the Near East. Its opponent controls Eastern Europe and two-thirds of Asia. The remainder of the world is in balance between them, although it appears that the United States has at the moment closer ties with India and other Southeast Asian neutrals (except Indonesia) and with most of the new states of Africa than does the Soviet Union.

A question of great import for the future of the West is whether or not this gradual whittling down of Western strength in accordance with the size principle is a now completed process. I do not believe that it is, for it seems to me that the West is still sufficiently confident of its winning strength to allow further losses of allies. The occurrences in Cuba are instructive in this respect. While the Cuban revolution was probably home-grown, still the revolutionaries have turned to the Soviet Union for protection. If the Soviet Union has not yet gained a firm ally, the United States has lost one. Will the United States attempt to regain it? To regain probably means fostering and financing another revolution, as we seem to have done on a much smaller scale in Guatemala. Whether or not we will pay such a relatively high price remains to be seen. If we do not, then we can, I assume, expect further such defections, even in the Americas. And outside the Americas further defections seem more likely still, especially if we should fail to maintain the status quo in Laos. The rest of the Indo-Chinese peninsula as well as Thailand and Burma seem likely candidates for defection. And if they should go, Indonesia, already aggressively neutral, may well prefer to plump openly for the other side. So it seems likely that the Soviet Union will continue to gain allies, both neutrals and former allies of the West, until in the world's opinion the two great coalitions are roughly equal in size.

In the journalism of the West the dominant interpretation of the events in the world society during the last fifteen years is that of an aggressive imperial power (i.e. the Soviet Union) constantly upsetting the status quo. In this theory, the main propulsion of change is the evil motive of the Communist leaders. In the interpretation offered here, on the other hand, a rational (rather than evil) motive is ascribed to the leaders of both sides. The changes in the relative strength of coalitions is viewed as a normal political process. In both theories, the Soviet

Union is interpreted as aggressive while the Western bloc is seen as a defender of the status quo. The difference between the theories is that, from the journalistic theory, one might infer that, were Communists to be replaced by liberals or democrats or aristocrats or kings, the aggression would cease. In the interpretation offered here, however, the aggression is a function of the total situation and would not be affected by a change of Eastern rulers except perhaps that kings might be less efficient aggressors than Communists.

## POLITICS IN AN AGE OF MANEUVER

The fifteen years since the Second World War may well be called the Age of Equalization. This is the period in which, in accordance with the size principle, the Western coalition has diminished and the Communist one expanded. How long this age may be expected to continue is not entirely clear. The United States has lost much power relative to the Soviet Union which suggests that the age may be nearly over; but since the two coalitions do not yet seem to be roughly equal, one can expect the equalization process to continue for an indefinite time.

It is possible, however, to suggest a standard by which one may know when the Age of Equalization has come to an end. The standard is an inference from the United States policy of "containment." The basic form of the political problem for the United States in the Age of Equalization has been to determine what final coalition to seek to hold. While few, if any, policymakers in the United States have had a broad enough view of the political process to realize that this was what they were doing, still in building the NATO, CENTO, and SEATO alliances, they were in effect deciding where to draw the line of their future coalition, what to attempt to retain, and what to abandon. In the period in which both the policy of containment (which, though the policymakers ordinarily did not realize it, contained both the United States and the Soviet Union) and the actual alliances were constructed, the main kind of political event was border warfare, or what the Communists euphemistically call "wars of national liberation." Such warfare was in effect a probe by the Communist alliance to find weak spots in the Western coalition (i.e., allies the West would not pay or fight to hold on to). The Korean action was the main instance of such border warfare, but the guerrilla wars in Vietnam, Laos, Burma, Iran, and Greece, as well as the political strikes in Italy and France were also instances of the same kind of border probing. The number of places where such probing may now continue is limited. A probe is worthwhile only if it is reasonably close to the borders of the Soviet bloc so that the guerrillas et al., can be adequately supplied. Since the West has now made firm alliances and commitments over most of the border territories, the occasion for border warfare has substantially disappeared. Of course, the probing is still going on in various parts of the Indo-Chinese peninsula and the position of India, especially Kashmir, is perhaps vague enough to occasion some probing. Further, the exact position of Afghanistan and Finland and even Sweden is somewhat ambiguous, although the United States acts as if it expects the first two to be absorbed ultimately into a Soviet alliance. Still, unless the Communists reopen border warfare in places in which it has been effectively settled, there are not very many places left for probing. When the few remaining ambiguities of border territory have been clarified, the Age of Equalization will be over.

At that point the character of world politics will change rather abruptly. We will pass from the Age of Equalization to the Age of Maneuver. And there will then be an entirely different tone to world politics.

The main features of the Age of Maneuver will, I submit, be the following:

1. The price asked by neutrals or marginal members for their allegiance to one side or the other will rise steadily.
2. The tone of politics will become more intense in the sense that each decision will seem to involve the entire future of each coalition.
3. As a result of the previous effect, the danger of general warfare will increase.
4. Finally, as a result of all three previous effects, the two main opposing powers will exhaust their resources in maintaining their alliances and other nations will come to the fore as world leaders.

Let us examine each of these effects in some detail.

The price asked by neutrals can hardly fail to rise as the border territories are worked into a tight set of alliances. That is, a reduction in the supply of neutrals will raise their individual prices, probably to the point that, for each side, the total bill for allegiance will be considerably greater than it is now. Up to the present time this rise in the price of side-payments has been obscured by the systematic dismemberment of the colonial holdings of the United States, Italy, Britain, France, Netherlands, and Belgium. Only the Portuguese empire remains for dismemberment, something which (judging from the events in Goa and the Congo) can be expected to occur fairly soon. In effect, there has been a constant increase in the supply of neutrals over the last fifteen years. But now the sources of neutrals in the system is about exhausted. From now on the supply may be expected to contract gradually as some neutrals are firmly drawn into one orbit or the other. Entirely apart from this kind of restriction on supply is another and essentially independent restriction, namely, the prospective tendency of ex-colonial nations to federate with each other. The boundaries of most of the new nations of Africa, the Near East, and Southeast Asia were drawn originally by the colonial powers for administrative or military convenience. No effort was made to ensure the viability of any particular colony inasmuch as viability was felt to be a feature not of the parts but of the colonial system as a whole. As a result, when, as often happened, the empires were dismembered in accord with the colonial boundaries, many new states were not large enough to develop either military or economic strength. Undoubtedly this result was intended by the colonial powers, for it permits a kind of sub rosa economic imperialism to flourish long after the political imperialism ostensibly ends. But in the long run the economic disadvantages for the too-small states of Africa and the Near East and Southeast Asia will probably be unsupportable. If so, then consolidation will occur on the pattern of the Canadian absorption of Newfoundland. In this way also, then, the supply of neutrals will probably contract.

On the other hand, the supply of neutrals may well be increased by occasional flurries of Titoism. The process can be visualized thus: Dependent members of each alliance, resentful of the fact that their foreign policies are actually made in either Washington or Moscow, and resentful also of the fact that the pattern of their domestic lives is deeply influenced by the foreign-made foreign policy, may declare themselves neutral. Often such declarations will fail (as in Hungary or Guatemala, for example); but often they will succeed (as in Yugoslavia or, provisionally at least, Cuba). As the possession of the technology of nuclear warfare spreads, such defections may well become more frequent. Thus, in the last few years, France, gaining confidence with each Saharan explosion and resenting more and more rabidly the part played by the United States in the dismemberment of the French empire, has become a less and less reliable member of NATO and the Western alliance generally. It is not too fanciful to suggest that France may neutralize itself, not by means of a Communist revolt—the French Communist party seems to be decreasingly effective—but rather by an independent rapprochement with the Soviet Union, a rapprochement reminiscent of numerous Franco-Russian treaties of friendship over the past several hundred years.

Titoist defections of this sort can, however, hardly be expected to occur frequently or in large numbers. Hence, the supply of neutrals may be expected to decline.

Along with the prospective decline in the supply of neutrals, an effect which alone will raise their price, an entirely independent force will probably operate on the demand for allies in such fashion as to raise the price from the demand side. If, as I shall try to show in subsequent paragraphs, the tone of world politics becomes more intense in the Age of Maneuver than it has been in the Age of Equalization, then allies will be more desperately needed than they are now. If the fate of world leaders is believed to hang on every decision, however minor, then allies must be acquired at any price in order to assure victory.

Anticipating, then, a shorter supply of prospective new allies and a greater demand for those available, one can also anticipate that the price will go up. In an auction in which the ultimate outcome determines life or death, it is unreasonable to suppose that there will be table stakes. Hence one can further anticipate that the total bill for allies will also increase for both sides. Not only will they have to continue to maintain the allegiance of already attracted ex-neutrals, but also they will have to pay inflated prices for new ones. In the United States there has been much resentment (which seems to me to have grown in recent years) of the large expenditure on allies in the Age of Equalization. If, as I suggest, the expenditures already made will appear minute in comparison with those needed in the Age of Maneuver, one of the great political problems of the Western alliance will be the persuasion of its own citizens to pay the necessary costs of leadership. Indeed, it may well be that a failure of the United States and Western Europe to solve that elementary problem within a democratic framework will result in either the abandonment of democracy or a total defeat for the West.

The second previously listed feature of the Age of Maneuver is a putative intensification of the tone of politics. It may seem to some who have lived through the recurrent crises of the Cold War in the Age of Equalization that the sense of crisis cannot be deepened. Yet, I suggest, exactly such deepening will occur. In the similar phases of equalization and maneuver in American politics of the last century and three-quarters the atmosphere of politics has been much more heated in ages of maneuver than in ages of equalization. The ages of maneuver have been those in which the two parties are approximately equal in voting strength, namely, the late 1790s, the 1840s, the late 1870s and the 1880s, the late 1930s and early 1940s and, possibly, the period we are entering now. Assuming that the participation of a large proportion of eligible voters is evidence of an intensity of emotion in politics, then the ages of maneuver are also the ages of greatest intensity of emotion. The proportion of eligible voters participating was at a high point for a generation on either side in the Presidential elections of 1840, 1888, and 1940. While we have no adequate record of voting in the 1790s, it seems likely from scattered evidence that the turnout in the election of 1800 was exceptionally high for its era. Even without the evidence from the amount of voting, however, there is much evidence that political life in the ages of maneuver was more vituperative than at other times. And excessive vituperation seems to me evidence of intensity of emotion. In the age of Jefferson the pattern of extreme vituperation was established by such journalists as Freneau, Bache, and Cobbett. It was revived in Jackson's day by Isaac Hill, Duff Green, and Nicholas Biddle. In the 1870s and 1880s one kind of vituperation was so common it acquired a special name, "waving the bloody shirt." And those who remember the late 1930s know well the vituperative emotions aroused by Franklin Roosevelt.

And so, arguing from the analogy of the ages of maneuver in American politics, I suggest that the coming age of maneuver in world politics will generate its own new levels of intensity of emotion. Nor, on reflection, is this surprising. If each side has a chance to win on even the interim decisions, then the energy that each side puts into trying to win will probably be much greater than the energy either has put into decisions likely to be won by the much weightier side. And the mutual expenditure of energy will undoubtedly generate intense emotion.

The third feature of the Age of Maneuver is that, owing to the increase of tension, the danger of general war becomes much greater. As emotions become more intense on each decision, as, increasingly, both sides believe that every decision, however trivial objectively, determines the pattern of the future, then the temptation to deploy all resources on a particular decision is seductive indeed. In previous ages, when the technology of warfare was simpler, governments could succumb to this temptation without serious consequences to the species. The total wars both of antiquity and modern times have been total only in the sense of involving all governments. But the total war of the forthcoming age of maneuver will involve, if it occurs, every complex living thing. Out of fear of this prospect reasonable men on both sides have sought for some way to control atomic weapons. But, unfortunately, safety for the species cannot be obtained by as simple an expedient as arms control. The dilemma is this: If men know about nuclear weapons and if they believe that their entire future is at stake, then they may use them regardless of all the elaborate plans for nuclear disarmament and the like. Hence, no matter how much reasonable men may wish to avoid the obliteration of mammals, they still may do so. If a government comes to believe that it may use nuclear weapons without totally destructive retaliation, then in the prospective tension of the Age of Maneuver, when emotions will probably run so much higher than they do now, the temptation to use these weapons may be irresistible. If the belief is correct that complete retaliation is impossible, then the species may survive; but if the belief is false (as it may well be) then the species will be obliterated—and probably not in as pleasantly romantic a fashion as depicted by Mr. Nevil Shute.

This is the main horror of the forthcoming Age of Maneuver. But there is another horror, not nearly so terrifying to all mankind, but unpleasant enough for people in the United States and the Soviet Union. This lesser horror is the prospect of systematic overpayment of allies or, alternatively, mutual self-destruction so that at the end of the age both nations are thoroughly enfeebled. If and when this comes about—and it is the fourth listed feature of politics in the Age of Maneuver—the United States and the Soviet Union will have been reduced to dismembered followers and other more vigorous peoples will take up the leadership of the world.

This lesser horror for the citizens of the two world-dominating nations is almost certain to come about. Assuming that the tone of world politics becomes increasingly intense and that the price of the allegiance of neutrals becomes greatly inflated, then both leading nations will feel compelled to pay the anticipated high prices for allies. Entirely apart from side-payments to allies, both the major powers will be required to continue to expend vast sums on armaments. Even if they can come to an agreement to restrict the production of nuclear weapons and even if they can agree on a practical and efficient system of inspection to enforce the agreement, they will still need to spend large amounts of money on both the technology of space travel and conventional military devices. Bases on natural or artificial satellites will unquestionably be of great military significance throughout the Age of Maneuver. It does not seem fanciful to suppose, should the emotions of this age concentrate competition on a race for space, that both nations might spend a quarter of their national income in the competition. And all this without reference to nuclear weapons. On a more mundane level, military equipment of the conventional sort will continue to be necessary in large quantities in order to fight such occasional limited wars as may arise and in order to keep one's allies properly awed. A curious phenomenon: One of the chief kinds of side-payments presently desired by neutrals and marginal allies is a supply of conventional arms. In most instances these are desired in order to awe or even to fight another neutral. But as the supply of them increases, each of the two main powers must increase its own supply simply in order to police those whom it has armed. And, of course, rapid technological change and obsolescence of conventional weapons is a necessary part of offering acceptable side-payments. So the supply of conventional weapons alone can be expected to be inordinately expensive.

Even if no wars occur, therefore, allies and armaments

will undoubtedly be a heavy drain on the resources of both leading powers. Their dependents, freed to some degree from these costs, may then be expected to grow rich and powerful at the expense of their leaders. If wars occur, either limited or total, it is, of course, the two leading powers that must bear the greater portion of the expense both in money and men. The leaders have most at stake and hence will be expected to stand most of the cost. And this will, in the long run, also favor the marginal allies at the expense of the leaders.

In the beginning of this chapter the fall of empires was attributed both to the size principle and to systematic overestimation by leaders of the objective value of decisions. In the Age of Equalization, it is the size principle that contributes most to the decline, but in the Age of Maneuver it will doubtless be the overpayment of followers and the excessive expenditure of energy on the maintenance of leadership. The end-product of both processes in both ages is, of course, the decline of the leaders. And that is what the United States and the Soviet Union have to look forward to toward the end of the Age of Maneuver.

## STRATEGY IN THE AGE OF MANEUVER

In the Age of Maneuver, for both the United States and the Soviet Union, the main strategic goal—albeit perhaps a goal unrecognized by one or both governments—is the prolongation of the age for the greatest possible duration. Inasmuch as the end of this age is likely also to be the end of the leadership of both powers, it is in the objective interests of both to forestall the end.

For the achievement of this goal, there are several obvious strategic policies.

First and foremost, each ought to take every possible

precaution to avoid nuclear war or even total war without nuclear weapons. If either such war occurs, neither of the leading powers can possibly be the winner, even though the wars are zero-sum. The winner will of course win the power that the loser loses. But soon after the war is over it will appear that marginal members of both sides are stronger than the original leaders. I do not know how such wars are to be avoided, except by the conscious intention of both powers. Indeed, both must recognize that they are playing not only a zero-sum game against each other but also are playing a sub rosa zero-sum game in which they are allies against the rest of the world. The main challenge to the diplomacy of both powers is to keep the other forever cognizant of the sub rosa game even when the tensions of the Age of Maneuver are at their most intense. Like parliamentary leaders who at heart have greater sympathy with the leaders of the parliamentary opposition than they have with their own back benchers, these two powers can only at their deepest peril forget that leadership itself is as much a value as winning.

In order to remember this point, both governments need institutional reminders. This is the chief role that the United Nations can play. Since the beginning of the Korean Conflict the U.N. General Assembly has been something of a covert American agent. But with the projection into it of African neutrals, it seems likely that the U.N. as a whole will revert to its intended function as a world parliament. As such it may be able to transmute military hostilities into verbal ones. If it is able to do so, then it may be a genuine institutional damper on the war-inducing tensions of the Age of Maneuver. Every institutional change that strengthens the U.N.—e.g., giving it responsibilities for, initially, controlling nuclear testing; giving it, subsequently, responsibility for arms control; giving it, ultimately, some of the powers of a genuine world government—will increase its effectiveness as a damper. Hence, it is in the best interests of both the United States and the Soviet Union now to strengthen the U.N. in preparation for the Age of Maneuver. Of course, in many daily ways, a strengthened U.N. appears to be a threat to both powers, especially when it is strengthened somewhat at the expense of one of them, as occurred in 1950 and as will occur when Red China gets its seat on the Security Council. But daily threats are, I think, less significant than the ultimate potentiality of this institution to dampen the tensions that may induce military action. Hence, it seems to me strategically correct, from the point of view of prolonging the Age of Maneuver, to strengthen the U.N. as much as possible.

A second obvious and basic strategy for the Age of Maneuver is to control in some way the prices paid for allies. If the free market price is allowed to prevail, it will, as I have earlier suggested, be extraordinarily high. There is no reason, however, why clever men cannot rig these prices just as prices of all other commodities have in one way or another been controlled to advantage. The Soviet Union has made most of its conquests in the Age of Equalization at a remarkably low price, that is, by infusing home-grown guerrillas with the Communist ideology and perhaps by supplying a rather small quantity of equipment for guerrilla warfare. It has been able to do this in so-called underdeveloped societies because the statist technique of modernization and industrialization, invented by Lenin and demonstrated to be practicable for a rural society by Stalin, has proved extraordinarily attractive to the intelligentsia of underdeveloped societies. By contrast, the liberal ideology of the West, which depends for its economic effectiveness on the existence of a large class of literate and cosmopolitan entrepreneurs, has seemed economically irrelevant in places where most of the people are illiterate peasants or tribesmen. On the other hand, the United States has retained some of its most secure allies at little cost simply because it was the main exponent of the liberal ideology of freedom. Freedom may be a somewhat defective ideal, for it is difficult to imagine the commitment the human psyche craves directed at so instrumental and morally empty a goal as freedom. Yet for those who do not have a bit of it, freedom can become an absolute. Those who remember a past tyranny have rejoicingly identified with the American standard of freedom, simply because it is freedom and regardless of its economic significance. Thus in two contrasting ways during the Age of Equalization the two main antagonists have bought allies with ideology, which costs very little. Doubtless they will continue to be able to do so.

But as the possibilities of the neutralist role are more thoroughly grasped and exploited, it may well happen that ideology is not enough to hold even thoroughly convinced allies. In the case of Yugoslavia, for example, neither devotion to Marxism nor gratitude for Soviet assistance were sufficient to maintain the alliance in the face of Stalinist tyranny. It seems likely that such Titoist behavior will be more common in the future than in the past and will involve defections from both sides. And it is at this point that the problem of price control becomes most pressing.

For the United States, presumably the leader of the leading coalition and presumably desirous of maintaining its lead, this poses an extraordinarily important strategic problem. Will it meet the price that neutrals and marginal and recalcitrant members of its coalition demand? If it meets every price asked, it may well squander its resources. So the strategic problem will necessarily be the establishment of a policy for dealing with high prices. Control of prices is, it seems to me, possible on the basis of a fine sense of necessity. In a world in which ultimate victory or defeat is controlled by the possession of nuclear warheads in intercontinental missiles, the allegiance of recalcitrant allies is neither desirable nor negotiable. Those allies attracted by our ideology—which, I believe, is more attractive than the Communist one to nations on what Rostow has called the "take off" level of development—and those attracted by a simple fear of Soviet imperialism should of course be welcomed. But those who must be coerced or heavily bribed need not be paid for at all, especially if they find the Soviet ideology deeply unpalatable (e.g., Spain). All this calls for very delicate calculations. The United States must pay heavily, but not too heavily.

In making these calculations, the most important consideration, it seems to me, is that the United States not be mesmerized by the need to maintain a weightier alliance than the Soviet Union. Let us suppose—what is not essentially unreasonable—that to win a nuclear or non-nuclear total war a leader must have a coalition comprising two-thirds the weight of the world. If so, the consistent maintenance of an alliance of considerably over half but somewhat less than two-thirds the weight of the world is overly expensive. Yet this is precisely what the United States is now doing. Without endangering its position it could allow the Soviet alliance to grow to a weight greater than half. Indeed, such action, if gradually and consciously but secretly taken, would tend to prolong the Age of Maneuver and at the same time to increase the costs of leadership for the Soviet Union while reducing them for the United States. This is, however, a difficult policy to follow and one requiring both delicacy and political maturity on the part of both government and citizenry. A democracy bedeviled by a McCarthyite demagoguery, for example, would probably be entirely unable to follow such a policy and would, therefore, be expected to exhaust itself in overpayments quite quickly. But if the American democracy can learn to transcend demagoguery of this and other sorts, it may actually be able to follow such a policy for a long period of years.

If it can establish a policy involving relatively little overpayment and if it can avoid great wars, then the Age of Maneuver may be prolonged indefinitely.

## CONCLUSION

This book started out as an essay on political science, as an effort to develop a theory of coalitions. And in the beginning of this chapter, the three main theoretical conclusions were summarily stated. But it turned out to be impossible to stop there. Politics is, as Aristotle long ago argued, a practical science in the sense that people study it not only to discover reality but also to manipulate it. Since this abstract political theory has practical implications, I have, in Aristotelian fashion, tried to spell them out in this final chapter for one area of action. But though these implications are practical, they are also propositions deduced from the theory and hence are subject to at least pragmatic verification. If politicians act upon them and the action is successful, as I am personally convinced would be the case, then in a pragmatic fashion the theory would be justified. This is part of the reason I have spelled out the implications here. Another part of the reason is, of course, that I, as a (possibly overoptimistic) citizen in the leader of a world-dominating coalition, would like to see both the leadership and the coalition survive in an Age of Maneuver lasting at least as long as the lifetime of my children.

# APPENDIXES

# APPENDIX I

# Derivation of the Size Principle

The concern of this Appendix is to limit in some way the range of possible outcomes for $n$-person, zero-sum games. The intent is, of course, to derive by deductive methods a nonobvious rule for rational behavior in the model so that one can in turn investigate empirically whether or not such behavior actually occurs. For this purpose we start with the notion of the characteristic function, explaining it and then placing some reasonable limits on it.

Since our concern is with $n$-person games, the powerful mathematics of two-person, zero-sum theory will not be discussed except to point out that, by means of Von Neumann's minimax theorem, it is possible to specify a value for every two-person, zero-sum game. That is, for every such game, $\Gamma$, there is a value, $v$, such that player 1 possesses a strategy that guarantees him a payoff of at least $v$ regardless of the second player's action and such that player 2 possesses a strategy that holds the first player to a payoff of no more than $v$ regardless of what player 1 does. This equilibrium point, $v$, is extraordinarily useful for it permits players to calculate payoffs in advance and, furthermore, provides a standard of "good" or "rational" play.

While it would be advantageous to transfer this notion of value directly to the $n$-person case, it does not immediately appear to be feasible, inasmuch as $n$-person games are concerned with coalitions rather than strategies. The absolute end product of coalition-formation is, however, a two-person game. That is, when a coalition is the size at which it can render a decision, there necessarily exists one winning coalition. The remaining members of the decision-making set, whether actually joined in alliance or not, may conventionally be regarded as members of a single losing coalition. Then follows a trivial two-person game in which coalitions are substituted for persons and in which there is only one move, the rendering of a decision by the winning side. On the basis of this interpretation, it is possible to specify a value for $n$-person games that is somewhat similar to value in two-person games. The players of $\Gamma$, who form the set $I: \{1, 2, \ldots, n\}$ are arranged in two complementary subsets, $S$ and $-S$, such that no player is in both $S$ and $-S$. Since $S \cap -S = 0$ (read: "the intersection of $S$ and $-S$ equals zero") and since $S \cup -S = I$ (read: "the union of $S$ and $-S$ equals $I$"), $\Gamma$ is a two-person game with players $S$ and $-S$.[1] Hence, there is a $v(S)$, which is the payoff $S$ can get regardless of what $-S$ does and which is what $-S$ can hold $S$ down to.

Assuming that all subsets of $I$ are conceivable coalitions in $\Gamma$, there are $2^n$ possible coalitions, for each of which $v(S)$ exists. Thus, $v$ is a real-valued set function, i.e., it is a real number that can be calculated for all members of the set $\bar{I}$, where $\bar{I}$ is the set of all $2^n$ subsets of $I$.[2] This function $v$, which Von Neumann and Morgenstern called the *characteristic function* of the zero-sum game $\Gamma$, has the following properties:

1. $v(\phi) = 0$, where $\phi$ is the empty set
2. $v(S) = -v(-S)$, for all $S$ in $\bar{I}$
3. $v(I) = 0$
4. $v(S \cup T) \geqq v(S) + v(T)$, where $S \cap T = \phi$
5. $v(S_1 \cup S_2 \cup \ldots \cup S_p) \geqq v(S_1) + v(S_2) + \ldots$

1. The *intersection* of two sets is the set of elements each of which belongs simultaneously to both sets and the *union* of two sets is the set of all elements each of which belongs to at least one of the two sets.
2. A basic theorem of the theory of sets is: For every set of $n$ members, there are exactly $2^n$ subsets, including the set itself and the empty set.

$+ v(S_p)$, where $S_1, S_2, \ldots , S_p$ are pairwise disjunct subsets of $I$.[3]

These properties may be regarded as matters of definition or as theorems to be deduced from the two-person case. Rigorous proofs are offered in McKinsey, *Introduction to the Theory of Games,* pp. 307 ff. Here, however, they will simply be interpreted verbally.

1. The empty set has a value of zero. Without members, presumably it cannot win or lose anything.

2. The second property is the zero-sum feature.

3. The third property is a direct consequence of the first two, inasmuch as $I$ is the complement of $\phi$. If property 2 is abandoned, property 3 must be also. Note that this property concerns only the whole coalition and says nothing about the division of payoffs inside the coalition.

4. The fourth property is superadditivity. This is, as Luce and Raiffa remark, the crucial assertion "which, on reflection, is extremely plausible." [4] Consider the play of $\Gamma$, when $I$ is partitioned into three subsets: $S$, $T$, and $-(S \cup T)$.[5] Thus $\Gamma$ has been transformed from an $n$-person to three-person game. But coalition-formation is not likely to cease at this point for it is still possible to form at least three more larger coalitions, that is $(S \cup T)$, $(S \cup -(S \cup T))$, and $(T \cup -(S \cup T))$. Suppose in fact that $S$ and $T$ combine so that the game is concluded as if it were a trivial two-person game with players $(S \cup T)$ and $-(S \cup T)$. One could hardly expect these successive transformations of coalitions unless $v(S \cup T)$ at least equals the sum of $v(S)$ and $v(T)$, since presumably rational players would not expend energy in realigning coalitions in order to obtain a loss in payoff. Hence it is never true that $v(S \cup T) < v(S) + v(T)$.

3. Two sets are said to be *disjunct* when they have no members in common, i.e., when their intersection is empty: $S \cap T = \phi$. A set, $\omega$, of other sets is said to be *pairwise disjunct* when all pairs of sets in $\omega$ are disjunct.

4. Luce and Raiffa, *Games and Decisions,* p. 191.

5. A set, $I$, is said to be *partitioned* into a set of subsets, $\omega$, when (1) all members of $I$ are members of some set in $\omega$ and (2) $\omega$ is a set of pairwise disjunct subsets of $I$.

Of course, $S$ and $T$ need not form $(S \cup T)$, but it cannot be supposed that any action at all will occur unless the foregoing proviso holds. Suppose, however, it were always true that $v(S \cup T) = v(S) + v(T)$. Again it would be difficult to imagine the occurrence of coalition-formation inasmuch as rational players would not expend energy to change position if the most they could expect would be the same payoff. Hence it must in some cases be true that $v(S \cup T) > v(S) + v(T)$. Combining, one gets the property of superadditivity, $v(S \cup T) \geqq v(S) + v(T)$, which is the fourth property.

It is clear that for a game in which $v(S \cup T) = v(S) + v(T)$ there is no point to forming coalitions. Indeed, if $\Gamma$ is larger than two-person there is not much of anything for players to do. Such games as this Von Neumann and Morgenstern labeled *inessential,* while all games for which $v(S \cup T) \geqq v(S) + v(T)$ holds they called *essential.*

5. The last property follows from repeated applications of the fourth.

Since an infinity of infinities of characteristic functions exist, the notion as it has so far been developed is not particularly useful for discussing games. Von Neumann and Morgenstern recognized this problem and partially solved it by their definition of strategic equivalence and normalization, which are here explained following Luce and Raiffa. There are many games that go under the name of bridge. While all are played in substantially the same way, they differ in the unit of payoff. It makes a difference in payoff—and in formal description—if one plays for dollars or rupees (about $\frac{1}{5}$ of a dollar). But in the actual play of these several games of bridge, one is—theoretically at least—influenced by exactly the same kinds of strategic considerations, regardless of the kind of money one uses. Transferring this observation from bridge to games generally, there may be two games, $\Gamma$ and $\Gamma'$, with characteristic functions $v$ and $v'$ which are exactly alike except that $v'(S) = cv(S)$, where $c$ is a positive constant (e.g., $\frac{1}{5}$, the ratio of dollars to rupees). Similarly, there may be two games in which the possibilities and inducements to form coalitions are identical except that the payoff to the same coalitions and persons varies by a fixed amount, as, for example, when the house exacts a payment from each player for the privilege of sitting in on a poker game. Designating these fixed amounts as $a_i$, where $a$ is the amount for player $i$, there can be two games with characteristic functions $v$ and $v'$ such that

$$v'(S) = v(S) + \sum_{i \text{ in } S} a_i.$$

Combining these multiplicative and additive constants, two games defined over the same set of players and having characteristic functions $v$ and $v'$ are *strategically equivalent* if there exist constants $a_1, a_2, \ldots , a_n$ and a positive constant $c$ such that, for every $S$ in $\bar{I}$

$$v'(S) = cv(S) + \sum_{i \text{ in } S} a_i.$$

The advantage of the notion of strategic equivalence is that it permits the division of games into equivalence classes from each of which one can pick out a particularly simple member for discussion. Von Neumann and Morgenstern have shown that it is possible to pick out of each equivalence class (except the class of inessential games [6]) one, and only one, zero-sum game in which each player acting by himself receives $-1$. That is, they showed that one and only one characteristic function in each class satisfied these conditions: [7]

(a)  $v(\{i\}) = -1$
(b)  $v(I) = 0.$

This characteristic function they called the "reduced form" of all characteristic functions in an equivalence class, although subsequent writers have preferred to call it the "$-1, 0$ normalization" of characteristic functions. Regardless of the name, however, it is an effective device to simplify discussion by stating characteristic functions in a readily comparable and standardized form.

6. All inessential games are strategically equivalent inasmuch as it is absolutely pointless to form coalitions in any of them.

7. The notation "$v (\{i\})$" signifies the value of a single player when he is considered as a single-member coalition.

By means of the notion of a normalized characteristic function which summarizes the gross strategic possibilities of alliances in *n*-person games, Von Neumann and Morgenstern created a tool by which the basic political activity of coalition-making could be discussed mathematically. And thus, as I have already indicated, they perhaps made possible a genuine science of politics. Some writers have, however, been less than impressed with the theory. McKinsey, for instance, has shown by means of a particularly devastating example that characteristic functions misrepresent two-person, non-zero-sum games. (His example involves a non-zero-sum, two-person game in which the characteristic function indicates that players are in identical positions, when in the extended form of the game it is perfectly clear that one has a great advantage over the other.) [8] However, as long as the use of characteristic functions is restricted to zero-sum games (as it will be here) and perhaps to non-zero-sum games of more than two players, this criticism is irrelevant. A more direct and significant criticism is one aimed at the zero-sum condition itself by Luce and Raiffa. They suggest that the assumption of $S$ and $-S$ prejudges "the theory by demanding that all conflicts of interest always reduce to two opposing coalitions." [9] While it is true that Von Neumann and Morgenstern do develop the notion of characteristic functions by use of $S$ and $-S$, it is not necessary to do so. As I have already shown, $-S$ may be a conventional fiction for all those opposed to $S$, whether these opponents be united in $-S$ or not. Aside from this minor technicality, however, it should again be pointed out in defense of the zero-sum condition that, whenever events like elections or wars are presented to the common imagination, they are interpreted as two-sided. This two-sidedness or sense of indivisible victory is, of course, what $S$ and $-S$ represent. While it is improper to use characteristic functions to describe what are clearly non-zero-sum situations, it seems to me legitimate to use them to describe those situations involving indivisible victory which make up so large a part of politics. At least, I shall so use it here leaving it to the reader to decide whether or not the use is legitimate.

8. McKinsey, *Introduction to the Theory of Games*, pp. 351–53.
9. Luce and Raiffa, p. 191.

## THE RANGE OF CHARACTERISTIC FUNCTIONS

Once the notion of characteristic functions is accepted, at least provisionally, a question of immediate interest concerns the range of possible values for $v(S)$ in normalized form. Von Neumann and Morgenstern discuss this question by means of the graph in Figure 6. It describes a zero-sum game with $n$ players. Along the abscissa is shown the number of members,

FIGURE 6

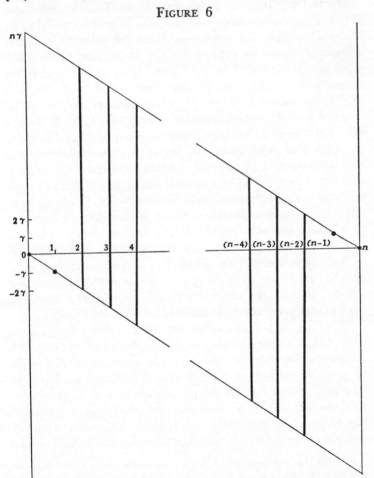

Source: Von Neumann and Morgenstern, *The Theory of Games*, p. 252.

$p$, in the set, $S$, where $0 \leqq p \leqq n$. Since normalized characteristic functions require that all one-person coalitions have the same value, this value can be set as $-\gamma$ so that $v(\{1\}) = v(\{2\}) = \ldots = v(\{n\}) = -\gamma$. The range of $S$ can then be measured on the ordinate in multiples of $\gamma$. The range of possible values for $v(S)$ is then shown by the boldface dots and lines: dots at $(0,0)$, $(0,n)$, $(1,-\gamma)$, and $((n-1), \gamma)$; and lines parallel to the ordinate through $(2,0)$, $(3,0)$, $\ldots$ , $((n-2),0)$.

The full explanation of Figure 6 follows: Since by definition of characteristic functions $v(\phi) = v(I) = 0$, the dots at $(0,0)$ and $(0,n)$ follow from the definition. Since the value of a single-member coalition is defined for the normalized form thus: $v(\{i\}) = -\gamma$, the dot at $(1,-\gamma)$ follows from this definition. By property 3 of characteristic functions $(v(S) = -v(-S))$, the $(n-1)$ member complement of a single-member coalition has a value of $\gamma$, which accounts for the dot at $((n-1), \gamma)$. In a decision system in which coalition formation is the essential activity, the worst that can happen to a person is to be completely left out. Therefore, if an attempt is made to assign a player in a coalition a greater loss than he will sustain alone, he can resign and form a single-member coalition, thereby guaranteeing himself a loss no greater than $-\gamma$. Since, presumably, all members of a losing coalition could do this, the maximum that any coalition $S_p$, where $2 \leqq p \leqq (n-2)$, can lose is $-p\gamma$. By reason of the zero-sum condition, where $S_{(n-p)}$ is the complement of $S_p$, the maximum gain of $S_{(n-p)}$ is $\gamma(n-p)$.[10] Hence, for $2 \leqq p \leqq (n-2)$, the range of $v(S)$ is: $-p\gamma \leqq v(S) \leqq (n-p)\gamma$, which range is expressed by the boldface lines on Figure 6.

This range of possible values for $v(S)$ is, unfortunately, quite wide. While one might wish to narrow this range, it is, as Von Neumann and Morgenstern point out, quite impossible to do so, given the definition of a normalized characteristic function. The only way to narrow the range is to impose additional restrictions on $v(S)$. Von Neumann and Morgenstern examined the effect of some possible restrictions with interesting, although not impressively consequential, results. Here I intend

10. Note that the subscript, $p$ or $(n-p)$, to the name, $S$, of a coalition identifies the size of the coalition. Note also that "$S_{(n-p)}$" means the same as "$-S_p$".

to re-examine their restrictions and introduce some others.

One obvious and, I believe, intuitively justifiable restriction arises out of the notions of winning and losing. In the zero-sum situation, the winning coalition must take something (presumably a positive amount) away from the losing coalition (which presumably therefore receives a negative payoff). This loose intuitive supposition will now be given numerical form.

Partition the set, $\bar{I}$, of all subsets of $I$ into three pairwise disjunct subsets:

> $W$ is the set of all winning coalitions.
> $L$ is the set of all losing coalitions.
> $B$ is the set of all blocking coalitions.

These definitions effect an immediate restriction on the range of $v(S)$ as shown in Figure 6, if one assumes that winning coalitions have a positive value, losing coalitions a negative value, and blocking coalitions a value of zero. The values for $\phi$ and $I$ do not fit into this scheme, however, and so it will be conventionally assumed that they are limiting cases, i.e., that $I$ is winning though it wins nothing and $\phi$ is losing though it loses nothing. Precisely:

$$\text{if } S_p \; \varepsilon \; W, \text{then } v(S) \geqq 0$$
$$\text{if } S_p \; \varepsilon \; B, \text{then } v(S) = 0$$
$$\text{if } S_p \; \varepsilon \; L, \text{then } v(S) \leqq 0.$$

As a complete partition, these sets have the following properties:

1. $W \cap L = \phi$, $W \cap B = \phi$, and $L \cap B = \phi$
2. $W \cup L \cup B = \bar{I}$.

That is, no set can be both losing and winning, etc.; and every set in $\bar{I}$ must belong to either $W$ or $L$ or $B$. Let us further postulate that, for any pair of complementary subsets, $S$ and $-S$, one and only one can belong to $W$ and the other belongs to $L$. That is, if $S \; \varepsilon \; W$ (read "$S$ belongs to $W$" or "$S$ is a member of $W$"), then $-S \; \varepsilon \; L$. However, if $S \; \varepsilon \; B$, so also $-S \; \varepsilon \; B$.

Presumably winning and losing have something to do with the size of the coalition.[11] Indeed, if one expresses size in terms

11. When Von Neumann and Morgenstern defined winning and losing, they carefully avoided any reference to size, except to say that any super-

of weights of the members of a coalition rather than in terms simply of the numbers—an expression I shall shortly undertake —then it seems intuitively obvious that the coalition with the greater weight should be defined as winning. To use the notion of size to discriminate among winning, losing, and blocking coalitions, it is necessary to use the rather imprecise notion of a majority. An essential element of this notion is that no coalition is winning unless it contains over half the membership or votes or weight in the decision-making system. But in many natural instances more than half is required to win. To render the notion of a majority general, one needs to establish a range for winning. For this purpose, assume a number $m$, the minimum size smaller than which no coalition is winning. Assume further that players are weighted equally. Then if $n$ is even, the lowest possible value for $m$ is $n/2 + 1$; and if $n$ is odd, this lowest value is $\frac{n+1}{2}$. The range for $m$ then is: $\frac{n}{2} + 1, \frac{n+1}{2} \leqq m \leqq n$.

In effect, the definition of $m$ has defined the members of $W$:

$$S_p \ \varepsilon \ W \text{ if and only if } m \leqq p.$$

Similarly, $m$ can be used to define $L$ and $B$:

$$S_p \ \varepsilon \ B \text{ if and only if } (n - m) < p < m$$
$$S_p \ \varepsilon \ L \text{ if and only if } p \leqq (n - m).$$

Note, with respect to $B$, no whole number occurs in the interval, $(n - m) < p < m$, when $n$ is odd and $m = \frac{n+1}{2}$. Since players are weighted equally $B$ cannot exist in this circumstance. Using these restrictions, the range of characteristic functions is reduced to that shown in Figure 7 by boldface dots and lines.

The foregoing definition of $W, L,$ and $B$ is in terms of members of $I$ who are assumed to have equal roles. This assumption is, of course, highly artificial. So in order to render the model

set of a winning coalition was also winning and any subset of a losing coalition was also losing (p. 241 et seq.). Presumably the avoidance was intended to permit them to retain the full generality of the analysis, but it also prohibited them from placing as much restriction as one might wish on the range shown in Figure 6.

more realistic, I shall introduce the notion of players of varying weights of power. This will necessitate some redefinition of $m$, $W$, $L$, and $B$ and, unfortunately, will somewhat increase the range of $v(S)$.

For the set $I$, let each player, 1, 2, . . . , $n$, be assigned a weight, $w_1$, $w_2$, . . . , $w_n$. (In the real world, assigning weights is sometimes simple, as in the case of stockholders in a corporation, and sometimes extremely difficult, as in international poli-

FIGURE 7

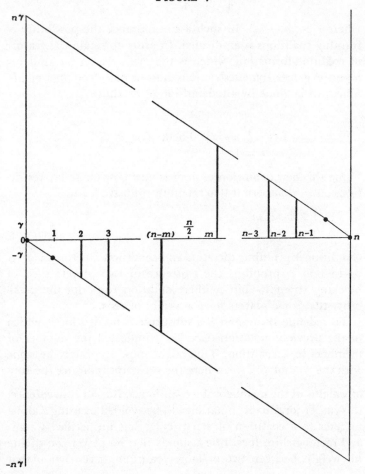

tics. Consequently, I shall simply leave the procedure for assigning weights vague and assume that some sort of procedure exists.) When players are weighted equally—as implicitly they were in the model as heretofore described—it was impossible for a dictator to occur. When players are weighted unequally, however, it is possible that, e.g., in a five-person game the weights be distributed thus: (1, 0, 0, 0, 0) or even

$$\left( \frac{1}{2} + \varepsilon, \; \frac{\frac{1}{2} - \varepsilon}{4}, \frac{\frac{1}{2} - \varepsilon}{4}, \frac{\frac{1}{2} - \varepsilon}{4}, \frac{\frac{1}{2} - \varepsilon}{4} \right),$$

where $\varepsilon > (m - \frac{1}{2})$. In such a circumstance the possibility of forming coalitions is eradicated. In order to retain the feature of coalition-formation, which is the main reason for studying $n$-person games, some restrictions must be placed on the weights. This will be done by a redefinition of $m$, thus:

$$\text{Let } \sum_{k=1}^{n} w_k = 1. \text{ Then, } \frac{1}{2} < m \leqq 1.$$

Using this new definition of $m$, it is now possible to lay restrictions on $w_k$ that permit $\Gamma$ to retain its collusive feature:

1. $0 \leqq w_k < m$
2. $(w_j + w_k) < 1$

Condition 1 prohibits dictators and condition 2 permits $v(S) > 0$—in that it prohibits the existence of two players each of blocking strength—but neither condition rules out the possibility that some players have a weight of zero.

To redefine $W$, $L$, and $B$ a substitute is needed for $p$, which in the previous notation (e.g., "$S_p$") indicated the number of members in a coalition. This might most accurately be done with the symbol: $S_{\sum_{k \text{ in } S} w_k}$, where the subscript indicates the sum of weights of the members of a coalition, $S$. But for convenience, this rather formidable notation will be avoided by using $S$ alone to refer to a coalition of a particular but unspecified weight and membership. It will be assumed that no player can divide his weight between two or more coalitions, a restriction that is perhaps unrealistic considering the way some people in real life hedge on membership as, for example, when paving contractors contribute to both political parties. Using this new notation and the concept of weighting, $W$, $L$, and $B$ are defined thus:

1. $S \varepsilon W$ if and only if $m \leqq \sum\limits_{k \text{ in } S} w_k$

2. $S \varepsilon L$ if and only if $\sum\limits_{k \text{ in } S} w_k \leqq 1 - m$

3. $S \varepsilon B$ if and only if $1 - m < \sum\limits_{k \text{ in } S} w_k < m$

This definition may be visualized by ordering the weights of all coalitions, $S$, numerically from $\phi$ to $I$. The range of $W$, $L$, and $B$ is then a definite distance on a line, as in Figure 8.

### FIGURE 8

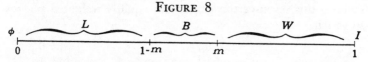

In order to use these new definitions to discuss the range of characteristic functions, it is desirable to introduce an additional change in notation. While $\gamma$, the unit of measurement on the ordinates in Figures 6 and 7 will still be used, it can no longer be interpreted as $v(\{i\}) = -\gamma$. Rather it shall be said that $v(\{a\}) = -\gamma$, where $a$ is the member of $I$ for whom, when in the single-member set, $w_a$ is the smallest positive number of any $w_i$.

The first change occasioned in the graph by the use of weights rather than persons is that the area in which $v(S)$ can fall is, contrary to our intention, expanded horizontally, but not vertically. While formerly $v(S)$ could lie only on certain points and lines, now it can lie on the boldface points and lines as well as in the shaded area in Figure 9. Specifically, possible locations for $v(S)$ are the points $(0,0)$, $(w_a, -\gamma)$, $((1 - w_a), \gamma)$, $(0,1)$ and many points lying on the abscissa in the closed interval $\langle (1 - m), m \rangle$ as well as many points in the entire areas $A\,B\,C\,D$ and $E\,F\,G\,H$ including the lines that form their boundaries.[12] (Note: While $D$ must coincide with $(1 - m)$ and $F$ with $m$, $A$ may coincide with $2w_a$ or lie to its right and $G$ may coincide with $(1 - 2w_a)$ or lie to its left. In Figure 9, I have for the sake of clarity chosen the latter alternatives for $A$ and $G$.) The use of weights does not, of course, render $v(S)$ a continuous function, although if $a$ is small and $n$ is large $v(S)$ may approach being continuous. Nevertheless, the use of weights does expand the range of $v(S)$ horizontally, but not vertically.

The reduction up to this point of the range of $v(S)$ may perhaps be interesting but it is hardly sufficient to be useful. For an additional restriction, which leads to the discovery of an interesting family of games, one can require that $v(S)$ lie on $0C$ and $E1$ in Figure 9. In a somewhat different form, this restriction was imposed by Von Neumann and Morgenstern, who called games whose characteristic functions invariably lay on $0K$ and $J1$ in Figure 9 *simple games*. An example of a simple game is this seven-person game with equally weighted players in which,

$$\text{if } \gamma = -1 \text{ and if } S \text{ has } \begin{Bmatrix} 0 \\ 1 \\ 2 \\ 3 \\ 4 \\ 5 \\ 6 \\ 7 \end{Bmatrix} \text{ members, then } v(S) = \begin{Bmatrix} 0 \\ -1 \\ -2 \\ -3 \\ 3 \\ 2 \\ 1 \\ 0 \end{Bmatrix}.$$

The outstanding feature of such games is that all coalitions receive multiples of $\gamma$. Losing coalitions, $S_p$, lose $-p\gamma$, the maximum that each player can lose.

Simple games are probably rare in nature, although, if many $n$-person parlor games existed, they would probably all be simple. Hence, little of practical value is likely to result from studying them. Nevertheless they possess an extremely interesting property which is immediately apparent from Figure 9.

12. A *closed interval*, symbolized "$\langle a,b \rangle$," includes points $a$ and $b$ and all intervening ones. An *open interval*, symbolized by "$(a,b)$," includes all the points between $a$ and $b$ but not $a$ and $b$ themselves.

If the set $B$ is undefined, as indeed it must be under Von Neumann and Morgenstern's definition of simple games, then the line on which $v(S)$ lies always slopes downward to the right. Even when the restrictions imposed by using numerical definitions of $W$ and $L$ are used, this property remains although, of course, the line on which $v(S)$ lies jumps from negative to positive at $m$ and, if $B$ is defined, some values of $v(S)$ lie on the abscissa between $D$ and $F$. Since this property leads to some

FIGURE 9

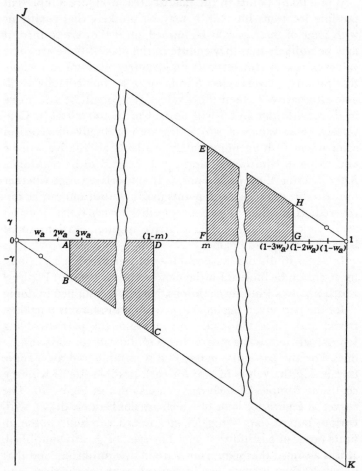

sociologically fascinating inferences, one immediately wonders
if it is just an accidental consequence of the diagonal structure
of *BC* and *EH* or if this property might hold inside *A B C D*
and *E F G H* as well. This question is of such importance that
further study of the range of $v(S)$ is indicated.

## EQUILIBRIUM POINTS IN THE RANGE OF
## CHARACTERISTIC FUNCTIONS

While many points in the shaded area in Figure 9 represent
possible locations for $v(S)$, it may be unlikely that coalitions
with some of these payoffs be formed, or, if they are formed, it
may be unlikely that they endure in the play. If there are some
values of $v(S)$ so unnecessarily disadvantageous for $S$ as a whole
that rational players reject $S$ in favor of an immediately available alternative $T$, then these values of $v(S)$ will be said to be
in *disequilibrium* and $S$ will be said to be *unrealizable*. Conversely, those values of $v(S)$ which are not disadvantageous in
comparison with an immediately available alternative will be
said to be in *equilibrium* and $S$ will be said to be *realizable*.
After uttering these definitions, it is apropriate to see whether
unrealizable coalitions and points in disequilibrium can be discovered. If so, then it will be possible to lay restrictions on
available coalitions and thus to arrive at generalizations about
behavior in $n$-person games.

In order to discuss the possibility of unrealizable coalitions,
let attention be limited for the moment to that part of Figure 9
which involves winning coalitions. No loss is sustained in doing
so for the part involving blocking coalitions is, for our purposes,
trivial and, since the games are zero-sum, the part involving
losing coalitions is the mirror image of the part for the winning
ones. For any particular game, $\Gamma$, it is possible to draw a curve
connecting the values of $v(S)$ for each possible size of winning
coalition. Samples of such curves are shown in Figure 10. The
curves in Figure 10, some of which are deliberately drawn with
curious bumps, flats, squiggles, etc., in order to indicate the infinite range of possibilities, may, however, be greatly simplified.
If it is assumed that some points are in disequilibrium and that
disequilibrium occurs when higher values are obtainable—and

both assumptions will be demonstrated in the subsequent argument—then it is possible to smooth the curve from its lowest

## FIGURE 10

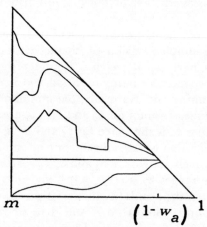

$m$     $\left(1 - w_a\right)$   $1$

to highest points, as is done in Figure 11. When this is done it is immediately apparent that the infinity of curves can be categorized into several simple patterns:

1. Those with negative slope throughout,
2. Those with positive slope in part,
3. Those with zero slope in part.

## FIGURE 11

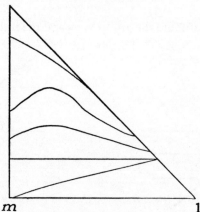

$m$      $1$

(Note, with respect to classes 2 and 3, that all curves have a negative slope in the range between points $(1 - w_a)$ and 1 on the abscissa.) Having created these classes of curves, it is possible to inquire by classes whether or not disequilibrium points exist on them.

For the sake of a heuristic discussion of these questions, let us return to the simpler version of characteristic functions in which players have equal weights. Consider the position of players in a two-member losing coalition and its complement, an $(n - 2)$ winning one. Naturally, the minimum value for $n$ is five. The range of values for $S_2$ and $S_{(n-2)}$ are portrayed in Figure 12, where $ac$ is the range for $S_2$ and $df$ is the range for $S_{(n-2)}$. The question is: Are all values on $ac$ and $df$ in equilibrium? Alternatively stated, are $S_2$ and $S_{n-2}$ realizable throughout the entire ranges $2\gamma \geqq v(S_{n-2}) \geqq 0$ and $0 \geqq v(S_2) \geqq -2\gamma$?

Consider, first, the possibility that $v(S_2) > -\gamma$, which locates it in the half-open interval $\langle a,b \rangle$ and that, since $S_{n-2}$ is the complement of $S_2$, $v(S_{n-2}) < \gamma$, which locates it in the half-open interval $\langle d,e \rangle$. By the definition of a normalized characteristic function, however, $v(S_{n-1}) = \gamma$, so that $v(S_{n-2}) < v(S_{n-1})$. In this circumstance $S_{n-2}$ can increase its value simply by increasing its membership. There are two possibilities of action: the members of $S_{n-2}$ may reject it entirely and, *de novo*, attempt to form $S_{n-1}$. This procedure does not, of course, guarantee that $S_{n-1}$ occur, but the alternative possibility does: Members of $S_{n-2}$ may retain their organization and play a curious sort of sub-game $\Gamma'$.

The players of $\Gamma'$ are the group $S_{n-2}$ and the individual mem-

FIGURE 12

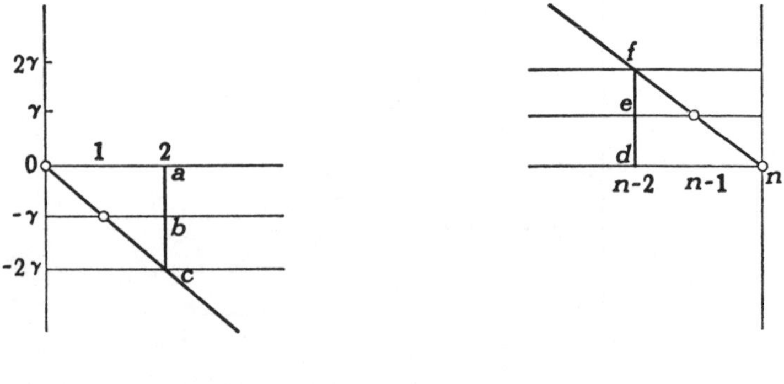

bers of $S_2$, whom we will call $i$ and $j$. The object is to form $S_{n-1}$ and thus to divide the additional amount $[\gamma - v(S_{n-2})]$ among themselves and either $i$ or $j$. This game is quite unsymmetric in the sense that only coalitions containing $S_{n-2}$ and some other player(s) are winning. Precisely, these are: $\{\{S_{n-2}\},\ I\}$, $\{\{S_{n-2}\},\ j\}$, and $\{\{S_{n-2}\},\ i,\ j\}$, although, since the third of these is $I$ with a value of zero, $S_{n-2}$ has a powerful incentive to prohibit its occurrence. (It must be assumed that members of a winning coalition, $S_p$, can control entry into any superset of $S_p$, else all losers could avoid loss by forcing the creation of $I$. While such evasions undoubtedly occur in nature, to admit them here would make $I$ the only realizable winning coalition and would render the whole theory of characteristic functions trivial.) Assuming, therefore, that $S_{n-2}$ can prohibit $I$, only two winning coalitions exist.

Since the player $S_{n-2}$ is a dictator, the bargaining features and payoffs in $\Gamma^v$ differ markedly from the symmetric three-person game studied so intensively by Von Neumann and Morgenstern. The first question about $\Gamma^v$ is whether or not it will be played. Naturally, $S_{n-2}$ has a strong incentive to play because, for it, the game is certainly profitable and absolutely riskless. But for $i$ and $j$, assuming they divide the cost of $S_2$ in a ratio of $q$ and $1 - q$, the certain loss of $qv(S_2)$ and $(1 - q)\ v(S_2)$ may be preferable to the risk of $-\gamma$, which is what the loser of $\Gamma^v$ is certain to obtain. The player $S_{n-2}$ can, however, induce $i$ or $j$ to play by offering one, say $i$, a final payoff of $u$, where $qv(S_2) < u < [\gamma - v(S_{n-2})]$. (It is assumed that players are honest and do not renege, but here honesty is partially enforced inasmuch as it is advantageous for $S_{n-2}$ to play and if $S_{n-2}$ tries to force $i$ to accept less than $u$, $i$ can resign and re-enter $S_2$.) Since two of the three players are thus assured of improving their position, it is certain that $\Gamma^v$ will be played. Stated alternatively, the coalitions $\{I\}$, $\{i,j\}$, $\{S_{n-2}\}$, and $\{\phi\}$ are ruled out.

The payoffs to each player (symbolized by "$\alpha_i$") can be specified within limits. The set of payoffs, which Von Neumann and Morgenstern interpreted as a vector in $n$-dimensional space is symbolized by "$(\alpha_1, \alpha_2, \ldots, \alpha_n)$" or more briefly by "$\overrightarrow{\alpha}$" and is called an *imputation*.

The coalitions $\{\{S_{n-2}\}, i\}$ or $\{\{S_{n-2}\}, j\}$ can occur. Assume the former. If $i$ and $j$ simply bid against each other for inclusion in $S_{n-1}$, then the player $S_{n-2}$ faces a pure problem of minimizing $u$. Since the player in $S_2$ who shifts a larger portion of its cost onto his partner thereby enables his partner to bid higher for inclusion in $S_{n-1}$, it appears that $q = \frac{1}{2}$ is an equilibrium point. Hence $u$ is a negative number approaching a minimum of $\frac{1}{2} v(S_2)$. If, however, $j$ bids to retain $i$ in $S_2$—as he well might, perhaps collusively, in order to drive up $u$—then $q$ has no equilibrium value and $u$ can range over the whole interval $qv(S_2) < u < [\gamma - v(S_{n-2})]$. In the general case $\vec{\alpha}$ is

$$\alpha_{S_{n-2}} = \gamma - u; \ \alpha_i = u; \text{ and } \alpha_j = -\gamma.$$

The outcome for $\{\{S_{n-2}\}, j\}$ is the same, except that $i$ and $j$ are reversed.

In both outcomes, at least two players improve their position. Hence $\Gamma'$ is certain to be played. And, since $S_{n-2}$ is invariably one of the winners, it has an incentive to initiate $\Gamma'$. From this it follows that $v(S_2) > -\gamma$ is in disequilibrium and $S_2$ is unrealizable in the range $\langle a,b \rangle$ in Figure 12.

Turning now to the ranges $\langle b,c \rangle$ and $\langle e,f \rangle$, the curious subgame $\Gamma'$ still exists, provided $v(S_2)$ is not at $c$ or $-2\gamma$, which is its limit. Now, however, rational players will not initiate it. Since $v(S_{n-2}) \geqq \gamma$, there is no immediate gain to $S_{n-2}$ from an increase in size. Hence, any payment, $u$, which $S_{n-2}$ might offer to $i$ or $j$ must come out of its present resources rather than its future gain. It is conceivable that $S_{n-2}$ might risk $u$ if it could count on an imputation in the range:

$$\alpha_{S_{n-2}} = \gamma - u, \text{ where } \gamma - v(S_{n-2}) > u; \ \alpha_i = u; \ \alpha_j = -\gamma.$$

But $S_{n-2}$ cannot be certain that $i$ will pay to form $S_{n-1}$. Since it is both costly and risky to start $\Gamma'$, $S_{n-2}$ has no clear incentive to do so. As for $i$, it is conceivable that he too could initiate $\Gamma'$ in the hope of obtaining $u$, where $u > q \ v(S_2)$. But since $S_{n-2}$ need not offer him anything, his action can only start a round of self-destructive bidding by $i$ and $j$ for inclusion in $S_{n-1}$, bidding which ends at the worst possible outcome for both $i$ and $j$:

$$\alpha_{S_{n-2}} = 2\gamma; \ \alpha_i = -\gamma; \ \alpha_j = -\gamma.$$

Since no player in $\Gamma'$ has an incentive to initiate it when $v(S_2) \leqq -\gamma$, it follows that it will not be played. Hence, in this case $v(S_2)$ is in equilibrium and $S_2$ is realizable.

This discussion of the special case of $S_2$ and $S_{n-2}$ can now be generalized in order to discuss equilibrium points on the three classes of curves of characteristic functions.

Assume $v(S) < v(S \cup i)$, where $\sum\limits_{k \, \varepsilon \, S} w_k < \sum\limits_{k \, \varepsilon \, (S \cup i)} w_k$.

Then there exists a subgame, $\Gamma'$, where the players are the group $S$ and the individual members of $-S$ and where the object is to form $(S \cup i)$ in order to divide $g$, when $g = v(S \cup i) - v(S)$. In $\Gamma'$ the only coalitions which can obtain $g$ are those which contain $S$ and one other player inasmuch as these coalitions are the only ones with sufficient weight to form $(S \cup i)$. Hence all winning coalitions are those which contain $S$ and some $i$, formerly of $-S$. Any outcome in the following range exists in $\Gamma'$ and all these outcomes are preferred by members of a winning coalition to any outcome for themselves in $\Gamma$:

$$\alpha_S = v(S) + g - u, \text{ where } q_i v(-S) < u < g, \text{ where } g > 0, \text{ and}$$
$$\text{where } q_1 + q_2 + \ldots + q_{(n-p)} = 1;$$
$$\alpha_i = u; \text{ and } \alpha_{-(S \cup i)} = -v(S \cup i).$$

All these imputations exist because $S$ can costlessly offer $u$ and simultaneously increase its own value and because $i$ can invariably better its position by changing sides. Furthermore, these are all the imputations in $\Gamma'$ for, if $u \geqq g$, then $S$ will refuse to play and, if $u < q_i v(-S)$, then $i$ will refuse to play. All outcomes in $\Gamma'$ are preferred because, for winning coalitions in $\Gamma'$, every imputation in $\Gamma'$ dominates every imputation in $\Gamma$, with respect to the same pair.[13] All sets $\{\{S\}, i\}$ are effective inasmuch as $\alpha_S + \alpha_j = v(S \cup i)$. Identify imputations in $\Gamma'$ by $\alpha_i$ and imputations in $\Gamma$ by $\beta_i$. If $\alpha_i = u$ and $\beta_i = q_i v(-S)$, where $u > q_i v(-S)$, then $\alpha_i > \beta_i$. If $\alpha_S = v(S) + g - u$ and $\beta_S = v(S)$,

13. Defining *dominance*, a set, $S$, which is a subset of $I$, is said to be *effective* for an imputation $\vec{\alpha}$ if $\sum\limits_{i \varepsilon S} \alpha_i = v(S)$. An imputation, $\vec{\alpha}$, is said to *dominate* an imputation, $\vec{\beta}$, if (1) $S$ is not $\phi$, (2) $S$ is effective for all $\vec{\alpha}$, and (3) $\alpha_i > \beta_i$ for $i$ in $S$.

where $g > u$ and $g > 0$, then $\alpha_S > \beta_S$. Since outcomes in $\Gamma'$ both exist and are preferred to those in $\Gamma$, it follows that $\Gamma'$ will be played and that $v(S)$ is not in equilibrium. By repeated applications of this argument, it can be shown that no point lying on a curve with positive slope is in equilibrium. Thus, for $v(S) < v(T)$, where $\sum\limits_{k\,\varepsilon\,S} w_k < \sum\limits_{k\,\varepsilon\,T} w_k$, the only point in equilibrium is $v(T)$, which is the maximum value of a point on a rising slope.

Assume $v(S) \geqq v(S \cup i)$. If $\Gamma'$ is played in this circumstance, it has the following range of imputations, owing to the possibilities of self-destructive bidding among the members of $-S$ for membership in $(S \cup i)$ and owing to the fact that $S$ has no leeway for negotiation:

$$v(S) \leqq \alpha_S \leqq \max v(S)$$
$$v(\{i\}) \leqq \alpha_i \leqq q_i v(-S)$$
$$v(\{i\}) - \max v(S) \leqq \alpha_{-(S\,\cup\,i)} \leqq (1 - q)v(-S).$$

Since $\alpha_i \leqq \beta_i$ for all winning coalitions in $\Gamma'$, imputations in $\Gamma'$ do not dominate imputations in $\Gamma$. Hence $\Gamma'$ is not played and $v(S)$ is in equilibrium, with respect to $v(S \cup i)$. By repeated applications of this argument, it can be shown that any point lying on a curve with a negative or zero slope is in equilibrium with respect to all other points on the curve to its right. But this argument says nothing about whether or not it is in equilibrium with respect to points lying to its left. To consider this question it is necessary to make a more detailed analysis.

Assume $v(S) = v(S \cup i)$. Recalling that $\alpha_k \geqq v(\{k\})$ and that $\sum\limits_{k\,=\,1}^{n} \alpha_k = 0$, consider the imputation with respect to $S$. Since $S$ is not $I$ (which it cannot be owing to the fact that we are considering the case when a coalition $(S \cup i)$ exists), $\sum\limits_{i\,\varepsilon\,S} \alpha_i > 0$.

For a particular $i$ in $S$, perhaps, $\alpha_i \leqq 0$. Still, there must exist some $j$ in $S$, for which $\alpha_j > 0$. If $w_j < w_S - m$, then the other members of $S$ can expel $j$ to form a new coalition, without endangering the receipt of $v(S)$, and thereby obtain an amount,

$\alpha_j$, to divide among themselves. Assuming $j$ is expelled, symbolize the new coalition by " $-(-S \cup j)$ ". The members of $-(-S \cup j)$ divide $\alpha_j$ by playing a new subgame $\Gamma'$, in which coalitions, members, payoffs, etc. will be identified with prime marks as superscripts. Since the members of $S'$ dare not expel their fellows beyond the point that $S'$ is also an $S$ in $W$ in $\Gamma$, it follows that the minimum winning weights in $\Gamma$ and $\Gamma'$ are the same, that is, $m' = m$. Assuming that a member expelled from $S$ and forced into $(-S \cup j)'$ may even sustain the maximum loss in that coalition and that at the other extreme the entire gain from the expulsion may be given to one member of $-(-S \cup j)'$, the range of payoffs in $\Gamma'$ is then, for $i = 1, 2, \ldots, n$, the following: $-\gamma \leqq \alpha'_{i'} = \alpha_i + \alpha_j$. Since the purpose of $\Gamma'$ is simply to divide $\alpha_j$ (rather than to rearrange payoffs already established in $S$), $\alpha'_{i'} \geqq \alpha_i$, for $i' \varepsilon -(-S \cup j)'$ and for $i \varepsilon S$. There exist, however, imputations in $\Gamma'$ such that for all members of $-(-S \cup j)$, it is the case that $\alpha'_{i'} > \alpha_i$, for example, $\alpha'_{i'} = \alpha_i + \alpha_j/p$, when $S$ has $(p + 1)$ members. If some such imputation, $\overrightarrow{\alpha'}$, can be agreed on, $\Gamma'$ is certain to be played, for, with respect to the effective set $-(-S \cup j)$, $\overrightarrow{\alpha'}$ dominates every $\overrightarrow{\alpha}$ in $\Gamma$.

There is considerable urgency for the players of $\Gamma'$ to arrive at a dominating imputation. Entirely aside from the postulated rationality on account of which players prefer to have more rather than less of whatever is being divided up, there is an urgency in the game situation itself. In $\Gamma$ there is only the amount $v(S)$, where $S$ is in $W$, to be distributed among the members of $S$. The members of $-S$, for one of whom necessarily $\alpha_i < 0$, may be able by offering appropriate side-payments to some member of $S$ to form $S^*$, a new winning coalition in $\Gamma$. In order to meet the offers tendered by $-S$ to $i$, $i \varepsilon S$, it may well be necessary for $S$ to expel some $j$. This is especially likely to occur when $-S$ aims at forming $S^* \varepsilon W^m$, that is a minimum winning coalition which is smaller than $S$ has been assumed to be. Considering the urgency of this incentive, therefore, one can expect that $-(-S \cup j)$ will agree on an imputation $\overrightarrow{\alpha'}$ that dominates all $\overrightarrow{\alpha}$ and hence that $\Gamma'$ will be played.

Repeated plays of $\Gamma'$ ensure that $S$ reduce itself in size to some coalition $T$, when either $T \, \varepsilon \, W^m$ or $v(\mathrm{T}) \neq v(-(-T \cup j))$. Hence when the slope of the characteristic function is zero, the only point in equilibrium is that point farthest to the left in the range of the zero slope.

Assume finally, $v(S) > v(S \cup i)$, that is, a negative slope. By an argument similar to the one used in the case of $v(S) = v(S \cup i)$, it can be shown that the incentive for $S$ to expel $j$ even more compelling than when the slope is zero. Hence in this case it follows that the only point in equilibrium is $v(S)$ when $\displaystyle\sum_{k \, \varepsilon \, S} w_k = m$, that is, when $S$ is a minimum winning coalition.

The foregoing arguments were undertaken in order to narrow down the number of realizable winning coalitions. This task has now been completed and the results may be summarized in terms of the three categories for shapes of characteristic functions:

1. Functions with a *negative* slope throughout the whole range for winning coalitions. For these games, there is a uniquely realizable size of winning coalition, namely the minimum size. While many different selections of players may each be this size and while infinitely many different imputations may be possible for each such selection, nevertheless coalitions of all other sizes have been identified as unrealizable.

2. Functions with a *positive* slope in part of the range of winning coalitions. Since the curves have all been smoothed, we know that they all have either a single peak or a truncated plateau at the top. If they are single-peaked, then the unique point in equilibrium is at the peak, owing to the fact that all lower points on both the positive and negative slopes are in disequilibrium. If they have a plateau at top, the unique point in equilibrium is $v(S)$, when $v(-(-S \cup i)) < v(S) = v(S \cup i)$, that is the point at the extreme left of the plateau. This follows from the fact that all other points on the positive and negative slope are in disequilibrium as well as all other points on the zero slope.

3. Functions with a *zero* slope throughout the range of winning coalitions except from the distance on the abscissa from $(1 - w_a)$ to 1. Here, as for the first class, the uniquely realizable winning coalition size is $m$.

These results permit us to say that realizable winning coalitions invariably occur when $v(S)$, $S \, \varepsilon \, W$, is at its maximum. For classes 1 and 3, the uniquely realizable coalitions have the size $m$. But for class 2, the size of uniquely realizable coalitions is larger than $m$. (This follows because, having smoothed out the curves to single-peakedness, no positive slope would be possible if the peak were at $m$.)

## CONDITION FOR EXISTENCE OF v(S) WITH A POSITIVE SLOPE IN PART OF THE RANGE OF WINNING COALITIONS

Having thus greatly simplified the range of sizes for winning coalitions, we are now in a position to distinguish between those games in which the equilibria values of their characteristic functions are at $m$ and those in which they are not. The condition for a game to display an equilibrium value of the characteristic function at a point larger than $m$ is:

While the size $m$ is in the rules stated to be a winning size, in actual play among rational and informed players $m$ is in fact unrealizable and some size larger than $m$ is invariably reached in the formation of winning coalitions.

Or, stated alternatively:

In the construction of winning coalitions, rational and informed players continue to add to their winning coalitions after they reach the size $m$, even though they know they have already won.

As the rather paradoxical forms of the statements suggest, this is an extraordinarily restrictive condition to meet in the construction of real games. Some of the paradoxical quality of such characteristic functions can perhaps be indicated by an examination of some of the commonly used rules for the allocation of winnings among the players in the winning coalition. For some rules, at least, and perhaps for all, the actual use of the rule renders $m$ the only realizable size of coalition, even though $S$, $S \varepsilon W^m$, has been shown to be unrealizable by the previous argument.

*Rule 1.* Suppose, to take the commonest rule, one that follows naturally from Shapley's value for $n$-person games and which probably is the one most frequently used in real political situations, that the players who start a coalition agree that they will pay each other the amount that each adds to the value of the coalition as it increases in size. If $v(S)$ has a negative slope throughout, as in the curve $0AB1$ in Figure 13, then this rule presents no problems for the unique $v(S)$ in equilibrium lies at point $B$ and the value that each new member adds can be calculated easily. Let player $j$ add $w_j$ to the weight of $S$, $S \varepsilon W^m$. Then the change in value attributable to player $j$ is $(a' - b')$. In the calculation of the distribution of the winnings of $S$, $j$ simply receives $-(a' - b')$ or $(a - b)$. But this rule is far less clear if $v(S)$ has some positive slope, as on curve $0CDEF1$ in Figure 13. What, in this latter case, might be considered the contributions and hence payoffs for players $k$ and $h$? The alternatives for $k$ are: $-(c' - d')$ or $(c - d)$; $-(e' - f')$ or $(e - f)$; or $-(g' - h')$ or $(g - h)$. The alternatives for $h$ are: $-(c''' - d''')$ or $(c'' - d'')$; $-(e''' - f''')$ or $(e'' - f'')$; or $-(g''' - h''')$ or $(g'' - h'')$.

*Rule 1a.* For $k$, $(c - d)$ and, for $h$, $(c'' - d'')$. While initially $(c - d)$ seems the most reasonable payoff for $k$ under this rule (in the sense that one might wish to follow the path of the characteristic function), this procedure leads to unreasonable consequences when applied to the contribution of $h$. The rule is to measure the contribution on $0C'EF$. But, by this rule, $h$, who brings the potentially winning coalition closer to victory than does $k$, still must receive a negative amount in the payoff, that is, $(c'' - d'')$. It is hard to imagine $S$, $S \varepsilon W$, being formed at all under such circumstances. One concludes, therefore, that decision and victory are impossible if the rule is interpreted in this way.

*Rule 1b.* For $k$, $(e - f)$ and, for $h$, $(e'' - f'')$. In this case, while the difficulty of the previous case disappears, another kind of paradox comes to light. While $h$ receives $(e'' - f'')$ for joining $S$ where $v(S)$ is maximum, the prospective members of $-S$ can afford to pay $h$ the amount $(e'' - c'')$ to remain outside of $S$. (Note that, by reason of the positive slope of $CD$—and hence of the negative slope of $C'E$—, it is always true that $(e'' - f'') < (e'' - c'')$.) It will be recalled that the argument by

FIGURE 13

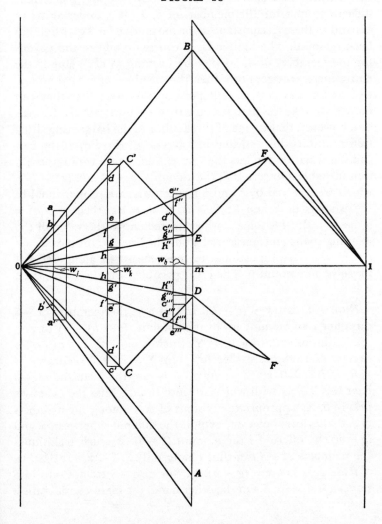

which it was shown that only maximum $v(S)$ was in equilibrium for $v(S)$ having a positive slope depended on the absence of restrictions on bargaining so that $S$ could, if necessary, outbid $-S$ for some member, $i$, of $-S$ to join $(S \cup i)$. But this particular imputation puts a limitation on the bargaining so that $S$ at max $v(S)$ is unrealizable.

*Rule 1c.* For $k$, $(g - h)$, and, for $h$, $(g'' - h'')$. In this case still a third kind of paradox appears. In the first place, it is difficult to imagine the members of $S$, $S \varepsilon W^m$, undertaking to expand in these circumstances, for the motive for expansion has been removed. The motive is, of course, to add to the payoffs for the members of $S$, $S \varepsilon W^m$, by forming $(S \cup i)$. But if the entire increment goes to $i$, then the members of $S$ have no motive to form $(S \cup i)$, except possibly the hope that they can induce $i$ to take less than the rule they are using allows. It turns out, however, that in one of three subcases the bargaining situation prohibits this and that in a second of three cases the bargaining situation renders the very existence of a winning coalition unstable. Observe that the amounts $(g - h)$ and $(g'' - h'')$, which are received by $k$ and $h$ respectively, are proportional to the weights of $k$ and $h$; that is, if $w_k = w_h$, then $(g - h) = (g'' - h'')$. But for some $i$, whose increment to the value of the winning coalition is measured along the line $EF$, the payoffs are not necessarily proportional to those measured along $0D$. Let $i$ receive an amount $x$. Then it is possible, when $w_i = w_k$, that: $x \gtreqless (g - h)$.

*Rule 1c1.* Let $x > (g - h)$. In this case the members of $-S$ can offer $i$ an amount up to the amount $((g - h) - x)$ to persuade him to withdraw from $S$, which is more than $S$ can offer to retain $i$. In this case, therefore, only $S$, $S \varepsilon W^m$, is realizable.

*Rule 1c2.* Let $x < (g - h)$. In this case the members of $-S$ have less leeway with which to work in attacking the cohesiveness of $S$. By appropriate divisions of cost among the members of $-S$, they can, however, exploit the difference between $x$ and $(g - h)$, by offering $i$ the amount $(g - h)$. By such techniques the members of $-S$ can thus render only $S$, $S \varepsilon W^m$, realizable.

*Rule 1c3.* Let $x = (g - h)$. In this case $-S$ cannot outbid $S$ nor can it disrupt $S$. On the other hand, the main consideration of this case, i.e., Rule 1c, is still operative. The members of $S$, $S \varepsilon W^m$, have no motive to expand because, if $-S$ plays rationally, the members of $S$ can get no benefit from the expansion.

*Rule 2.* Suppose, however, that the rule of division among members of a winning coalition is that suggested by Von Neumann and Morgenstern as part of their notion of a solution, namely, equal division among the winners. There is a powerful motive behind a rule such as this inasmuch as it is intended to prevent defections from $S$ to $(-S \cup i)$ by reducing the temptations of the underprivileged members of $S$ to find greater rewards for themselves elsewhere. But this rule leads to paradoxical results also. Consider these possibilities: $\sum_{i \varepsilon S} \alpha_i \gtreqless \sum_{i \varepsilon (S \cup j)} \alpha_i$, where $S \varepsilon W^m$ and where $v(S)$ and $v(S \cup j)$ both lie on the part of the curve with a positive slope. These possibilities are diagrammed in Figure 14. If $\sum_{i \varepsilon S} \alpha_i > \sum_{i \varepsilon (S \cup j)} \alpha_i$, then $0A$ lies above $0B$, as is the case for $v(S)$ in Figure 14. If, however, $\sum_{i \varepsilon S} \alpha_i = \sum_{i \varepsilon (S \cup j)} \alpha_i$, then $0A$ is superimposed on $0B$, as is the case for $v'(S)$ in Figure 14. Finally, if $\sum_{i \varepsilon S} \alpha_i < \sum_{i \varepsilon (S \cup j)} \alpha_i$, then $0A$ lies below $0B$, as is the case for $v''(S)$ in Figure 14.

*Rule 2a.* Let $\sum_{i \varepsilon S} \alpha_i \geqq \sum_{i \varepsilon (S \cup j)} \alpha_i$. It is difficult to imagine, if this situation exists, why the members of $S$ would undertake to expand to $(S \cup j)$. Indeed, with this rule of division and this shape(s) for $v(S)$ and $v'(S)$, the characteristic functions are in equilibrium only when $S$ is at size $m$. Hence in this case $(S \cup j)$ is unrealizable.

*Rule 2b.* Let $\sum_{i \varepsilon S} \alpha_i < \sum_{i \varepsilon (S \cup j)} \alpha_i$. In this case $S$ at the maximum $v''(S)$ appears to be realizable. But still there are paradoxical elements to the result. Suppose $S$, $S \varepsilon W^m$, is formed and is thoroughly cohesive—a reasonable assumption, since there is small motive for an already winning coalition to break up. Since perfect information is assumed, this high degree of cohesiveness is known to the members of $-S$. Suppose further that $S$ attempts to form $(S \cup j)$ by attracting $j$ from $-S$. Following the rule of equal division, the offer they must make is calculated as follows: Let $a = v(S \cup j) - v(S)$, that is, $a$ is the

FIGURE 14

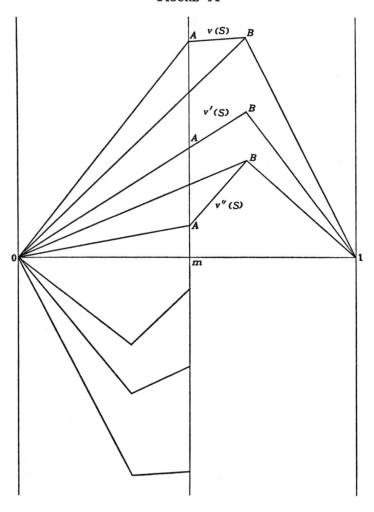

gain to the winning coalition from adding $j$. To render $\alpha_j \underset{j \,\varepsilon\, (S \,\cup\, j)}{} = \alpha_i \underset{i \,\varepsilon\, (S \,\cup\, j)}{}$, which is required by this rule of division, it is necessary to divide $a$ into two parts thus:

$$b = v(S)/p, \text{ where } S \text{ has } p \text{ members}$$
$$c = v(S \cup j) - v(S) - b = a - b.$$

Then the offer to $j$ is as follows: $\alpha_j \underset{j \,\varepsilon\, (S \,\cup\, j)}{} = b + \dfrac{c}{p+1}$. Of course, the gain by $j$ is greater for it is $\left( \alpha_j \underset{j \,\varepsilon\, (S \,\cup\, j)}{} - \alpha_j \underset{j \,\varepsilon\, -S}{} \right)$. But $-S$ can better both the offer and the actual gain. Suppose the members of $-S$ other than $j$ consider their position in $-(S \cup j)$. They will by themselves be forced to undergo the loss of $a$, in addition to what they are losing in $-S$. Hence, to avoid this loss, they can afford to pay $j$ an amount $d$, where $a > d > \left( b + \dfrac{c}{p+1} \right)$. They can, for example, pay $j$ as much as $d'$, where $d' = \left( b + \dfrac{pc}{p+1} \right)$, and still be better off than they are if $(S \cup j)$ forms. In short, under this rule the original winners (members of $S$) try to take too much of the increment produced by $j$ when he joins them—and by their greediness they are undone. Thus, $(S \cup j)$ is unrealizable under the rule of equal division and only $v(S)$, $S \,\varepsilon\, W^m$ is in equilibrium.

*Rule 3.* Let members of $S$, $S \,\varepsilon\, W$, divide the payoff in proportion to their weights. This rule involves exactly the same considerations as Rule 2 and leads to the same paradoxical results.

*Rule 4.* Let the members of $S$, $S \,\varepsilon\, W$, divide thus: When $S$ is $(S' \cup S'')$, where $S' \,\varepsilon\, W^m$ and $S'' \,\varepsilon\, L$, let members of $S'$ divide $v(S')$ and the members of $S''$ divide $(v(S) - v(S'))$. This rule involves exactly the same considerations as Rule 1c and leads to the same paradoxical results.

There may be other rules for the division of winnings among the winners that do not lead to paradoxical results when $v(S)$ has in part a positive slope. But the paradoxical results encountered in applying these four rules, all of which are common in practice and in the theoretical literature, at least hint at the essentially paradoxical nature of such games. I, at least, have not been able to find a rule which avoids a paradoxical result and it may well be that the paradox is inherent in the nature of the rules about payoffs when $v(S)$ has in part a positive slope.

While paradox may not be inherent in games in which the slope of $v(S)$ is in part positive, the fact that the four most obvious rules for the division of winnings cannot be used to obtain the maximum value for $v(S)$ suggests that, if such games do exist in nature, they are quite rare—so rare, indeed, that we may leave them out of consideration in our analysis. If we do omit them on these grounds, then the size principle obtains.

# APPENDIX II

# Strategically Unique Positions of
# Proto-Coalitions

The task of this Appendix is to develop in detail the argument
standing back of the construction of Tables 1, 2, and 3 in Chapter 6. For this purpose, it is necessary

1. To utter precise definitions of kinds of uniqueness;
2. To analyze each possible case of relationships of weights
   among proto-coalitions and each possible kind of shape
   of characteristic functions to determine the existence
   or nonexistence of uniqueness; and
3. To examine in detail the meaning of Tables 1, 2, and 3.

We shall proceed immediately with these projects.

### DEFINITIONS OF UNIQUENESS

While "$P$", "$Q$", . . . , are names of proto-coalitions, it is
not unreasonable to extend their application to coalitions.
Thus, "$P^1$" is equivalent to "$I$", the name of the grand coalition, and "$P^2$" and "$Q^2$" are the names of winning and losing
coalitions (or of two blocking coalitions) when $I$ is partitioned
into two subsets. If "$P^2$" is the name of a winning coalition,
its reference is ambiguous, for it may refer to many coalitions

in the range $m \leqq w(P^2) \leqq w(I)$. In order to distinguish among these coalitions, arrange the winning coalitions in size from $w(P^2) = m$ to $w(P^2) = w(I)$. For $w(P^2) = m$, give $P^2$ the rank of 1 and write "$P^2_1$" to signify a minimal winning coalition. For $w(P^2) = m + a$, where $a$ is the weight of player $i$ such that $0 < w(i) \leqq w(j)$, for $i, j \, \varepsilon \, I$, give $P^2$ the rank of 2 and write "$P^2_2$". And so forth, to the point at which $w(P^2) = w(I)$ and there are $s$ ranks, write "$P^2_s$". Since it does not appear to be necessary to rank blocking coalitions, where $P^2 < m$, give $P^2$ the rank of zero and write "$P^2_0$". The ranks of $Q^2$ are the negative of those of $P^2$. Hence, for blocking coalitions, write "$Q^2_0$" and, for losing coalitions, write "$Q^2_{-1}$", "$Q^2_{-2}$", . . . , "$Q^2_{-s}$". Of course, $Q^2_{-s}$ is the null coalition. Where $i, j, \ldots , s$, are numbers of ranks, conventionally assume $i < j < \ldots < s$.

Recalling that the symbol "$\alpha_i$" was used to designate the payoff to a player, $i$, and that an imputation in a zero-sum game was defined as a set of numbers $(\alpha_1, \alpha_2, \ldots , \alpha_n)$ such that $\sum\limits_{i=1}^{n} \alpha_i = 0$, the symbol "$\alpha_{X^k}$" will be used to designate the payoff to a particular proto-coalition, $X^k$, and an imputation will now be a set of numbers $(\alpha_{P^k}, \alpha_{Q^k}, \ldots , \alpha_{T^k})$ such that $\sum\limits_{X^k = P^k}^{T^k} \alpha_{X^k} = 0$.

An *initial expectation* is an imputation in the $r^{\text{th}}$ stage anticipated by a proto-coalition situated in the $(r-1)^{\text{th}}$ stage. For the $r^{\text{th}}$ stage, assume that $m$ is at its minimum value, that is, $m = w_i + \frac{1}{2} \sum\limits_{j=1}^{n} w_j$, where $0 < w_i \leqq w_j$. Assume also $X^k \, \varepsilon \, P^2_i$. Then there is (if $k = 3$ and may be if $k > 3$) at least one proto-coalition, $Y^k$, such that $Y^k \notin P^2_i$ and $w(X^k \cup Y^k) \geqq m$. Assume that in the coalition $(X^k \cup Y^k)$, $Y^k$ will accept $\alpha_{Y^k} = 0$. Then in $(X^k \cup Y^k)$, $\alpha_{X^k} = v(X^k \cup Y^k)$. Define an initial expectation, $E(X^k)$, for a proto-coalition, $X^k$, thus: given a partition in the $(r-1)^{\text{th}}$ stage such that $P^2_i, P^2_j, \ldots$ may exist in the $r^{\text{th}}$ stage and such that $v(P^2_i) > v(P^2_j)$ and given a selection of $Y^k$ to maximize $\alpha_{X^k}$ in $E(X^k)$, then $E(X^k)$ is an imputation for $P_i^2$ such that in $E(X^k)$

$$\alpha_{X^k} = v(X^k \cup Y^k \cup \ldots)$$
$$\alpha_{Y^k} \leqq -v(X^k \cup Y^k \cup \ldots)$$

for $X^k \varepsilon P_i^2$ and $Y^k \notin P_i^2$.

It is now possible to define a uniquely preferable winning coalition thus: Given a partition in the $(r-1)^{\text{th}}$ stage such that $P_i^2, P_j^2, \ldots$ may exist in the $r^{\text{th}}$ stage, then a *uniquely preferable winning coalition, $P_i^2$*, is a coalition such that

1. $v(P_i^2) > v(P_j^2)$, and
2. $P_i^2$ may have an imputation $(\gamma_{X^k}, \gamma_{Y^k}, \ldots)$ such that, for $X^k$ and $Y^k \varepsilon P_i^2$, $\gamma_{X^k} \geqq \alpha_{X^k}$ and $\gamma_{Y^k} \geqq \beta_{Y^k}$, where $E(X^k) = (\alpha_{X^k}, \alpha_{Y^k}, \ldots)$ and $E(Y^k) = (\beta_{X^k}, \beta_{Y^k}, \ldots)$.

Verbally, a uniquely preferable winning coalition is one that, if it forms, will win more than any other conceivable coalition and, furthermore, will win enough to satisfy the initial expectations of all of its members.

A *uniquely favored proto-coalition* is a proto-coalition, $X^k$, such that

1. for $P_i^2$, where $X^k \varepsilon P_i^2$, and for $P_j^2$, where $X^k \notin P_j^2$, then $v(P_i^2) > v(P_j^2)$; and
2. for $X^k, Y^k, \ldots$ satisfying condition 1, some $P_k^2$ is possible such that $X^k \varepsilon P_k^2$ and $Y^k \notin P_k^2$.

When only one winning coalition is possible, it will be referred to as a *unique* coalition. Manifestly, if in a three-set partition of $I$ only one conceivable coalition is winning, then necessarily $m$ is higher than its minimum value, that is, an extraordinary majority is required.

When one proto-coalition appears in all winning coalitions (again a possibility only when $m$ is higher than its minimum value) and when no other coalition is so favored, the invariably winning proto-coalition will be referred to as *uniquely essential*.

Finally, define a *strategically weak proto-coalition* as a proto-coalition, $X^k$, such that, if the partition in the $(r-1)^{\text{th}}$ stage admits the arrangements of the coalitions in the $r^{\text{th}}$ stage into ranks where $v(P_i^2) > v(P_j^2)$, then $X^k \notin P_i^2$.

## THE $(r - 1)^{\text{th}}$ STAGE

With the vocabulary supplied by the foregoing definitions, it is possible to analyze the $(r - 1)^{\text{th}}$ stage according to the number of subsets in the partition of $I$ at this point in time. *Case 1 and 2:* $w(P^1) = w(I)$ and $w(P^2) \geqq w(Q^2)$. These cases are those of grand and winning (or blocking) coalitions and are outside the framework of the present investigation. If these exist, the $r^{\text{th}}$ stage has been reached. In the $(r - 1)^{\text{th}}$ stage, $w(P^k) < m$. *Case 3:* three set partitions of $I$: $m > w(P^3) \geqq w(Q^3) \geqq w(R^3)$. In cases 3A through 3D following it assumed that the value of $m$ is such that any coalition is a winning one. *Case 3A:* $w(P^3) > w(Q^3) > w(R^3)$. Ignoring the possibility of grand and empty coalitions in the $r^{\text{th}}$ stage, it is possible for these proto-coalitions to pass into the $r^{\text{th}}$ stage by one of these three moves:

1. $R^3$ joins $Q^3$ to form $(Q^3 \cup R^3)$ which is $P_i^2$.
2. $R^3$ joins $P^3$ to form $(P^3 \cup R^3)$ which is $P_j^2$.
3. $Q^3$ joins $P^3$ to form $(P^3 \cup Q^3)$ which is $P_k^2$.

Identify the values of the resulting coalitions thus:

$$v(Q^3 \cup R^3) = a = v(P_i^2) \qquad v(P^3) = -a = v(Q_{-i}^2)$$
$$v(P^3 \cup R^3) = b = v(P_j^2) \qquad v(Q^3) = -b = v(Q_{-j}^2)$$
$$v(P^3 \cup Q^3) = c = v(P_k^2) \qquad v(R^3) = -c = v(Q_{-k}^2).$$

Assuming, of course, that $i$, $j$, $k \neq 0$, then, by reason of the size principle and the relative weights assumed in this case, $a > b > c$. The question now is: Do uniquely preferable winning coalitions exist in this case? Manifestly, since $a > b > c$, the coalition $(Q^3 \cup R^3)$ satisfies the first condition of a uniquely preferable winning coalition. The coalition $P^3$ is strategically weak for it is excluded from the most valuable coalition. But does $(Q^3 \cup R^3)$ satisfy the second condition? Since $P^3$ is strategically weak, it can be assumed to be willing to accept a payment of zero in order to avoid a payment of $-a$. Hence, in the bargaining between $Q^3$ and $R^3$, the initial expectations (based on what each might expect in alliance with $P^3$ when $P^3$ accepts zero) are

$E(Q^3)$: $\alpha_{P^3} = -a$, $\alpha_{Q^3} = c$, $\alpha_{R^3} = a - c$, or simply $(-a, c, a-c)$

$E(R^3)$:        $(-a, a-b, b)$.

There are three possible relationships among these expectations and each relationship constitutes a subcase.

*Case 3A1.* $c = a-b$ and $b = a-c$. Here, as I will show, $(Q^3 \cup R^3)$ is a uniquely preferable winning coalition. Since it has already been shown that the first condition is satisfied, the question is whether or not the second condition is satisfied, that is, whether or not both $Q^3$ and $R^3$ can in $(Q^3 \cup R^3)$ achieve their initial expectations. One important consequence of the fact that $a > b > c$ is that $P^3$ cannot offer either $Q^3$ or $R^3$ enough to break up their incipient coalition. Suppose that $Q^3$ and $R^3$ have tentatively agreed on their fairly obvious division of the payoff to $P_i^2$, that is an imputation of $(-a, c, b)$, and suppose further that $P^3$ attempts to break up this prospective coalition by offering one of the members, say $R^3$, an amount $d$, where $b < d < a$. Proto-coalition $Q^3$ can invariably outbid $P^3$ for the allegiance of $R^3$ by offering to accept zero, that is, an imputation of $(-a, 0, a)$. Similarly, if $P^3$ attempts to seduce $Q^3$, then $R^3$ can also always outbid $P^3$ by offering to accept $(-a, a, 0)$. While it might be supposed that $R^3$, for example, would welcome such bids from $P^3$ in order to take advantage of $Q^3$, still, in fact, if $R^3$ behaves rationally, it must refuse unconditionally to listen to the blandishments of $P^3$. Suppose $R^3$ does listen and thereby forces $Q^3$ to acquiesce in an imputation of $(-a, 0, a)$. Then either $Q^3$ may approach $P^3$ with an offer of $(0, c, -c)$ or $P^3$ may switch tactics and approach $Q^3$ with this same obvious offer. (Note that offers are contingent on the formation, at least tentatively, of the coalition. Hence, if $Q^3$ is bound by ethical restrictions from approaching $P^3$, still $P^3$, which is left out certainly is not precluded from approaching $Q^3$.) Since $(0, c, -c)$ satisfies $\alpha_{Q^3}$ in $E(Q^3)$, it follows that $R^3$ can break up $(P^3 \cup Q^3)$ only by such offers as $(b, -b, 0)$ or $(-a, d, a - d)$, where $c < d \leqq a$. Since, in $E(R^3)$, $\alpha_{R^3} = b > (a - d) \geqq 0$, the conditional consequence of the fact that $R^3$ encouraged $P^3$ to make it an offer is simply that $R^3$ is worse off than if it had stuck resolutely to its alliance with $Q^3$. Of course, this is not necessarily a final consequence for a cycle of offers and counteroffers may ensue (a cycle which may well include the original imputation of $(-a, c, b)$, which is the only point at which the cycle can be expected to stop naturally). But if a decision is reached at some point in the cycle other than an agreement on $(-a, c, b)$, $R^3$ is likely to be worse off inasmuch as most of the imputations likely to appear in the cycle are less favorable to $R^3$ than $(-a, c, b)$. In short, $R^3$, in alliance with $Q^3$, can guarantee the receipt of its initial expectation, while outside this alliance $R^3$ runs the risk of receiving less. Hence $R^3$ has a powerful motive to remain in $(Q^3 \cup R^3)$. A similar argument applies to the situation of $Q^3$ in $(Q^3 \cup R^3)$. Hence, both $Q^3$ and $R^3$ have rational grounds to agree on $(-a, c = a - b, b = a - c)$, which satisfies the second condition in the definition of a uniquely preferable winning coalition. In general, it is the case that, when the second condition is satisfied, proto-coalitions in the uniquely preferable winning coalition are urgently impelled to form it with the appropriate imputation. Hence, when a uniquely preferable winning coalition can be observed in the $(r - 1)^{th}$ stage, its occurrence in the $r^{th}$ stage can be predicted, if the leaders of the proto-coalitions in it behave rationally.

Note, also, that, in this case, $R^3$ satisfies the definition of a uniquely favored proto-coalition. While this is an interesting fact about this case, still it does not affect the action, for the overwhelming consideration is the existence of a uniquely preferable winning coalition. Discussion of the significance of a uniquely favored proto-coalition will, therefore, be deferred until cases 3A3 and 3C, wherein this is the main determinant of action.

*Case 3A2.* Here $c < a - b$ and $b < a - c$. As in all case 3A circumstances, the first condition for a uniquely preferable winning coalition is satisfied. The question for this case is, therefore, whether or not the second condition is satisfied. Note that, if $(Q^3 \cup R^3)$ agree on $(-a, a - b, b)$, which is a conceivable imputation for it, then $Q^3$ does better than its initial expectation (inasmuch as $c < a - b$), while $R^3$ obtains $b = \alpha_R{}^3$ in $E(R^3)$. Similarly, if $(Q^3 \cup R^3)$ agree on $(-a, c, a - c)$, which is also a conceivable imputation, then $R^3$ does better than its initial expectation and $Q^3$ does at least as well as $\alpha_Q{}^3$ in $E(Q^3)$. Both $Q^3$ and $R^3$ have the same compelling motives to form $(Q^3 \cup R^3)$ as in Case 3A1, although the exact imputation is not precisely determined, as it was in the previous case. Despite this difference, $(Q^3 \cup R^3)$ is a uniquely preferable winning coalition. Furthermore, as in 3A1, $R^3$ is a uniquely favored proto-coalition.

*Case 3A3*. Here $c > a - b$ and $b > a - c$. While $(Q^3 \cup R^3)$ satisfies the first condition, it does not satisfy the second. Since $Q^3$ expects $c$ and $R^3$ expects $b$ and since $b + c > a$, it is clearly impossible for both to obtain their initial expectations. The effect of this situation is that all coalitions are rendered unstable. It is of course true that, should $P^3$ offer $R^3$ more than $Q^3$ offered, still $Q^3$ can outbid $P^3$ offering $(-a, 0, a)$. Still $R^3$ and $Q^3$ have no obvious bench mark for agreement. If $Q^3$ offers $R^3$ the amount $a - c$, which seems reasonable in light of $E(Q^3)$, then $R^3$ must reject it in favor of an alliance with $P^3$ wherein it can obtan $b > a - c$. Conversely, if $R^3$ offers $Q^3$ the amount $a - b$ which seems reasonable in light of $E(R^3)$ then $Q^3$ must reject it in favor of alliance with $P^3$ wherein it can obtain $c > a - b$. For $(Q^3 \cup R^3)$ to form, one or both must modify their original expectations. One may in fact do so in order to outbid $P^3$, but there is no guarantee that this will happen. Furthermore, if one modifies its expectation, the one which does so is entirely determined by the chance of the course of the bargaining, especially by the chance of which $P^3$ approaches first. And since $P^3$ expects at best zero from either one, there is no reason to suppose it will prefer to approach one rather than the other. In short, the effect of the fact that $(Q^3 \cup R^3)$ satisfies the first, but not the second, condition for a uniquely preferable winning coalition is that, while $(Q^3 \cup R^3)$ is highly probable (owing to the possibility of either $(-a, 0, a)$ or $(-a, a, 0)$), still there is no imputation that assures the formation of $(Q^3 \cup R^3)$.

On the other hand, there is some assurance that either $(P^3 \cup R^3)$ or $(Q^3 \cup R^3)$ will form. Should $(P^3 \cup Q^3)$ be tentatively formed with any imputation between the extremes of $(c, 0, -c)$ and $(0, c, -c)$, still $R^3$ can break it up by offering either $P^3$ or $Q^3$ an amount $d$, where $c < d \leqq a, b$. Hence, while we cannot be certain that $(Q^3 \cup R^3)$ will form, we can be certain that any coalition actually formed will include $R^3$. Of course, $R^3$ satisfies the definition of a uniquely favored proto-coalition and our assurance about its probability of success is a consequence of the fact that it does satisfy this definition.

*Case 3B.* $m > w(P^3) > w(Q^3) = w(R^3)$. Ignoring the grand and null coalitions, identify the values of possible winning and losing coalitions thus:

$$v(Q^3 \cup R^3) = v(P_i^2) = a; \qquad v(P^3) = v(Q_i^2) = -a$$
$$v(P^3 \cup R^3) = v(P^3 \cup Q^3) \qquad v(Q^3) = v(R^3) = \mathrm{v}(Q_k^2) = -b$$
$$= v(P_k^2) = b;$$

By the size principle and the weights assumed, $a > b$. Hence $(Q^3 \cup R^3)$ satisfies the first condition for a uniquely preferable winning coalition. The question then is: Does it satisfy the second? In order to answer, one must know the initial expectations, which are:

$$E(Q^3) : (-a, b, a - b)$$
$$E(R^3) : (-a, a - b, b).$$

There are three possible relationships among these expectations, each of which constitutes a subcase.

*Case 3B1.* $b = a/2$. If $b = a/2$, then $b = a - b$ and with the imputation $(-a, b, b)$ the coalition $(Q^3 \cup R^3)$ qualifies as uniquely preferable.

*Case 3B2.* $b < a/2$. If $b < a/2$, then $b < a - b$ and with the imputation $(-a, b + \varepsilon, b + \varepsilon)$, where $0 \leqq \varepsilon \leqq a - 2b$, the coalition $(Q^3 \cup R^3)$ qualifies as uniquely preferable.

*Case 3B3.* $b > a/2$. If $b > a/2$, then $b > a - b$. Hence, if $E(R^3)$ is met, $E(Q^3)$ is not and vice versa. As in case 3A3, $Q^3$ and $R^3$ have no obvious bench mark for agreement and, although $(Q^3 \cup R^3)$ is highly probable, it is not certain to form.

*Case 3C.* $m > w(P^3) = w(Q^3) > w(R^3)$. Ignoring the grand and null coalitions, identify the values of the winning coalitions thus:

$$v(P^3 \cup R^3) = v(Q^3 \cup R^3) = v(P_i^2) = a$$
$$v(P^3 \cup Q^3) = v(P_j^2) = b.$$

By the weights assumed and the size principle, $a > b$. Here the first condition for a uniquely preferable winning coalition cannot be met, for there are two coalitions equally preferable to a third. Although no uniquely preferable winning coalition can be found, there may be a uniquely favored proto-coalition. It will be recalled that this latter was defined as the one proto-coalition such that coalitions of which it was a member were invariably more valuable than coalitions of which it was not a member. The rationale of this definition may be explained by reference to the facts of this case. Suppose $P^3$ and $Q^3$ negotiate to form $(P^3 \cup Q^3)$, their initial expectations must be $(b/2, b/2, -b)$. Any deviation from $\alpha_P^3 = b/2$ renders the less rewarded member of $(P^3 \cup Q^3)$ especially sympathetic to offers from $R^3$. Hence, $b/2$ is a kind of equilibrium point in the bargaining between $P^3$ and $Q^3$. Hence, also, in either $(P^3 \cup R^3)$ and $(Q^3 \cup R^3)$, $R^3$ can initially expect $\alpha_R^3 = a - (b/2)$, while $P^3$ and $Q^3$ expect $b/2$, the amount they could obtain in $(P^3 \cup Q^3)$. Hence, $R^3$ is in an exceptionally strong position. It can offer one of the others, say $P^3$, an amount $c$, where $b/2 < c \leq b$ and thus be certain of outbidding $Q^3$ for alliance with $P^3$. Thus, $R^3$ and $R^3$ alone is certain of winning. Furthermore, rather than $R^3$ bidding for an ally, it is much more likely that $Q^3$ and $P^3$ bid against each other for the allegiance of $R^3$ so that, while $\alpha_R^3$ may be as low as $a - (b/2)$, it may also be as high as $a$. A uniquely favored proto-coalition, such as the $R^3$ of this case, is thus in a much stronger position than a member of a uniquely preferable winning coalition, provided, of course, that a uniquely preferable winning coalition does not simultaneously exist.

*Case 3D.* $m > w(P^3) = w(Q^3) = w(R^3)$. When $m$ is at its minimum value, this case is the same as the essential three-person game discussed by Von Neumann and Morgenstern. There is little that one can add to their discussion. Neither a uniquely preferable winning coalition nor a uniquely favored proto-coalition exist and any one of $(P^3 \cup Q^3)$, $(P^3 \cup R^3)$, and $(Q^3 \cup R^3)$ is equally profitable and probable.

*Case 3E.* $m > w(Q^3 \cup R^3)$ or $w(P^3 \cup R^3)$. Here $m$ is necessarily larger than its minimum value, that is, an extraordinary majority is required. What is important about this case, however, is not that $m$ is above the minimum (for that may occur in cases 3A through 3D also) but rather that the value for $m$ restricts the number of winning coalitions.

*Case 3E1.* $w(P^3 \cup R^3) \geqq m > w(Q^3 \cup R^3)$. Here there are only two winning coalitions, ignoring, of course, the grand coalition. Identify their values, thus:

$$v(P^3 \cup R^3) = a$$
$$v(P^3 \cup Q^3) = b.$$

Note that only $P^3$ can calculate an initial expectation, which is $(b, -a, a - b)$. If $w(Q^3) > w(R^3)$, then $a > b$. Hence $(P^3 \cup R^3)$ is uniquely preferable and $P^3$ is uniquely essential. (Note that $P^3$ is not uniquely favored for it cannot satisfy the first condition of the definition of uniquely favored.) By reason of the fact that it is essential, $P^3$ may reasonably expect to do better than its initial expectation. If, on the other hand, $w(Q^3) = w(R^3)$, no coalition is preferable and $Q^3$ and $R^3$ may be expected to bid against each other quite ardently for alliance with $P^3$. Doubtless, to be uniquely essential is the greatest advantage any proto-coalition can have.

*Case 3E2.* $w(P^3 \cup Q^3) \geqq m > w(P^3 \cup R^3)$. Here, aside from the grand coalition, only $(P^3 \cup Q^3)$ is winning, which is to say it is unique. This fact probably does not endow either of the members with a great advantage, however, for the fact that they are forced to each other gives them no choices in bargaining. Furthermore, while they may be certain of winning, they cannot be certain of winning much, owing to the small size of the loser, $R^3$.

The information gathered in the discussion of cases 3A through 3E is summarized in tabular form in Table 1 of Chapter 6.

*Case 4.* $m > w(P^4) \geqq w(Q^4) \geqq w(R^4) \geqq w(S^4)$.
*Case 5.* $m > w(P^5) \geqq w(Q^5) \geqq w(R^5) \geqq w(S^5) \geqq w(T^5)$.

It is probably unprofitable to discuss these cases in the same kind of detail as case 3. Case 4 involves at least 60 subcases and case 5 involves at least 250 subcases (even after much grouping of conditions in order to simplify the analysis). In Tables 2 and 3 of Chapter 6, however, the results of a detailed analysis are set forth in summary fashion analogous to the presentation in Table 1. Several features of Tables 2 and 3 deserve comment.

### THE MEANING OF TABLES 1, 2, AND 3

Note, first, that Tables 2 and 3 do not contain exactly the same information as Table 1. While Table 1 identifies, under *all* the relevant conditions, those proto-coalitions that are either uniquely favored or members of uniquely preferable winning coalitions, Tables 2 and 3 do not go into such fine detail. They show only the variations possible in size of coalitions and (in contrast to Table 1) do not relate the conditions of size to conditions of the shape of the characteristic function. Hence the entries in the cells of these tables are those proto-coalitions which either are uniquely favored or are members of coalitions that satisfy the first condition for uniquely preferable winning coalitions. To render the information in Tables 2 and 3 into the same form as Table 1, each cell containing the names of two or more proto-coalitions must be divided into two cells, one of which assumes that the second condition for unique preference can be satisfied and the other of which assumes it cannot. The former of the new cells then contains the same names as the original cell, while the latter new cell contains either (1) a blank or (2) the name of any proto-coalition appearing in boldface in the original cell (i.e., uniquely favored proto-coalitions). Since this transformation is easily made by the reader, I have for convenience of presentation omitted consideration of the second condition for unique preference from these two tables.

Furthermore, the right half of Table 1 is not repeated in Tables 2 and 3. In these latter tables it is assumed that $m$ is at its minimum value or that, even if an extraordinary majority is required, still all the coalitions that are winning when $m$ is at its minimum are also winning when $m$ is larger. With all these omissions, therefore, Tables 2 and 3 are strictly analogous to column 1 of Table 1. For some purposes, it may be desirable to extend Tables 2 and 3, but their general tenor is clear enough as they stand.

It should be understood, of course, that the absolute size of the weights in a decision-making body determines whether or not actual instances of the cases in the cells exist. For example, if the sum of the weights of all the members of the body is 15 (according to some numerical scale) and if 15 is partitioned by integers, then there are some cells in Table 2 which are necessarily empty of instances (e.g. cell (1,1)—read "row 1, column 1"—is empty because no partition of 15 can satisfy these conditions). On the other hand, if the sum of the weights is sufficiently large, at least one instance of partition of this sum is to be found in each unshaded cell. (Using $\sum_{X=P}^{T} w(X^k) = 100$, 101, and varying $k$ over the numbers 3, 4, and 5, I have satisfied myself that some instance of a partition can be found for each unshaded cell and further I have shown deductively that no instance can be found regardless of the size of the sum of the weights for any shaded cell.) In general, as the sum of the weights increases, the number of instances falling in each cell increases, although I am not able to observe a regular pattern in the increase. In general also, though in an even less regular fashion, as $m$ increases and the sum of the weights is held stable, the cells in Tables 2 and 3 are emptied, for the instances of partitions are transferred to other columns not shown but analogous to the two right-hand columns in Table 1.

Finally it should be observed that no suggestion is implied in the tables about the relative frequency of occurrences of instances of partitions. If one regards all partitions as equally probable (and there is certainly no historical reason for such an assumption), then it is probably true that as the sum of the weights increases, the proportion of instances falling in the first row increases. Students of combinatorial analysis do not seem to have studied partitions in a way that gives direct mathematical assurance on this point, but I have made some calculations that suggest the assumption is probably correct. These calculations are reported in Table 4. Let "$p(k)$" stand for the number of distinct partitions into $k$ subsets. Then, let

$$a = p(k), \text{ where } w(P^k) \leq \tfrac{1}{2} \sum_{X=P}^{T} w(X^k), \text{ and where } w(X^k)$$

$$\neq w(Y^k), \text{ and}$$

$$b = p(k), \text{ where } w(P^k) \leq \tfrac{1}{2} \sum_{X=P}^{T} w(X^k).$$

That is, $b$ is the number of partitions appearing in all cells in Table 1 (or 2 or 3) and $a$ is the number of partitions appearing in the first row of Table 1 (or 2 or 3). More precisely, $b$ is the number of partitions into $k$ sets when no one of the sets is larger than $m$; and $a$ is the number of such partitions which, in addi-

TABLE 4

| $\sum_{X=P}^{T} w(X^k)$ | Ratio of $a$ to $b$ | | | |
|---|---|---|---|---|
| $k$ | 10 | 20 | 25 | 100 |
| 3 | 2/4 | 8/13 | 10/16 | 207/233 |
| 4 | 1/7 | 15/41 | 31/67 | ... |
| 5 | 0/6 | 6/66 | 24/128 | ... |

tion, have unequal parts. As Table 4 clearly indicates, the ratio of $a$ to $b$, that is the proportion of instances falling in the cells of the first row to the whole number of instances, increases as the sum of the weights increases. If instances of partitions are equally probable, therefore, only the first row of these tables holds much interest when the sum is fairly large.

It seems unlikely, however, that instances are equally probable. For example, regardless of the sum of the weights, for every sum divisible by three, there is one instance of $w(P^3) = w(Q^3) = w(R^3)$. If the sum is 9, and the instances are equally likely, this partition has a $\frac{1}{3}$ chance of occurring. If the sum is 15, this partition has a $\frac{1}{7}$ chance. Experience with real decision-making bodies of this size indicates that partitions of (3,3,3) and (5,5,5) do not occur as frequently as $\frac{1}{3}$ or $\frac{1}{7}$ of the time. Indeed, it seems quite possible that in nature there is a preference for partitions in the first row of Tables 1, 2, and 3; and if this is true then the first row is more important than the others, even when the sum of the weights is small.

# Index